RED, WHITE, AND BLUE

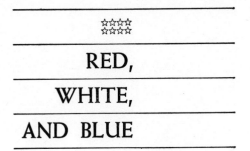

RED,
WHITE,
AND BLUE

MEN, BOOKS, AND IDEAS
IN AMERICAN CULTURE

John William Ward

New York · Oxford University Press · 1969

FOR HENRY NASH SMITH:
Teacher, Pattern, and Friend

PREFACE

In his *Autobiography*, skeptical, old Ben Franklin tells a story on himself to draw the moral that the nice thing about being a reasonable man is that one can always find a principle to justify one's inclination. The obvious danger in publishing a book of essays is the temptation to sound terribly high-minded about the whole thing. So I am willing to accept the most immediate reason: Sheldon Meyer, my editor, and Oxford University Press were willing to publish the essays as a book.

Each of the following essays was occasional, in the sense that the occasion of an invitation to deliver a talk, or a paper at a conference, or an essay on a writer or a book gave rise to each. Yet, simply because they were written by the same person, certain lines of connection run between them. There are other essays, but I have selected those which fall into the two major areas of my own interests, the way in which history and the imagination shape each other, and the meaning of individual freedom in American history. The division is largely artificial and anyone who is kind enough to read all of the essays in Parts Two and Three will see readily enough how one might shift a particular essay from one section to the other. What most holds them all together is a certain way of looking at things, which is the subject of Part One. Part Four, on the transmission of values in American culture, is to suggest that the meaning of American culture is shaped by the demands of the present as much as by the examples of the past. Since each essay was meant to stand by itself, there are two instances where I have repeated two paragraphs from one essay in another. Even though I have brought them together, I still wish each essay to be self-existent, so I have let the repetition stand. Further, I decided to omit such paraphernalia as footnotes, since any reader who wishes to pursue them may by reference to the place of an essay's first appearance in the list of acknowledgments at the end.

Finally, over the years in which I have written these essays, I have been fortunate enough to run myself deeply into debt to others, debts both material and intellectual. To name them all would make a considerable essay in itself, but at the risk of slighting so many I wish to name only one, Professor Henry Nash Smith, of the University of California at Berkeley, to whom I have dedicated this book.

J. W. W.

Amherst, Massachusetts
January 1969

CONTENTS

ix

PART IV: THE VALUES OF AMERICAN
CULTURE: THE INTELLECTUAL AND
THE UNIVERSITY

☆☆☆☆
☆☆☆☆

PART I

HISTORY AND CULTURE

1

HISTORY AND THE CONCEPT OF CULTURE

I AGREE WITH the remark of that fine historian, Mr. Robert R. Palmer, when he says that "history should be written in the ordinary language." Yet Mr. Palmer's remark occurred in the course of a discussion of the concept of culture in an article on the problem of generalization in the writing of history. One suspects Mr. Palmer was finally able to write so well in the ordinary language because he first gave thought to such arid matters as the nature of history and the method of the historian. My own instinctive preference is for the descriptive and the concrete, rather than the abstract and the conceptual. The reader whose instincts run in the same direction may simply turn to the essays which follow, but I have chosen to begin with some discussion of the job of the cultural historian (which is what I choose to call what I choose to do) because the one element which all the following essays share is a common method. Method is, perhaps, too strict a word. A common perspective, a way of looking at things, is more accurate.

My purpose is tendentious. I have an end in view, beyond the more obvious one of self-justification. I wish to argue that a certain perspective on man and his actions, a perspective implicit in the concept of culture as developed in the work of modern cultural anthropologists, would be fruitful for the writing of history. To do so, however, requires two definitions, the definition of "history," and the definition of "culture." Like all definitions, which are gestures toward order and control, these two have implicit in them the conclusion I wish to reach.

First, History. History is the study of the actions of men in the past, however recent that past may be. The difference between the study of men and the study of nature is that the study of nature deals with events, not actions. The history of the study of nature may be described, as in Mr. Charles Gillispie's book, *The Edge of Objectivity*, as the movement toward greater objectivity, that is, the willingness to dispense with notions of purpose and intention behind the phenomenal events which the scientist studies. Whatever the particular scientist may feel when he is at church, if he happens to go there, he has, as the Frenchman said, no need for that hypothesis in his work. Unlike the scientist in his study of nature, however, the historian deals not with events but with actions, and action implies an actor. The proper subject of the historian is not the fact of an action (the event, if one will), but the processes of thought which go on in the mind of the actor which are disclosed in, and establish the meaning of, that action.

To use the simple example which appears in many of the handbooks on the meaning of history: Caesar crossed the Rubicon. To describe that action in so simple a sentence involves other determinations, of course: the existence and location of a river, the existence and identity of a man named Caesar. But to say, "Caesar crossed the Rubicon," after having established the accuracy of such a statement about the event, says nothing of interest. That is, it says nothing about what the action means, and to say what the action means involves the historian in a consideration of Caesar's intention in crossing the Rubicon, and so defying a convention in his society, a convention derived from the authority of republican law over the soldiers of the state.

So, the interest of the historian is properly not with the spectacle of events, but with the thought within them. He must, of course, get his events, his facts, straight, as so many historians like constantly to insist. That is elementary. But that is the beginning, not the proper end of his work. As R. G. Collingwood put it, history has an inside. The inside of history, the thought disclosed in action, *is* history. In this sense (one need not, I think, go all the way with Collingwood in order to go this far), one can say with Collingwood that all history is the history of thought. Even those events not the result of human action, say a terrible plague visited upon human society by the invasion of infected rats, derive their meaning in history from the way men act in response to them. In some societies, the toll of death will be understood as the wrath of an angry god, and men will fast and pray for deliverance; in others, men will look to the conditions of sanitation and get to work to arrest the disaster.

So, for the definition of "history," one may amend the statement that history is the study of actions of men in the past to read more directly, *history is the study of the consciousness of men in the past.* But if one sets out to study the consciousness of men in the past, one immediately confronts the problem of what one means by the consciousness of men and, especially when one deals with a moment other than the immediate past, what materials are appropriate to the study of that subject. Both these questions, if pursued, lead to the concept of culture, the second word in need of definition.

I tread lightly here, not simply because I am an amateur,

but because so many have been here before me and with such bewildering results. The anthropologists, Messrs. Kroeber and Kluckhohn, have, with the collaboration of others, compiled a considerable monograph, *Culture: A Critical Review of Concepts and Definitions*. Their analytical description of what scholars have meant when they have used the word "culture" falls into six main categories (with twelve sub-categories), and Mr. Kroeber and Mr. Kluckhohn still felt the need for an omnibus seventh category of "incomplete definitions." In their monographic treatment, Mr. Kroeber and Mr. Kluckhohn present and discuss more than three hundred definitions, but suggest that one may reduce these to 164. Having finished their compendious critical review, they decline to add number 165 to that long list. So, in offering a definition of the concept of culture, I am intensely aware of the presumption, and do so largely for the pragmatic purpose of getting on with what I have to say.

One may define "culture" as *the organization of social experience in the consciousness of men made manifest in symbolic action*. The immediate objection to this definition is that it is elliptical to the extreme and requires some comment.

The word "social" carries a heavy burden. First, it implies that without society we have no human consciousness. To put it shortly, to be human is a social achievement. Without society, man is not the human animal, he is simply animal. Exploration has cast some doubt on the authenticity of Mr. Gesell's story of the wolf-children, abandoned at an early age, reared in a wolf-pack, who when captured in their teens proved unadaptable to the erect carriage of human posture and incapable of learning human speech. The story now looks to be an apocryphal version of the Romulus and Remus legend rather than an authentic account of an historical event. But if Mr. Gesell's instance is only story rather than history, research into comparable situations has confirmed the truth of that imaginary account, and the meaning seems to be accepted now by all. Individual consciousness emerges from the group; the group is not the association of individuals with consciousness already formed.

Further, the word "social" implies that the perception of experience is itself mediated by conventions or categories derived from the historical experience of the group. That is, the individual mind is not simply a passive recipient of the experience which impinges upon the individual, but rather that the individual apprehends experience through modes which he derives from his social history. As Mr. Kingsley Davis puts it, "the normative order makes the factual order of human society possible." Which is to say that we see, think, and react by means of socially inherited norms. Obviously the biological self has imperious demands. Man seeks sexual satisfaction, food, and protection against the rude weather. Yet the universality of these appetites and necessities seems less important than the conventions through which their satisfaction is mediated. That comment points to one major item which I have omitted from my compressed definition: the process by which the individual internalizes the conventions derived from social experience. To put it more simply: the learning process, which would take one in the direction of social and individual psychology, which is important, but not critical, to the meaning of the definition.

The other item in the definition of "culture" which requires some amplification is the phrase, "made manifest in symbolic action." Again, like the word, "social," the words carry a heavy burden of meaning. The word, "manifest," may seem to require no comment, but I chose it with Freud in mind in the hope that, along with the word "symbolic," one might be a'e.t to the fact that action may have a latent as well as more than a single meaning. Further, the phrase, "symbolic action," is an attempt to bridge the gap between the material and intellectual aspects of culture, a division between mind and matter which has a long tradition behind it in Western epistemology, a division which troubles nearly every definition which Mr. Kroeber and Mr. Kluckhohn have gathered.

Normally, when we speak of ideas or values we think of the word, whether spoken or written. Rightly so, since the word is our chief, most flexible, and richest resource for the expression of consciousness. But things, too, speak for us. The material objects we create, the institutions we devise, the gestures of our manners, all these are expressive. They are, in other words, symbolic embodiments or presentations of subjective attitudes. As George Kubler, the art historian at Yale, says in a book I much admire, *The Shape of Time: Remarks on the History of Things,* "the 'history of things' is intended to reunite ideas and objects under the rubric of visual forms: the term includes both artifacts and works of art . . . both tools and expressions —in short all materials worked by human hands under the guidance of connected ideas. . . . From all these things a shape in time emerges. A visible portrait of the collective identity . . . comes into being. This self-image reflected in things is a guide and a point of reference to the group for the future, and it eventually becomes the portrait given to posterity."

In the history of the word, "culture," there is the constant association with the word, "civilization." One is used to point to intellectual, moral, and spiritual phenomena; the other to the material dimension of social organization. German usage tends to prefer "culture" for the intellectual and moral realm, the "higher" level of social existence, while the French reverse the meanings and tend to use "civilization" for such estimable activity. The intention behind the phrase, "symbolic activity," is to unite the two modes of activity, not simply to avoid the confusions of terminology (although there may be a certain advantage to that), but to suggest that the polarization between the work of our minds and the work of our hands is a false polarization and feeds too easily into the derogation of either, depending upon one's particular bias. The low-brow (or, when he is self-conscious, the materialist) can offer us a decerebrated view of human history with his insistence on the hard facts of life, forgetful that the material context of human association is itself the product and the image of human intentions. The high-brow (or, when he is self-conscious, the idealist) can offer us an elegant withdrawal from the mundane facts of life because they do not participate in his elevated realm. The consequence has been especially acute in America. It defines what Santayana named the "genteel tradition," the split between coarse and brutal action, on the one hand, and lofty and noble idealism, on the other. It vitiates both the material environment in which we live as well as the intellectual environment in which we do our work.

But to finish with the abstract matter of definition, one may see, readily enough, that if history is the study of the con-sciousness of men in the past, and that if culture is the organi-zation of social experience in the minds of men made manifest in symbolic action, then one may say that history is, ideally, the study of past culture. Or, as Mr. Stuart Hughes put it, the historian is a retrospective cultural anthropologist. Since I name my own interest as that of a "cultural historian," there is an obvious imperialism lurking in my attempt to relate, by definition, the study of history to the study of culture.

At this point, an example may help, a small example of what the historian does when he works from the perspective inti-mated so far in my abstract definitions. My purpose is to make the general concrete, but also to raise two problems implicit in the perspective of the cultural historian which are, perhaps, troublesome for the traditional habits of the discipline of his-tory.

My example begins with the second annual message of President Andrew Jackson of December 6, 1830. In the course of his message, Jackson announced with pleasure plans for the final removal of the Cherokee Nation from its traditional home in the Old Southwest, especially the state of Georgia. The Indians had memorialized the Congress to respect their treaty rights with the Federal government so they might live out their lives near the graves of their fathers, so they might continue their tribal ways on the land they held in severalty, so they might not suffer the fatal consequences that dislocation held for their venerated way of life. Their appeals met a blank lack of comprehension on Jackson's part. The result of Jackson's action was to satisfy the rapacity of land-hungry white settlers in the State of Georgia, but for present purposes, as writers like to say, what is interesting is Jackson's reason for his action, for his rejection of the arguments of the Cherokees and for their expulsion from within the borders of the settled states.

After obeisance to the sentiments of good men who weep over the fate of the American aborigine, Jackson asks, rhetorically, "Doubtless it will be painful to leave the graves of their fathers, but what do they more than our ancestors did or than our children are now doing? To better their condition in an unknown land our forefathers left all that was dear in earthly objects. Our children by thousands leave the land of their birth to seek new homes in distant regions. Does Humanity weep at these painful separations from everything, animate and inanimate, with which the young heart has become entwined? Far from it. It is rather a source of joy," said Jackson, "a source of joy that our country affords scope where our young population unconstrained in body or in mind, [develop] the powers and faculties of men in their highest perfection."

Jackson's few words represent a dramatic moment in the conflict between two cultures, two systems of values which share no point in common. Jackson simply cannot comprehend the nature of the Indian's position because it violates the assumptions of his own culture. Jackson cannot admit the worth of a patriarchal, authoritarian, tribal culture, where land is held in common and where action is determined by reference to the past of one's ancestors and tradition. To do so would call into question the triumph of his own culture, which Jackson obviously assumes to be superior, and which more importantly, is defined by an ideal where man is, as Jackson puts it, "unconstrained in body or in mind."

The measure of the worth of American culture in Jackson's time is held by him to be the degree to which society liberates the individual person from all external restraint, whether the traditions of the past or the institutions of the present, even that elemental and basic institution, the family. The atomic, self-propelled individual, moving freely through space and society, stands at the center of Jackson's image of the good society.

Now, let me place beside Jackson's speech the words of another American of his time, an intellectual who had deeply ambivalent feelings about Jackson himself and about the Democratic party which he headed, and who opposed the Indian policy for which Jackson spoke. These are the words of Ralph Waldo Emerson in his essay on "Politics" in 1840. "That which all things tend to educe," argued Emerson, "which freedom, cultivation, intercourse, revolutions, go to form and deliver, is character; that is the end of Nature, to reach unto this coronation of her king. To educate the wise man the State exists, and with the appearance of the wise man the State expires. The appearance of character makes the State unnecessary. The wise man is the State. He needs no army, fort, or navy,—he loves men too well; no bribe, or feast, or palace, to draw friends to him; no vantage ground, no favorable circumstance. He needs no library, for he has not done thinking; no church, for he is a prophet; no statute-book, for he has the lawgiver; no money, for he is value; no road, for he is at home where he is; no experience, for the life of the creator shoots through him. . . . He has no personal friends."

Emerson's celebration of his lonely hero, god-like in his self-existence, presents a chilling ideal, unless, of course, one can share the assumptions about the nature of man from which it derives. But rather than pursue the basis of Emerson's trust which allows him to embrace his solitary hero, I want only to point to the obvious fact that Jackson and Emerson share the same assumption about the genius of American culture. The ideal of their culture has for its hero the individual, unconstrained in body or in mind, free from all adventitious circumstance, steering his way unaided through the world.

For a third and final quotation, let me place alongside those of Jackson and Emerson one taken from a magazine of the time, from the level of "popular culture." The author is unknown and his subject, in 1839, is "The Course of Civilization." "The history of humanity," says the author, "is the record of a grand march . . . at all times tending to one point —the ultimate perfection of man. The course of civilization is the progress of man from a state of savage individualism to that of an individualism more elevated, moral and refined. Personal separation and independence were the beginning, as they will be the end, of the great progressive movement, with this difference—that in its last and more perfectly developed condition, the sense of justice shall have supreme control over the individual will."

Our anonymous journalist here speaks in the same accent as Jackson and Emerson. He assumes that the measure of the advance of civilization is the degree to which it moves toward a condition, to use his words, of "personal separation and independence," supported—as is Emerson's sanguine string of negatives—by the assumption that the single person internalizes within his own personality the moral order and the demands of justice which then need no external sanctions. One who knows the history of evangelical Protestantism in early nineteenth century America will recognize that this was also the millennial expectation of the fervid revivalism of the period.

One may see readily enough what my brief example suggests. Whether we regard the state paper of an American President, an essay of the leading spokesman for American Transcendentalism, the journalistic article of a magazine writer, or the message of the major religious practice of the time, we discover a common assumption about the central value of American culture: the assertion of the worth of the totally liberated, self-sufficient, atomistic, single individual. It would be possible to show how the expression of this cultural ideal is presented in other idioms of the time, other modes of "symbolic action," from general acts of incorporation in the economic institutions of the society to landscape gardening and architecture, as I have tried to suggest in my remarks on Andrew Jackson Downing in the essay, "The Politics of Design."

But rather than pursue the pervasive expression of this cultural ideal in other forms of action in early American democratic culture, I would like to turn instead to two problems which are perhaps troublesome for the conventional practices of the historian. First, the angle of vision of the cultural historian looks upon a moment in time, abstracts it from the flux of change, and presents it in rather static terms. Such a way of writing history departs from the genetic emphasis of the usual historical mode. Second, it begs the whole question of cause and effect, at least for the moment, while it seeks an understanding of the cultural pattern, the image of reality which men carry about in their heads and act out in the different areas of their experience. If history is to be restricted, by a different definition of history, to a sequential narrative of events through time, and if history must, again by some other definition, engage the question of causation, then the analysis of the cultural historian which I have just briefly intimated will have little appeal for some historians.

One needs to be careful here. I am *not* saying that a genetic account of Jacksonian political theory, or Transcendental idealism, or the religious doctrine of the perfect law of liberty for the righteous will not lead to a considerable understanding of any of these subjects as they fall more readily into the traditional organization of knowledge in the various specialties of advanced learning. What I am saying is that to remain in the confines of one idiom of action, whether it be politics or literature, religion or painting, will not readily lead us to an apprehension of the basic pattern of values which is implicit in the many forms of "symbolic action" of a culture. In other words, if we are to seek, as Alfred North Whitehead asked the intellectual historian to do, the "fundamental assumptions" of an epoch, we will do so more readily by an examination of the general culture than by a single part of it. Or, conversely, when we examine the particular, we should, so far as possible, be sensitive to the larger pattern in which it is implicated and from which it derives the full amplitude of its meaning. The essay, "The Ideal of Individualism and the Reality of Organization," is a sketch of the first prescription, but since these are essays most are examples of the second. The essay on Lindbergh's flight is, perhaps, the clearest instance of the attempt to move through a particular action to the general culture.

Further, to speak of the "many forms" of symbolic action in a culture leads ultimately to the troublesome problem of causation. In his examination of the many forms of expression in a culture in order to arrive at a grasp of the general and pervasive meaning of that culture, the cultural historian gives no precedence to one mode of activity over another. For the moment, at least, the cultural historian does not assign relative weights of importance to the actions he examines, an assignment which implies that one area of activity is more important and more dynamic in society and, therefore, the locus of change. So long as one's attention is toward an analysis of the cultural pattern of a single moment in time (however narrowly or broadly we define the limits of that "moment"), the matter of causation is not pressing. It becomes pressing only when one takes two widely separate moments in time, say Jacksonian

America and the twentieth century, and asks the difficult question how the later moment developed out of the conditions of the earlier. Then cause raises its troublesome questions.

I have tried, then, to suggest how the concept of culture bears upon the definition and the practice of history. In conclusion, I would like to reverse direction and turn history back upon the concept of culture. It, too, has a history. The relation of history to the emergence of culture and to the genesis of the idea of culture is important—as an historian, one would like to say crucial—in two respects.

First, and again as an amateur, as I read the writings of cultural anthropologists, there stands out one central notion. It is that what sets man off from other animals is man's capacity to symbolize his experience and, thus, to transmit it extra-somatically rather than biologically. The animal becomes the human animal by the capacity to free itself (himself?) from physiological and instinctive response by the astonishing creation of a symbolic and transmissible non-biological system of meaning. Man, in other words, makes himself by making culture.

If this notion is as central as I take it to be, then surely the most exciting moment in man's long history lies at the origins of history, in pre-history as historians like curiously to name the reaches of time before the appearance of records on which to base written history. Since culture itself has a history, one of the more fascinating directions in the development of cultural anthropology will surely come with the work of scholarship which tries to penetrate the blackness of the past which covers the emergence of culture and humanity.

Second, there is the parallel fact that if culture has a history, so does the concept of culture, the use and meaning of the idea of culture. My remarks here are speculative and are meant to lead to the most important use the concept of culture may have for the writing of history. There are two major periods in the history of the development of the idea of culture, one in Germany in the eighteenth century, the other in England and the United States in the latter part of the nineteenth century. Professor Sir Isaiah Berlin's excellent essay on Herder has demonstrated how Herder with his relativistic emphasis on the unique qualities of German *Kultur* is a clear anticipation of what Messrs. Kroeber and Kluckhohn call the modern "scientific" concept of culture. Alfred Meyer has suggested that "these *Kultur* theories are a typical ideological expression . . . of the rise of backward societies against the encroachment of the West on their traditional cultures." They consist, Mr. Meyer writes with emphasis, "*they consist in asserting the reality of something which is just about to be destroyed.*"

Later, in the United States and especially in England, as Raymond Williams has shown so well in *Culture and Society*, the concept of culture emerged gradually in the ongoing public debate about the consequences of industrialism and the results of mass democracy for traditional institutions and ways of life. Mr. Williams summarizes his history of the idea of culture: "The idea of culture is a general reaction to a general and major change in the conditions of our common culture. . . . The change in the whole form of our common life produced, as a necessary reaction, an emphasis on attention to this whole form. . . . General change, when it has worked itself clear, drives us back on our general designs, which we have to learn to look at again, and as a whole. The working-out of the idea of culture is a slow reach again for control."

The conditions present in both moments in the emergence of the concept of culture share one similarity: both are moments of awareness of the need to establish general order in a society threatened by disorder and discontinuity. The idea of culture is itself a response to historical moments of challenge to the conditions which support a generally shared system of meaning and ideals in human community.

The historical context of the idea of culture brings me back to the reason I suggested at the start I would give to support my desire to see the writing of history go in the direction I have described. As protection against the real world which often wonders what he is up to, the intellectual, wisely enough, tends to take a mildly ironic, self-depreciating view of his role in the world's work. But it is still true that a considerable part of the role of the intellectual in society is, to use the words of Edward Shils, to "elicit, guide, and form the expressive dispositions within society." If this is at all true, then it demands considerable care, and demands that historians be sensitive to the simple fact that the subject of history is always and finally what it means to be a human being. If the concept of culture is to be understood as a "slow reach again for control" over the centrifugal forces of social change in history, then its ultimate value for written history may be to remind historians of the need for general order in their work. It may even remind all of us of the need for general order in our divided culture.

PART II

AMERICAN CULTURE AND
THE AMERICAN IMAGINATION

1

THE MEANING OF
LINDBERGH'S FLIGHT

On Friday, May 20, 1927, at 7:52 a.m., Charles A. Lindbergh took off in a silver-winged monoplane and flew from the United States to France. With this flight Lindbergh became the first man to fly alone across the Atlantic Ocean. The log of flight 33 of "The Spirit of St. Louis" reads: "Roosevelt Field, Long Island, New York, to Le Bourget Aerodrome, Paris, France. 33 hrs. 30 min." Thus was the fact of Lindbergh's achievement easily put down. But the meaning of Lindbergh's flight lay hidden in the next sentence of the log: "(Fuselage fabric badly torn by souvenir hunters.)"

When Lindbergh landed at Le Bourget he is supposed to have said, "Well, we've done it." A contemporary writer asked "Did what?" Lindbergh "had no idea of what he had done. He thought he had simply flown from New York to Paris. What he had really done was something far greater. He had fired the imagination of mankind." From the moment of Lindbergh's flight people recognized that something more was involved than the mere fact of the physical leap from New York to

Paris. "Lindbergh," wrote John Erskine, "served as a metaphor." But what the metaphor stood for was not easy to say. The *New York Times* remarked then that "there has been no complete and satisfactory explanation of the enthusiasm and acclaim for Captain Lindbergh." Looking back on the celebration of Lindbergh, one can see now that the American people were trying to understand Lindbergh's flight, to grasp its meaning, and through it, perhaps, to grasp the meaning of their own experience. Was the flight the achievement of a heroic, solitary, unaided individual? Or did the flight represent the triumph of the machine, the success of an industrially organized society? These questions were central to the meaning of Lindbergh's flight. They were also central to the lives of the people who made Lindbergh their hero.

The flight demanded attention in its own right, of course, quite apart from whatever significance it might have. Lindbergh's story had all the makings of great drama. Since 1919 there had been a standing prize of $25,000 to be awarded to the first aviator who could cross the Atlantic in either direction between the United States and France in a heavier-than-air craft. In the spring of 1927 there promised to be what the *New York Times* called "the most spectacular race ever held—3,600 miles over the open sea to Paris." The scene was dominated by veteran pilots. On the European side were the French aces, Nungesser and Coli; on the American side, Commander Richard E. Byrd, in a big tri-motored Fokker monoplane, led a group of contestants. Besides Byrd, who had already flown over the North Pole, there were Commander Davis, flying a ship named in honor of the American Legion which had put up $100,000 to finance his attempt, Clarence Chamberlin, who had already set a world's endurance record of more than fifty-one hours in the air in a Bellanca tri-motored plane, and Captain René Fonck, the French war ace, who had come to America to fly a Sikorsky aircraft. The hero was unheard of and unknown.

He was on the West Coast supervising the construction of a single-engined plane to cost only ten thousand dollars.

Then fate played its part. It seemed impossible that Lindbergh could get his plane built and east to New York in time to challenge his better equipped and more famous rivals. But in quick succession a series of disasters cleared his path. On April 16, Commander Byrd's "America" crashed on its test flight, crushing the leg of Floyd Bennett who was one of the crew and injuring Byrd's hand and wrist. On April 24, Clarence Chamberlin cracked up in his Bellanca, not seriously, but enough to delay his plans. Then on April 26, Commander Davis and his co-pilot lost their lives as the "American Legion" crashed on its final test flight. In ten days, accidents had stopped all of Lindbergh's American rivals. Nungesser and Coli, however, took off in their romantically named ship, "The White Bird," from Le Bourget on May 8. The world waited and Lindbergh, still on the West Coast, decided to try to fly the Pacific. But Nungesser and Coli were never seen again. As rumors filled the newspapers, as reports came in that the "White Bird" was seen over Newfoundland, over Boston, over the Atlantic, it soon became apparent that Nungesser and Coli had failed, dropping to their death in some unknown grave. Disaster had touched every ship entered in the trans-Atlantic race.

Now, with the stage cleared, Lindbergh entered. He swooped across the continent in two great strides, landing only at St. Louis. The first leg of his flight established a new distance record but all eyes were on the Atlantic and the feat received little notice. Curiously, the first time Lindbergh appeared in the headlines of the New York papers was Friday, the thirteenth. By this time Byrd and Chamberlin were ready once again but the weather had closed in and kept all planes on the ground. Then, after a week of fretful waiting, on the night of May 19, on the way into New York to see "Rio Rita," Lindbergh received a report that the weather was breaking over the ocean. He hurried back to Roosevelt Field to haul his plane out onto a wet, dripping runway. After mechanics painfully loaded the plane's gas by hand, the wind shifted, as fate played its last trick. A muddy runway and an adverse wind. Whatever the elements, whatever the fates, the decisive act is the hero's, and Lindbergh made his choice. Providing a chorus to the action, the *Herald Tribune* reported that Lindbergh lifted the overloaded plane into the sky "by his indomitable will alone."

The parabola of the action was as clean as the arc of Lindbergh's flight. The drama should have ended with the landing of "The Spirit of St. Louis" at Le Bourget. That is where Lindbergh wanted it to end. In *"WE,"* written immediately after the flight, and in *The Spirit of St. Louis*, written twenty-six years later, Lindbergh chose to end his accounts there. But the flight turned out to be only the first act in the part Lindbergh was to play.

Lindbergh was so innocent of his future that on his flight he carried letters of introduction. The hysterical response, first of the French and then of his own countrymen, had been no part of his careful plans. In *"WE,"* after Lindbergh's narrative of the flight, the publisher wrote: "When Lindbergh came to tell the story of his welcome at Paris, London, Brussels, Washington, New York, and St. Louis he found himself up against a tougher problem than flying the Atlantic." So another writer completed the account in the third person. He suggested that "the reason Lindbergh's story is different is that when his plane came to a halt on Le Bourget field that black night in Paris, Lindbergh the man kept on going. The phenomenon of Lindbergh took its start with his flight across the ocean; but in its entirety it was almost as distinct from that flight as though he had never flown at all."

Lindbergh's private life ended with his flight to Paris. The drama was no longer his, it was the public's. "The outburst of unanimous acclaim was at once personal and symbolic," said the *American Review of Reviews*. From the moment of success there were two Lindberghs, the private Lindbergh and the public Lindbergh. The latter was the construction of the imagination of Lindbergh's time, fastened on to an unwilling person. The tragedy of Lindbergh's career is that he could never accept the role assigned him. He always believed he might keep his two lives separate. But from the moment he landed at Le Bourget, Lindbergh became, as the *New Republic* noted, "*ours.* . . . He is no longer permitted to be himself. He is US personified. He is the United States." Ambassador Herrick introduced Lindbergh to the French, saying, "This young man from out of the West brings you better than anything else the spirit of America," and wired to President Coolidge, "Had we searched all America we could not have found a better type than young Lindbergh to represent the spirit and high purpose of our people." This was Lindbergh's fate, to be a type. A writer in the *North American Review* felt that Lindbergh represented "the dominant American character," he "images the best" about the United States. And an ecstatic female in the *American Magazine*, who began by saying that Lindbergh "is a sort of symbol. . . . He is the dream that is in our hearts," concluded that the American public responded so wildly to Lindbergh because of "the thrill of possessing, in him, our dream of what *we* really and truly want to be." The act of possession was so complete that articles since have attempted to discover the "real" Lindbergh, that enigmatic and taciturn figure behind the public mask. But it is no less difficult to discern the features of the public Lindbergh, that symbolic figure who presented to the imagination of his time all the yearnings and buried desires of its dream for itself.

Lindbergh's flight came at the end of a decade marked by social and political corruption and by a sense of moral loss. The heady idealism of the First World War had been succeeded by a deep cynicism as to the war's real purpose. The naïve belief that virtue could be legislated was violated by the vast discrepancy between the law and the social habits of prohibition. A philosophy of relativism had become the uneasy rationale of a nation which had formerly believed in moral absolutes. The newspapers agreed that Lindbergh's chief worth was his spiritual and moral value. His story was held to be "in striking contrast with the sordid unhallowed themes that have for months steeped the imaginations and thinking of the people." Or, as another had it, "there is good reason why people should hail Lindbergh and give him honor. He stands out in a grubby world as an inspiration."

Lindbergh gave the American people a glimpse of what they liked to think themselves to be at a time when they feared they had deserted their own vision of themselves. The grubbiness of the twenties had a good deal to do with the shining quality of Lindbergh's success, especially when one remembers that Lindbergh's flight was not as unexampled as our national memory would have it. The Atlantic was not unconquered when Lindbergh flew. A British dirigible had twice crossed the Atlantic before 1919 and on May 8 of that year three naval seaplanes left Rockaway, New York, and one, the NC-4 manned by a crew of five, got through to Plymouth, England. A month later, Captain John Alcock, an Englishman, with Arthur W. Browne, an American, flew the first heavier-than-air land plane across the Atlantic nonstop, from Newfoundland to Ireland, to win twice the money Lindbergh did, a prize of $50,000 offered by the London *Daily Mail.* Alcock's and Browne's misfortune was to land in a soft and somnolent Irish peat bog instead of before the cheering thousands of London or Paris. Or perhaps they should have flown in 1927.

The wild medley of public acclaim and the homeric strivings of editors make one realize that the response to Lindbergh involved a mass ritual in which America celebrated itself more than it celebrated Lindbergh. Lindbergh's flight was the occasion of a public act of regeneration in which the nation momentarily rededicated itself to something, the loss of which was keenly felt. It was said again and again that "Lindy" taught America "to lift its eyes up to Heaven." Heywood Broun, in his column in the *New York World*, wrote that this "tall young man raised up and let us see the potentialities of the human spirit." Broun felt that the flight proved that, though "we are small and fragile," it "isn't true that there is no health in us." Lindbergh's flight provided the moment, but the meaning of the flight is to be found in the deep and pervasive need for renewal which the flight brought to the surface of public feeling. When Lindbergh appeared at the nation's capital, the *Washington Post* observed, "He was given that frenzied acclaim which comes from the depths of the people." In New York, where 4,000,000 people saw him, a reporter wrote that the dense and vociferous crowds were swept, as Lindbergh passed, "with an emotion tense and inflammable." The *Literary Digest* suggested that the answer to the hero-worship of Lindbergh would "throw an interesting light on the psychology of our times and of the American people."

The *Nation* noted about Lindbergh that "there was something lyric as well as heroic about the apparition of this young Lochinvar who suddenly came out of the West and who flew all unarmed and all alone. It is the kind of stuff which the ancient Greeks would have worked into a myth and the medieval Scots into a border ballad. . . . But what we have in the case of Lindbergh is an actual, an heroic and an exhaustively exposed experience which exists by suggestion in the form of poetry." The *Nation* quickly qualified its statement by observing that reporters were as far as possible from being poets and concluded that the discrepancy between the fact and the celebration of it was not poetry, perhaps, but "magic on a vast scale." Yet the *Nation* might have clung to its insight that the public meaning of Lindbergh's flight was somehow poetic. The vast publicity about Lindbergh corresponds in one vital particular with the poetic vision. Poetry, said William Butler Yeats, contains opposites; so did Lindbergh. Lindbergh did not mean one thing, he meant many things. The image of itself which America contemplated in the public person of Lindbergh was full of conflict; it was, in a word, dramatic.

To heighten the drama, Lindbergh did it alone. He was the "lone eagle" and a full exploration of that fact takes one deep into the emotional meaning of his success. Not only the *Nation* found Sir Walter Scott's lines on Lochinvar appropriate: "he rode all unarmed and he rode all alone." Newspapers and magazines were deluged with amateur poems that vindicated one rhymester's wry comment, "Go conquer the perils / That lurk in the skies— / And you'll get bum poems / Right up to your eyes." The *New York Times*, that alone received more than two hundred poems, observed in trying to summarize the poetic deluge that "the fact that he flew alone made the strongest impression." Another favorite tribute was Kipling's "The Winners," with its refrain, "He travels the fastest who travels alone." The others who had conquered the Atlantic and those like Byrd and Chamberlin who were trying at the same time were not traveling alone and they hardly rode unarmed. Other than Lindbergh, all the contestants in the trans-Atlantic race had unlimited backing, access to the best planes, and all were working in teams, carrying at least one co-pilot to share the long burden of flying the plane. So a writer in the New York *Sun*, in a poem called "The Flying Fool," a nickname that Lindbergh despised, celebrated Lindbergh's flight: ". . . no kingly plane for him; / No endless data, comrades, moneyed chums; / No boards, no councils, no directors grim— / He plans ALONE . . . and takes luck as it comes."

Upon second thought, it must seem strange that the long distance flight of an airplane, the achievement of a highly advanced and organized technology, should be the occasion for hymns of praise to the solitary unaided man. Yet the National Geographic Society, when it presented a medal to Lindbergh, wrote on the presentation scroll, "Courage, when it goes alone, has ever caught men's imaginations," and compared Lindbergh to Robinson Crusoe and the trailmakers in our own West. But Lindbergh and Robinson Crusoe, the one in his helmet and fur-lined flying coat and the other in his wild goatskins, do not easily co-exist. Even if Robinson Crusoe did have a tidy capital investment in the form of a well-stocked shipwreck, he still did not have a ten thousand dollar machine under him.

Lindbergh, in nearly every remark about his flight and in his own writings about it, resisted the tendency to exploit the flight as the achievement of an individual. He never said "I," he always said "We." The plane was not to go unrecognized. Nevertheless, there persisted a tendency to seize upon the flight as a way of celebrating the self-sufficient individual, so that among many others an Ohio newspaper could describe Lindbergh as this "self-contained, self-reliant, courageous young man [who] ranks among the great pioneers of history." The strategy here was a common one, to make Lindbergh a "pioneer" and thus to link him with a long and vital tradition of individualism in the American experience. Colonel Theo-dore Roosevelt, himself the son of a famous exponent of self-reliance, said to reporters at his home in Oyster Bay that "Cap-tain Lindbergh personifies the daring of youth. Daniel Boone, David Crocket [sic], and men of that type played a lone hand and made America. Lindbergh is their lineal descendant." In *Outlook* magazine, immediately below an enthusiastic endorse-ment of Lindbergh's own remarks on the importance of his machine and his scientific instruments, there was the statement, "Charles Lindbergh is the heir of all that we like to think is best in America. He is of the stuff out of which have been made the pioneers that opened up the wilderness, first on the Atlantic coast, and then in our great West. His are the qualities which we, as a people, must nourish." It is in this mood that one sus-pects it was important that Lindbergh came out of the West and rode all alone.

Another common metaphor in the attempt to place Lind-bergh's exploit was to say that he had opened a new "frontier."

To speak of the air as a "frontier" was to invoke an interpretation of the meaning of American history which had sources deep in American experience, but the frontier of the airplane is hardly the frontier of the trailmakers of the old West. Rather than an escape into the self-sufficient simplicity of the American past, the machine which made Lindbergh's flight possible represented an advance into a complex industrial present. The difficulty lay in using an instance of modern life to celebrate the virtues of the past, to use an extreme development of an urban industrial society to insist upon the significance of the frontier in American ilfe.

A little more than a month after Lindbergh's flight, Joseph K. Hart in *Survey* magazine reached back to Walt Whitman's poem for the title of an article on Lindbergh: "O Pioneer." A school had made Lindbergh an honorary alumnus but Hart protested there was little available evidence "that he was educated in *schools*." "We must look elsewhere for our explanation," Hart wrote and he looked to the experience of Lindbergh's youth when "everything that he ever did . . . he did by himself. He lived more to himself than most boys." And, of course, Lindbergh lived to himself in the only place conceivably possible, in the world of nature, on a Minnesota farm. "There he developed in the companionship of woods and fields, animals and machines, his audaciously natural and simple personality." The word, "machines," jars as it intrudes into Hart's idyllic pastoral landscape and betrays Hart's difficulty in relating the setting of nature upon which he wishes to insist with the fact that its product spent his whole life tinkering with machines, from motorcycles to airplanes. But except for that one word, Hart proceeds in uncritical nostalgia to show that "a lone trip across the Atlantic was not impossible for a boy who had grown up in the solitude of the woods and waters." If Lindbergh was "clear-headed, naïf, untrained in the ways of cities," it was because he had "that 'natural simplicity'" which Fenimore Cooper used to attribute to the pioneer hero of his Leatherstocking Tales." Hart rejected the notion that any student "bent to all the conformities" of formal training could have done what Lindbergh did. "Must we not admit," he asked, "that this pioneering urge remained to this audacious youth because he had never submitted completely to the repressions of the world and its jealous institutions?"

Only those who insist on reason will find it strange that Hart should use the industrial achievement of the airplane to reject the urban, institutionalized world of industrialism. Hart was dealing with something other than reason; he was dealing with the emotion evoked by Lindbergh's solitude. He recognized that people wished to call Lindbergh a "genius" because that "would release him from the ordinary rules of existence." That way, "we could rejoice with him in his triumph, and then go back to the contracted routines of our institutional ways [because] ninety-nine percent of us must be content to be shaped and moulded by the routine ways and forms of the world to the routine tasks of life." It is in the word, "must," that the pathos of this interpretation of the phenomenon of Lindbergh lies. The world had changed from the open society of the pioneer to the close-knit, interdependent world of a modern machine-oriented civilization. The institutions of a highly corporate industrial society existed as a constant reproach to a people who liked to believe that the meaning of its experience was embodied in the formless, independent life of the frontier. Like Thomas Jefferson who identified American virtue with nature and saw the city as a "great sore" on the public body, Hart concluded that "certainly, in the response that the world—especially the world of great cities—has made to the performance of this midwestern boy, we can read of the homesickness of the human soul, immured in city canyons and routine tasks, for the freer world of youth, for the open spaces of the pioneer, for the joy of battling with nature and clean storms once more on the frontiers of the earth."

The social actuality which made the adulation of Lindbergh

possible had its own irony for the notion that America's strength lay in its simple uncomplicated beginnings. For the public response to Lindbergh to have reached the proportions it did, the world had by necessity to be the intricately developed world of modern mass communications. But more than irony was involved. Ultimately, the emotion attached to Lindbergh's flight involved no less than a whole theory about American history. By singling out the fact that Lindbergh rode alone, and by naming him a pioneer of the frontier, the public projected its sense that the source of America's strength lay somewhere in the past and that Lindbergh somehow meant that America must look backward in time to rediscover some lost virtue. The mood was nostalgic and American history was read as a decline, a decline measured in terms of America's advance into an urban, institutionalized way of life which made solitary achievement increasingly beyond the reach of ninety-nine per cent of the people. Because Lindbergh's ancestors were Norse, it was easy to call him a "Viking" and extend the emotion far into the past when all frontiers were open. He became the "Columbus" of another new world to conquer as well as the "Lochinvar" who rode all alone.

But there was always the brute, irreducible fact that Lindbergh's exploit was a victory of the machine over the barriers of nature. If the only response to Lindbergh had been a retreat to the past, we would be involved with a mass cultural neurosis, the inability of America to accept reality, the reality of the world in which it lived. But there was another aspect, one in which the public celebrated the machine and the highly organized society of which it was a product. The response to Lindbergh reveals that the American people were deeply torn between conflicting interpretations of their own experience. By calling Lindbergh a pioneer, the people could read into American history the necessity of turning back to the frontier past. Yet the people could also read American history in terms of progress into the industrial future. They could do this by emphasizing the machine which was involved in Lindbergh's flight.

Lindbergh came back from Europe in an American man-of-war, the cruiser *Memphis*. It seems he had contemplated flying on, around the whole world perhaps, but less adventurous heads prevailed and dictated a surer mode of travel for so valuable a piece of public property. The *New Republic* protested against bringing America's hero of romance home in a warship. If he had returned on a great liner, that would have been one thing. "One's first trip on an oceanliner is a great adventure— the novelty of it, the many people of all kinds and conditions, floating for a week in a tiny compact world of their own." But to return on the *Memphis*, "to be put on a gray battleship with a collection of people all of the same stripe, in a kind of ship that has as much relation to the life of the sea as a Ford factory has! We might as well have put him in a pneumatic tube and shot him across the Atlantic." The interesting thing about the *New Republic*'s protest against the unromantic, regimented life of a battleship is that the image it found appropriate was the Ford assembly line. It was this reaction against the discipline of a mechanized society that probably led to the nostalgic image of Lindbergh as a remnant of a past when romance was possible for the individual, when life held novelty, and society was variegated rather than uniform. But what the Ford Assembly Line represents, a society committed to the path of full mechanization, was what lay behind Lindbergh's romantic success. A long piece in the Sunday *New York Times*, "Lindbergh Symbolizes the Genius of America," reminded its readers of the too obvious fact that "without an airplane he could not have flown at all." Lindbergh "is, indeed, the Icarus of the twentieth century; not himself an inventor of his own wings, but a son of that omnipotent Daedalus whose ingenuity has created the modern world." The point was that modern America was the creation of modern industry. Lindbergh "reveres his 'ship' as a noble expression of mechanical wisdom. . . . Yet in this reverence . . . Lindbergh is not an exception. What he means by the Spirit of St. Louis is really the spirit of America. The mechanical genius, which is discerned in Henry Ford as well as in Charles A. Lindbergh, is in the very atmosphere of [the] country." In contrast to a sentiment that feared the enforced discipline of the machine there existed an attitude of reverence for its power.

Lindbergh led the way in the celebration of the machine, not only implicitly by including his plane when he said "we," but by direct statement. In Paris he told newspapermen, "You fellows have not said enough about that wonderful motor." Rarely have two more taciturn figures confronted one another than when Lindbergh returned to Washington and Calvin Coolidge pinned the Distinguished Flying Cross on him, but in his brief remarks Coolidge found room to express his particular delight that Lindbergh should have given equal credit to the airplane. "For we are proud," said the President, "that in every particular this silent partner represented American genius and industry. I am told that more than 100 separate companies furnished materials, parts or service in its construction."

The flight was not the heroic lone success of a single daring individual but the climax of the co-operative effort of an elaborately interlocked technology. The day after Coolidge's speech, Lindbergh said at another ceremony in Washington that the honor should "not go to the pilot alone but to American science and genius which had given years of study to the advancement of aeronautics." "Some things," he said, "should be taken into due consideration in connection with our flight that have not heretofore been given due weight. That is just what made this flight possible. It was not the act of a single pilot. It was the culmination of twenty years of aeronautical research and the assembling together of all that was practicable and best in American aviation." The flight, concluded Lindbergh, "represented American industry."

The worship of the machine which was embodied in the

public's response to Lindbergh exalted those very aspects which were denigrated in the celebration of the flight as the work of a heroic individual. Organization and careful method were what lay behind the flight, not individual self-sufficiency and daring romance. One magazine hailed the flight as a "triumph of mechanical engineering." "It is not to be forgotten that this era is the work not so much of brave aviators as of engineers, who have through patient and protracted effort been steadily improving the construction of airplanes." The lesson to be learned from Lindbergh's flight, thought a writer in the *Independent*, "is that the splendid human and material aspects of America need to be organized for the ordinary, matter of fact service of society." The machine meant organization, the careful rationalization of activity of a Ford assembly line, it meant planning, and, if it meant the loss of spontaneous individual action, it meant the material betterment of society. Lindbergh meant not a retreat to the free life of the frontier past but an emergence into the time when "the machine began to take first place in the public mind—the machine and the organization that made its operation possible on a large scale." A poet on this side of the matter wrote, "All day I felt the pull / Of the steel miracle." The machine was not a devilish engine which would enthrall mankind, it was the instrument which would lead to a new paradise. But the direction of history implicit in the machine was toward the future, not the past; the meaning of history was progress, not decline, and America should not lose faith in the future betterment of society. An address by a Harvard professor, picked up by the *Magazine of Business*, made all this explicit. "We commonly take Social Progress for granted," said Edwin F. Gay, "but the doctrine of Social Progress is one of the great revolutionary ideas which have powerfully affected our modern world." There was a danger, however, that the idea "may be in danger of becoming a commonplace or a butt of criticism." The speaker recognized why this might be. America was "worn and disillusioned after the Great War." Logically, contentment should have gone with so optimistic a creed, yet the American people were losing faith. So Lindbergh filled an emotional need even where a need should have been lacking. "He has come like a shining vision to revive the hope of mankind." The high ideals of faith in progress "had almost come to seem like hollow words to us—but now here he is, emblematic of heroes yet to inhabit this world. Our belief in Social Progress is justified symbolically in him."

It is a long flight from New York to Paris; it is a still longer flight from the fact of Lindbergh's achievement to the burden imposed upon it by the imagination of his time. But it is in that further flight that lies the full meaning of Lindbergh. His role was finally a double one. His flight provided an opportunity for the people to project their own emotions into his act and their emotions involved finally two attitudes toward the meaning of their own experience. One view had it that America represented a brief escape from the course of history, an emergence into a new and open world with the self-sufficient individual at its center. The other said that America represented a stage in historical evolution and that its fulfillment lay in the development of society. For one, the meaning of America lay in the past; for the other in the future. For one, the American ideal was an escape from institutions, from the forms of society, and from limitations put upon the free individual; for the other, the American ideal was the elaboration of the complex institutions which made modern society possible, an acceptance of the discipline of the machine, and the achievement of the individual within a context of which he was only a part. The two views were contradictory but both were possible and both were present in the public's reaction to Lindbergh's flight.

The Sunday newspapers announced that Lindbergh had reached Paris and in the very issue whose front pages were covered with Lindbergh's story the magazine section of the *New York Times* featured an article by the British philosopher, Bertrand Russell. The magazine had, of course, been made up too far in advance to take advantage of the news about Lindbergh. Yet, in a prophetic way, Russell's article was about Lindbergh. Russell hailed the rise to power of the United States because he felt that in the "new life that is America's" in the twentieth century "the new outlook appropriate to machinery [would] become more completely dominant than in the old world." Russell sensed that some might be unwilling to accept the machine, but "whether we like this new outlook or not," he wrote, "is of little importance." Why one might not was obvious. A society built on the machine, said Russell, meant "the diminution in the value and independence of the individual. Great enterprises tend more and more to be collective, and in an industrialized world the interference of the community with the individual must be more intense." Russell realized that while the co-operative effort involved in machine technology makes man collectively more lordly, it makes the individual more submissive. "I do not see how it is to be avoided," he concluded.

People are not philosophers. They did not see how the conflict between a machine society and the free individual was to be avoided either. But neither were they ready to accept the philosopher's statement of the problem. In Lindbergh, the people celebrated both the self-sufficient individual and the machine. Americans still celebrate both. We cherish the individualism of the American creed at the same time that we worship the machine which increasingly enforces collectivized behavior. Whether we can have both, the freedom of the individual and the power of an organized society, is a question that still haunts our minds. To resolve the conflict that is present in America's celebration of Lindbergh in 1927 is still the task of America.

2

LINDBERGH, DOS PASSOS, AND HISTORY

Remarks made in an American Studies
Seminar at Carleton College.

WHAT I wish to do, finally, is to raise the matter of the relation of literature to history, but rather than confront that general problem in abstract terms let me begin with two particular literary events, one in Scott Fitzgerald's *The Great Gatsby*, the other in John Dos Passos's *USA*. The moment in *The Great Gatsby* is that lyrical conclusion when Nick Carraway, the narrator, through whose intelligence we see the action of the book, comes to Gatsby's house and stands there and ruminates on the meaning of what has happened:

> Most of the big shore places were closed now and there were hardly any lights except the shadowy, moving glow of a ferry-boat across the Sound. And as the moon rose higher the inessential houses began to melt away until gradually I became aware of the old island here that flowered once for Dutch sailors' eyes—a fresh, green breast of the new world. Its vanished trees, the trees that had made way for Gatsby's house, had once pandered in whispers to the last and greatest of all human dreams; for a transitory enchanted moment man must have held his breath in the

presence of this continent, compelled into an aesthetic contemplation he neither understood nor desired, face to face for the last time in history with something commensurate to his capacity for wonder.

And as I sat there brooding on the old, unknown world, I thought of Gatsby's wonder when he first picked out the green light at the end of Daisy's dock. He had come a long way to this blue lawn, and his dream must have seemed so close that he could hardly fail to grasp it. He did not know that it was already behind him, somewhere back in that vast obscurity beyond the city, where the dark fields of the republic rolled on under the night.

Nick asks us at this point to identify Gatsby's story with the whole story of the discovery and the meaning of America. Gatsby's story and the meaning of his failure are somehow linked to the meaning of the American experience. The critical matter is that it is the imagery of greenness which connects Gatsby's story with the American story. Greenness becomes the physical symbol of an enchanted moment, a transitory moment when man had something commensurate to his capacity for wonder. For the discoverers, it points to a fresh and open new world; for Gatsby, to Daisy. For Nick, and for us, it points to the past, the loss of an ideal, of a vanished dream. If Jay Gatsby has failed in the pursuit of some ideal vision, so (we are made to feel) has America.

The second literary episode I would like to use is the Sacco-Vanzetti sequence in *The Big Money* at Camera Eye 49 and 50, where (in a stream of consciousness) the narrator ruminates, like Nick, on the meaning of the action.

The Camera Eye (49)

walking from Plymouth to North Plymouth through the raw air of Massachusetts Bay at each step a small cold squudge through the sole of one shoe

looking out past the gray frame houses under the robin'segg
April sky across the white dories anchored in the bottleclear
shallows across the yellow sandbars and the slaty bay ruffling to
blue to the eastward

this is where the immigrants landed the roundheads the sack-
ers of castles the kingkillers haters of oppression this is where
they stood in a cluster after landing from the crowded ship that
stank of bilge   on the beach that belonged to no one   between
the ocean that belonged to no one and the enormous forest that
belonged to no one that stretched over the hills where the deer-
tracks were up the green rivervalleys where the redskins grew
their tall corn in patches forever into the incredible west

for threehundred years the immigrants toiled into the west

and now today

walking from Plymouth to North Plymouth suddenly round
a bend in the road beyond a little pond and yellowtwigged wil-
lows hazy with green you see the Cordage   huge sheds and
buildings companyhouses all the same size all grimed the same
color a great square chimney long roofs sharp ranked squares
and oblongs cutting off the sea the Plymouth Cordage   this is
where another immigrant worked hater of oppression who
wanted a world unfenced

Another immigrant is, of course, Bart Vanzetti, an Italian
fish-peddler, yet a "founder" of Massachusetts because he believes in the "old" words grown slimy in the mouths of lawyers
and college presidents and judges. What happens to language
and the meaning of words is important for an understanding of
USA, but for the moment I want to stress the landscape of
defeat and betrayal. In the next Camera Eye, the "I" of the
novel, the consciousness which moves through the book, accepts defeat.

Camera Eye (50)

all right we are two nations
America our nation has been beaten by strangers who have
bought the laws and fenced off the meadows and cut down the
woods for pulp and turned our pleasant cities into slums and
sweated the wealth out of our people and when they want to
they hire the executioner to throw the switch

In *USA*, just as in *The Great Gatsby*, the betrayal of the
meaning of America, the corruption of words and values, is
dramatized by the movement from "a world unfenced" to the
monotonous, ranked squares of the factory which shut one off
from nature. Just as we are asked by Fitzgerald to identify
Gatsby's personal dream with the historical promise of a green
new world, so Dos Passos asks us to feel the defeat of Sacco and
Vanzetti as the defeat of America, again linked to the violation
of nature, the fencing of the meadows and the closing of the
openness of the continent. Both *The Great Gatsby* and *USA*
are sad books, books of defeat. *USA* is not only that; it is, I
think, the coldest, most mercilessly despairing book in our literature. As far apart as they are in other ways, however, both
books at climactic moments, project the sense of loss, of failure, of betrayal, through the violation of greenness, of meadows, of open, inviting, unravaged nature.

But so much has been written about *The Great Gatsby*, let
me speak more to *USA*.

USA is generally placed in the tradition of naturalism in
our literature, but naturalism is one of those large abstractions
which threatens to conceal reality rather than disclose it or define it. So, let me say that, for me, literary naturalism is not a

technique or a style, it is a point of view, a definition of the author's perspective on his subject matter. It implies some species of determinism; the human beings in the action are determined by some force outside their own personalities, whether that force be God, or biology, or the instincts of sex, or class in the Marxist version. In the United States, industrialism and the sudden passage into an urban world led in our literature to the stress on the overpowering and mastering force of the environment which reduces the individual to a function of a power, the dynamics of which lie outside the determination of human personality.

Let me emphasize a literary problem in naturalism. The subject of a work of fiction written from a naturalistic premise is that the individual does not count. You cannot have a hero in the traditional sense. You cannot have a hero who dominates the action because the whole point of naturalistic fiction is that the environment, or force, however defined, transcends and dominates the individual. The environment, in other words, is your subject; individual human beings, your characters, become simply shadows of environmental force. The point is simple and obvious enough, but the American writer, responding to a sense of the fatality of society, who wanted to write about society itself, the whole complex structure of relationships rather than about a single human being—a hero—had no developed tradition at hand to assist him in the technical problem of organizing his fiction.

Let me make the general specific by drawing your attention to two books, William Dean Howells' *A Hazard of New Fortunes* (1890) and Henry Blake Fuller's *The Cliff-Dwellers* (1893), which are attempts to solve the problem. I say attempts because both fail and it was left, I think, to Dos Passos to succeed, but Howells and Fuller are instructive because of what they fumblingly tried to do.

As one stands back from *A Hazard of New Fortunes*, its scope, when we think of Howells' other fiction, is astonishingly large. Among its many characters, there is a representative of nearly every shade of opinion in the America of its time: we find a *fin de siecle*, alienated artist, a speculating capitalist, a brash entrepreneur in the new field of mass journalism, a courtly and reactionary southern agrarian, a German anarchist, an idealistic representative of the social gospel movement, and many more. Clearly what Howells wants to do is to bring together a variety of figures, representing a variety of responses to the conditions of industrial society, and make the interplay of these figures his subject. But the only way Howells could imagine bringing this off was by the device of a literary magazine whose various contributors provide the spectrum of characters we discover.

Although there are strikes and violence in the book, though we know Dryfoos spends his days at the Stock Exchange, and though Basil March takes walks through the ghastly slums of New York, all this is rather off-stage. A literary magazine was closer to Howells' personal experience, but the device does not fit his purpose. Further, Howells' imagination did not reach beyond the sentimental, middle-class love story as a way of organizing his fiction and a number of these provide the dynamics of his plot rather than the apparent subject-matter, the way in which a number of individuals are functionally related to the anonymous and controlling forces of society.

Henry Blake Fuller's novel, *The Cliff-Dwellers*, is a much bolder attempt than Howells'. Fuller seized upon the modern expression of the complexity of a great city, William LeBaron Jenney's Home Insurance Building, our first skyscraper. With one masterful stroke, Fuller cut through the problem of how to write a novel about society itself rather than about the self in society, finding his controlling image in the anonymous forces of the economy embodied in a soaring office building whose occupants are related one to another only through the nexus of institutional roles in a complex economy.

The Cliff-Dwellers fails to become a fully successful book because Fuller is unable to manage his structural device. Despite his assertion that he will not wander far or often from inside his building, Clifton, by the sixth chapter he begins to wander away from what should have remained his controlling strategy and by the end of the novel we have spent more pages away from Clifton than in it. Like Howells', his book becomes a love-story, the dominant convention for the organization of the novel in American fiction unless one shipped aboard a whaler or lit out on a raft.

We can now better appreciate what Howells and Fuller were trying to do, that is, to create a structural device for a novel about society, because we can look back at their problem from the vantage point of the novel which solved the technical problem by a brilliant *tour de force*, John Dos Passos's *USA*. *USA* is, as I have said already, an icy, despairing book and it has been criticized because it presents no character with whom we can identify. The observation is a valid one but used for a mistaken conclusion. There are no people in the book, only automata walking stiffly to the beat of Dos Passos's despair. But the point of the novel, as we like to say, is that there are no individuals in American society. Dos Passos's "hero" is USA, that monstrous abstraction, Society itself. Society is the hero—or the villain—of the piece. In Dos Passos's vision, society has become depersonalized and abstract and there are no human beings, no human relations, in it. The style, as Alfred Kazin put it, is like some "conveyor belt carrying Americans through some vast Ford plant of the human spirit." As if on feeder lines in an assembly plant, lives connect one with another, but no human connection is made. We have the staccato juxtaposition of snatches of songs and headlines, historical figures and fictional characters, all observed by the passive eye of the camera, all making a bitter montage of nothingness.

Dos Passos is a difficult man to talk about. In 1932, he was one of those who signed a public statement supporting the presidential candidacy of William Z. Foster, the Communist

candidate for President; twenty years later, in 1952, he supported Robert A. Taft against Eisenhower for the Republican
nomination and he now writes for Mr. Buckley's *National Review*. The shift from left to right may look contradictory, but
I think is not. Dos Passos is a man always opposed to power. He
saw power in the hands of capitalistic businessmen in the 30s
and was, therefore, on the radical left; he sees power today in
the hands of liberal intellectuals, allied with labor, and is now
on the conservative right. I would, of course, stress the fact
that Dos Passos is responding to his own sense of where power
lies in our society; we can make sense out of his position, but to
accept his position would require an analysis into the accuracy
of his location of power. But Dos Passos has always been a
negative function of power; that is, one finds him always at the
opposite pole of where he conceives power to be. In this sense,
he is more an anarchist, and always was, than a socialist or a
conservative.

What Dos Passos achieved in *USA* was the creation of a
form appropriate to the theme of the overwhelming, impersonal force of society, a structure which would carry the
meaning of the primacy of society and make the anonymous
processes of society the very stuff of a fictional world. As an
aside, I might say that if the student of American culture, or
American civilization, assumes that there is a relationship between literature and history, he must take that assumption as
seriously as it deserves and examine the way in which history
enters not just the overt subject matter of literature but is there
in language, imagery and, to penetrate to the heart of the matter, the very ordering of the literary object, its very structure.

The ultimate despair we confort in *USA* relates closely to
what happens to language in the book. From the preface where
the voice of the Camera Eye sections first identifies the meaning of America with American speech and the meaning of
words, there is a constant concern, dramatically as well as explicitly, with the corruption of language. As we have seen, the

betrayal of the promise of America is that words have grown slimy in the mouths of the ruling classes who have perverted old ideals. At the end of *The Big Money*, coming appropriately after William Randolph Hearst, is Richard Ellsworth Savage, the advertising man, corrupted like everyone else by the big money, who creates a campaign to sell the quack nostrums of a patent medicine fraud and to fend off pure food and drug legislation by appealing to American individualism and self-reliance and self-help. The meaning of America has been lost because all the words have been turned inside out. The last Camera Eye section ends before the biography of Insull and one has to see the page to catch the connection:

we have only words against

Power Superpower

Not only have words lost their meaning, they have lost their efficacy. They prove incapable of stinging people into awareness. Power Superpower finally overwhelms even the language which creates the identity of America and if Dos Passos could say "we stand defeated," the defeat was particularly keen for the writer, the man who depends on words and his belief in the efficacy of language to sustain his personal identity. I would even speculate wildly and suggest that the vision of society Dos Passos presents in *USA* was a defeat for him personally and that is perhaps why he seems, to me at least, less estimable a writer after *USA* than before it. He had ceased to believe in the power of words.

Dos Passos comes to the same conclusion as Fitzgerald. The meaning of America, its initial promise, has been lost as Americans have gone whoring after false gods. The potentiality of America, the possibility of creating the good society, has been lost as Americans have fastened their ambitions on some meretricious goal, Daisy or the Big Money. Not only do both see a perversion of the ideal meaning of America, both associate that

ideal with greenness and meadows and the vast fields of the
republic and place the historical possibility of realizing that
ideal somewhere in the past, in some irrecoverable moment
whose memory haunts the meaninglessness of a debased and
sordid present. As I said at the outset, both are sad books, one a
mournful threnody, the other outraged despair.

My quick reference to *The Great Gatsby* and *USA* is to
suggest that they are related because both participate in a common way of apprehending the meaning of American history,
and this meaning is not a literary matter but a cultural matter.
To amplify my point, I would like to use here a book, a superb
book, I happen to think, by Leo Marx, *The Machine in the
Garden* (Oxford). The title and the cover get the theme rather
well: the sudden intrusion of a machine into a green landscape.
Almost twenty-five years ago now, when F. O. Matthiessen
wrote *American Renaissance*, dealing with those remarkable
five years from 1850 to 1855 which encompass *Representative
Men, The Scarlet Letter, The House of the Seven Gables,
Moby-Dick, Pierre, Walden* and *Leaves of Grass*, he pointed to
the book he was not writing. The book he was writing concerned itself primarily with *"what* these books were as works
of art," but Matthiessen pointed to another kind of treatment
which would concern itself with why this sudden outburst of
literary energy took place when it did. Unless one thinks that
acts of the human imagination are random and unrelated to
their historical moment, one can ask the question what was
happening in society which might make us better understand
why a literary renaissance occurred when it did. I think Leo
Marx has written the book F. O. Matthiessen saw but did not
choose to write.

Leo Marx constructs his book around the repeated appearance, in literary and popular culture, of a typical event, an event implicit in nearly every major work of the American imagination, but especially in the middle years of the nineteenth century among the writers of the American Renaissance. The event is the sudden intrusion of a machine into a green and pastoral setting. Mr. Marx begins with Hawthorne, but *Walden* is perhaps the most readily available example. In the chapter on "Sounds," where Thoreau is sitting in a timeless moment of self-contemplation, on the alert for the eternal, we get the shattering intrusion of the railroad engine and the moment of stillness and quiet and timelessness, bordering on the miraculous, is gone.

To leap in time, if you think of *The Education of Henry Adams*, you will remember in the chapter on Quincy when Adams describes the loss of the eternal verities of his eighteenth century heritage, he says that in 1844 when he was six years old "the old universe was thrown into the ash-heap and a new one created." Adams and his eighteenth century world were, he writes, "cut apart—separated forever," and he carefully lists the forces which traumatically expelled him from his old world: the railroad, the steamship, and the telegraph.

Since Mr. Marx has written his book, I leave it to you to discover how pervasive the pattern is in the American imagination, especially in the middle of our nineteenth century, the "take-off" period, to use W. W. Rostow's metaphor, in our economic history from an agrarian economy of self-subsistence to a self-sustaining economy of industrial power built upon the machine.

To come back to the question asked by F. O. Matthiessen to which I think Leo Marx's book is an answer: what happened in American society was the sudden transition from one kind of world to another, each with its different symbols, its different dynamics, its different heroes. From the simple world of Jefferson's agrarian republic we move to a world of cities and machines and power. The moment of transition brings two radically different worlds into conflict and arrays them dramatically one against the other. The moment may be a difficult one for society, but it seems to be an auspicious one for the literary imagination. History presents the writer with the very stuff of conflict and drama. One thinks of Theodore Spencer's account in *Shakespeare and the Nature of Man* where he accounts for the English Renaissance in comparable terms; Shakespeare's age was suspended between two worlds, divided in its cosmology between Ptolemy and Copernicus, in its politics between anointed kings and Machiavelli, in its psychology between religious injunction and Montaigne's naturalism. The prevalence of Southern writers in our fiction today, so Allen Tate has argued, derives from a comparable fact, that the South is still emotionally committed to a social order in conflict with a new way of life which challenges the old at every point. So these peaks in the history of the imagination seem to come at moments of deep and pervasive shifts in historical direction in a culture, and Leo Marx has suggested that the dominant shift in our culture has been from an image of America organized around a green and pastoral landscape to an image of the artificial landscape of technology and the machine.

Perhaps the most influential reading of the meaning of the American experience, Frederick Jackson Turner's frontier interpretation of American history, is involved in the same polarity which Marx discovers in our best imaginative writers. Henry Nash Smith, in *Virgin Land*, has made us see how deeply Turner was divided between two ways of reading American history. One view had it that the meaning of America was the advance of civilization into a rude and savage continent and that the history of the United States is a record of progress from simple, primitive beginnings to an advanced, complex, civilized society. That interpretation is present in Turner's famous essays, but it is an opposite emphasis for which Turner is famous and remembered. Turner's "thesis," put bluntly at first in his essay on the significance of the frontier in 1893, was that "the existence of an area of free land, its continuous recesssion, and the advance of American settlement westward, explain American development." Turner asserted:

> American development has exhibited not merely advance along a single line, but a return to primitive conditions on a continually advancing frontier line, and a new development for that area. American development has been continually beginning over again on the frontier. This perennial rebirth, this fluidity of American life, this expansion westward with its new opportunities, its continuous touch with the simplicity of primitive society, furnish the forces dominating American character. The true point of view in the history of this nation is not the Atlantic Coast, it is the Great West.

For Turner, the promise of American life implied the constant opportunity to escape from history, from society, to go backward in time to a new beginning. But it is important to remember the moment in which Turner spoke. The frontier was closed. History had, so to speak, caught up with the frontier. The American landscape now displayed factories and machines and great cities and people no longer shaped by the experience of pioneer life. There was a pessimistic fatalism in Turner's interpretation of our history. If the democratic values and the meaning of America had arisen from experience with a succession of frontiers, then the end of the frontier implied the weakening of democracy and a degeneration in American values.

Without going further with Turner, you can see how one might say that *The Great Gatsby* and *USA* are "Turnerian" books. America, meant to be the garden of the world, has become a wasteland, its landscape dominated by the factories of the machine. The image of the garden as a symbol of human felicity is not, of course, an American phenomenon; one need only remember the Bible and the long tradition of pastoralism in literature. What was an American phenomenon was belief in the possibility of realizing in history, in time, what had always been and had remained a utopian and literary figure. That is, with the settlement of America many people believed that in the new world it might be possible to make actual in history what had theretofore been a dream, that is, a society of a pastoral middle ground between nasty, brutish, and savage nature and decadent, corrupt, and oppressive civilization. At least Jefferson seems to have thought so. We may now think the notion sentimental, but the emotion still moves our collective memory and it is from this emotion that *The Great Gatsby* and *USA* derive much of their power. *USA* looked like a Marxist book to many of its contemporaries, but it is not. It is an American book in the agrarian tradition which sees the defeat of America in the victory of a mechanized society worshipping power and money over a society of simplicity devoted to the needs of human beings and individual felicity. As in the story of Jay Gatsby, the pastoral motive is only ironic. It stands for something lost, for paradise lost.

In the broad sense in which I have been talking so far, one can then assert a relation between literature and history. One can see how our best writers are involved in a widely shared, hence cultural, response to the meaning of our national experience. But that is a terribly general and rather distant relationship. I think we can bring the relation of literature to history closer to home by considering the article I have written which you have read, "The Meaning of Lindbergh's Flight."

Since you have read it, you may find some interest in how I came to write it. A university where I once taught was involved in a weekly TV show, and a senior professor asked me to give him a hand on two programs dealing with the 20s and the 30s. The bulk of the material on the 20s dealt with what was called "the flight of the expatriates." I suggested that there were two flights in the 20s and that it would be interesting to see what the public response was to Lindbergh's flight and discover how it compared or contrasted with the reasons of the expatriates. I worked out the idea but the producer kept chopping away at the Lindbergh material until finally there was no more than a flash of a film clip of Lindbergh's plane, *The Spirit of St. Louis*.

In my original script, I had some business about the fact that when Lindbergh landed at Le Bourget he was taken to Ambassador Herrick's home where the reporters finally caught up with him. Among them was a diligent *Herald-Trib* reporter who described the bedroom in which Lindbergh sat eating a sandwich and drinking milk and talking. On the bedside table lay a copy of Ernest Hemingway's *The Sun Also Rises*. Now, for a show about the flight of the expatriates and the flight of Lindbergh, to have the arcs of the two flights connect in Paris that way is perfect; sometimes history delights the historian this way and cooperates fully.

After we had shot the TV show on tape, I was still muttering about the loss of all that Lindbergh material when the producer remarked that an audience would not buy all that jazz. Jazz? Yes, he said. Who is going to believe all that made-up stuff about Hemingway's novel and Lindbergh in the same room and the two flights coming together? He thought I had simply made up the whole Lindbergh sequence! I told him it was all "fact," as historians like to say, but he was still dubious. He thought intellectuals would fabricate anything to make a point. Most depressing man I ever met.

The Lindbergh material continued to nag at me. So I did the article the next summer. I wanted to call it "The Public Meaning of Lindbergh's Flight," but the word "public" got lost somewhere in the process.

Like my book, *Andrew Jackson: Symbol for an Age*, the piece on Lindbergh is an attempt to get at the public mind; that

is, through a study of the themes implicit in the public celebration of the event, Lindbergh's flight, to get at what was on
society's mind. What I found is what you have read, namely,
that Lindbergh's public used the occasion of his flight to project
two different readings of the meaning of American history.
The two, contradictory one to the other, existed uneasily side
by side and I separate them out for purposes of analysis. Lindbergh's role was finally a double one. His flight provided an
opportunity for the people to project their own emotions onto
his act and their emotions finally involved two attitudes toward
the meaning of their own experience. One view, emphasizing
the fact that Lindbergh flew alone and by naming him a pioneer, had it that America represented a brief escape from the
course of history, an emergence into a new and open world
with the self-sufficient individual at its center. The other view,
emphasizing the machine and the elaborate technology which
made it possible, said that America represented a stage in historical evolution, "progress," and that America's fulfillment lay
in the development of a powerful and complex society. For
one, the meaning of America lay in the past; for the other in
the future. For one, the American ideal was an escape from
institutions, from the forms of society, and from the limitations society imposes upon the self; for the other, the American ideal was the elaboration of the complex social institutions
which make modern society possible, an acceptance of the discipline of the machine and the enjoyment of its advantages, the
achievement of the individual, not alone, but as a functioning
part of society. The two views were contradictory, but both
were possible and both were present in the public's reaction to
Lindbergh's flight.

You will have arrived by yourselves at my conclusion. All I
wish to point out is that in the emotions which the public projected onto Lindbergh's flight in 1927, one discovers the same
conflict in the reading of the meaning of American history
which is the stuff of Fitzgerald's and Dos Passos's fiction. In the

ephemeral popular material about Lindbergh, the problem is not clearly articulated and not resolved one way or the other. The function of the historian is to disclose the polarity which is implicitly there. That is the function of an intellectual: to bring to the level of consciousness the themes which are implicit in the culture of his time. It is also what an artist does and that is one reason I think literature a good way of entering the thought of the past.

I came to be interested in the meaning of Lindbergh's flight because of my interest in the writers of the 20s, Hemingway, Faulkner, Fitzgerald, Dos Passos. For me, and this admission may get me in trouble with historians, the discovery of an historical problem generally comes through the reading of literature. I mean that the formulation of a question which I ask of non-literary material generally comes from reading literary material.

Now every historian, when he looks at the past, has to have some question in mind; otherwise he has no criterion of relevance for the infinite mass of facts which stare him in the face. When historians write about history as an art, they generally have a simple relation in mind, something like writing well or dramatically. But the historian treats the past the way the artist constructs an imaginary world. The historian throws reality into shape, he gives it order so we can comprehend it and make sense out of the world in which we live.

Let me use a simple example. If when you are, say, nineteen years old you write an autobigraphy, you would recount those events which make sense out of where you are at nineteen, say at college. There might be a greater or lesser degree of sophistication in your analysis of how you came to be where you are, but your biography would attempt to discover a pattern of meaning which would make your present seem a part of your past. Now, when you came to be forty years old, unless you were so unlucky as not to change at all, and wrote another autobiography, the odds are considerable that a different sequence of events *before age nineteen* would enter into it; for the simple reason that time would have passed, you would have changed, and other "facts" would be more important in the formulation of your self-identity, your sense of yourself.

This homely example, if pursued, will land us in a thicket of thorny philosophical questions about self and identity and sub-jectivism. To talk this way leads people to think one means we are free to think what we want to think, but history does not tolerate that kind of caprice. As William James says some-where about reality: ignore it and it will break your neck. There are fellow-practitioners all too happy to remind you of neglected evidence and one must always consult the evidence with skepticism about his own intuitions, however derived. When I did the essay on Lindbergh, and before it was pub-lished, I had a rare opportunity. I was teaching a seminar with Robert Spiller at the University of Pennsylvania and he al-lowed me to turn the students loose on the material and the results were confirmatory. More interestingly, we had in that seminar a student from India and a student from France. From what native papers there were in the Philadelphia area, each did a short essay on how France and India responded to Lind-bergh's flight. What Americans saw in the flight was absent. The French celebrated it as a gay example of the sporting life, the carefree abandon of youth, the grandiloquent gesture of daring. The Indians used it to cudgel England, to suggest the decadence of Europe and, hence, the decline of the British Em-pire. They simply attributed Lindbergh's success to his mem-bership in a new, young country, and went on from there to say the future lay with the new nations of the world, such as India, of course.

These two examples point clearly to the fact that there was nothing coercive about the event itself, nothing coercive about its meaning. Lindbergh flew the Atlantic. There is a fact. But the meaning of that fact lies in the meaning imputed to the fact to make sense out of it. In America, as I say in the article itself

and have already said here, the meaning embodied two conflicting interpretations, one organized about nature, one about the
machine. The public, I am trying to argue, was involved in its
response to Lindbergh's flight in the very subject of Dos Passos's novel, *USA*.

Student: I was wondering about the relationship of the
hero and the ideas which are current: which makes which?

This gets us into the problem I pointed to: how free are we
to think what we want to think. In Lindbergh's case there was
a considerable degree of latitude because he was so taciturn and
left it to others to talk about the meaning of the flight or his
intentions. Also he was clean-cut; he didn't smoke and didn't
run around with girls. He looked and acted like the all-Ameri-
can boy. Most importantly, he said "No" to the big money. He
made money eventually through shares in Curtis-Wright and
opportunities in the aviation industry, but he did not cash in;
he did not take the quick buck. It was offered to him. Some
American businessmen made up a huge purse and offered it to
him, no strings attached, so he would not have to endorse
products and do sordid things like that. But he didn't take the
money because he had no intention of cheapening his flight by
exploiting it commercially. You will notice that in *USA* Lindbergh appears only fleetingly in two of the newsreels in *The
Big Money*. He runs counter to Dos Passos's point (although
I would stress again that Lindbergh's public, in their reaction
to his flight was grappling with Dos Passos's point). I have always wondered whether Charley Anderson in *The Big Money*
is not a conscious inversion by Dos Passos of Charles A. Lindbergh: the names, of course; both fliers; both Minnesota boys.
Except that Charley Anderson is, in his personal attributes, the
opposite of Lindbergh.

So Lindbergh was close to what society ideally admired,
and his close-mouthed nature made it easier to interpret his

flight without embarrassment from him. But that seems to me not so important and perhaps I should speak more directly to what I think goes on in a phenomenon like the public celebration of Lindbergh. Society has certain values; some individual or some event captures attention; society projects its values onto the event and then sees the event as verification, as proof, of the meaning imputed to it. For example, Lindbergh grew up on a farm; accounts of his life then place him in an idyllic world, close to nature, removed from the corruptions of city and society: Lindbergh becomes a symbol of the empowering force of nature. But he also flew an airplane and said, "We," not "I." On this side of his exploit, suggestions of Prometheus and the marvels of technology cluster about him. The public, in other words, imputes meaning to Lindbergh's flight and then Lindbergh's function is to affirm the truth of these meanings by his success. In Lindbergh's case, two different evaluations are involved and, analytically, they are irreconcilable; if we run either interpretation to its logical conclusion, it negates the other. But I doubt if any society has a single, coherent, one-dimensional system of values; there is always a tension, a potential polarity, between opposing ideals. A definition of reality as a field of tensions between poles which define each other seems closer, at least to my own experience, than the frame of mind which says it has to be one or the other.

Since we are talking generally about the theory behind such an article as my own on Lindbergh, perhaps I should mention the book which most influenced me and the way I look at ideas and attitudes in history: Bronislaw Malinowski, the functional anthropologist, and his little book, *Myth in Primitive Psychology*. Malinowski points out that a society's beliefs needs sanctions; they need miracles to prove them true. If a society is going to believe in its ideals, it must believe they are efficacious, that they produce results. Reality is interpreted in terms of cultural norms, not to verify reality but to verify the norms, to validate them. Malinowski has a wonderful phrase in which he says that the myths and symbols of society provide "a dog-matic backbone" to culture.

I think that even in our modern, rational culture much the same sort of process is still at work. I am not saying that values are nothing but wish-fulfillment, but I am saying that when people deeply cherish a way of looking at the world they will see the world in that way, proving to themselves the validity of their beliefs.

Question: But isn't there a danger in books like yours and Marx's and in articles like the one you wrote on Lindbergh, a danger of *imposing* a pattern on history?

Yes, that's the beast that haunts all artifice. But let me say what I think happens. As historian, you are dealing with a mass of disparate material about things and events and you are try-ing to make sense out of it. Your first responsibility, I think, is to abide quietly that anxious period of muddled suspension when you are not quite sure what it is you are doing. If you are willing, though, to immerse yourself in your material long enough, and if you are lucky, a pattern will begin to emerge; you will start to find lines of connection. Once you start to see how things hang together, then you can move fairly quickly and dispense with all that material which the historian blithely names "irrelevant." I do not think that the pattern, the shape, is there in the evidence; the pattern in the historian's account of history is *his* pattern. He creates it. But the pattern is poten-tially there in reality.

Let me give you a better example, rather than talk about history and meaning in the abstract. When I was a graduate student at the University of Minnesota, there was a scientist there doing research on the function of the adrenal cortex in mice, observing responses to multiple sensory stimuli. His scien-tific colleague was a European and their work together was like an international game of chess; that is, the scientist at Minnesota would run a series of experiments and summarize them by a graphic description of his results and ship them off to his friend in Europe, in Austria, I believe. By repeating the experience under similar controlled conditions, the partner in Europe would verify his results. Which is what we mean by the objectivity of the scientist: that is, not that the scientist himself is objective, but that science as an institution is objective because it is governed by public rules of verification. This process of exchange and testing back and forth would, of course, take some months. Finally, the two collaborators published an article on their work and this brings me to the point of my story.

A few days after publication, I had luncheon with the scientist at Minnesota. Himself a European by birth, he was a precise and proper gentleman and the day I met him he was severely upset. He had that day received a letter from a biochemist in Belgium who, having seen the joint article by him and his collaborator, wrote to say that innocent of their work he had been doing comparable work and sent them the results of some of his experiments. My acquaintance at Minnesota was visibly upset because, as he said, "This man is a fraud." Since I knew how long it took him to check the work of his own colleague, I asked him how he could possibly arrive at so serious a judgment so quickly. For a simple reason.

Imagine a graph with a sinuous line drawn upon it. That was, say, the kind of "statement" one scientist sent the other; the graphic line represents the truth; that is, a statement about the behavior of reality under certain conditions. Now what that line is, as any scientist knows, is a symbolic, shorthand representation of a multitude of particular observations. The particulars, as recorded experimentally, fall around and about that elegant line. The line is not a record of reality; the line abstracts from the multitudinous particulars of reality and presents the modal distribution of the message received in answer to a carefully framed question.

Now, the communication received from the unknown biochemist in Belgium presented data and a graphic description of that data which came very close to the graph presented in the published article, so close to the graph presented in the published article that my scientist friend knew at a single glance that they had to be forged and false. He did not expect that reality would ever conform to his symbolic statement of reality; he did not even expect reality to come very close. As soon as it did, he looked somewhere else for a reason, to the untrustworthiness of his correspondent, because he never expected brute nature to conform to his ideal description of it. So it proved to be. His correspondent did prove to be a fraud.

Now, when a historian describes reality, he too makes a construct of the evidence available to him and you can always find many things that seem to have no relevance to his construction. For example, I would not imagine handing my book on Jackson to someone interested in anything other than the popular ideology of the time. For example, when George Rogers Taylor writes about the transportation revolution, it would never occur to me to say querulously to him, "But you never discuss the ideas of nature, providence and will, George." Nor would he read my book and protest that I don't say how many miles of track were laid down. There are objections as well as facts which are irrelevant. Irrelevant in the sense Henry James has in mind in his preface to *Portrait of a Lady* when he says you must give the writer his *donnée*, his given, his subject matter. Look at the world from his perspective and then you can quarrel about the ordering of the evidence, the reading of material, the weighing of evidence.

So when you ask whether one *imposes* a pattern on reality, on history, I think that is a false way to put the question. One exposes himself to his evidence; he discovers a potential order and realizes it. That is what I meant when I said the historian throws the past into shape. He constructs the pattern which allows reality to make its meaning evident. A dangerous position, I know, but no less dangerous than the position of the historian who thinks he is the amanuensis of time. Of course, no historian thinks that. . . . Well, I'll take that back, I do know a couple who *say* that the job of the historian is to put down in chronological sequence every fact he can get his hands on. You couldn't do it for a day! Think of all the facts you could find from 1815 to 1845 which is the period of my book on Jackson. The notion that the historian records the sequence of events derives from a simple-minded Baconian notion of experience that if you put all the facts down the meaning will (like a jack-in-the-box) just pop up. It's the ghost-in-the-file-cards theory of history, a decerebrated view of the nature of history in which meaning exists outside the minds of men.

But, then, I remember a lecture once at the University of Minnesota by a great teacher, Samuel Holt Monk, lecturing on Pope and eighteenth century British aesthetics, when he was talking away, looking out the window, and suddenly turned to see all those heads down and all those pencils going and blurted out, "For God's sake, don't write any of this down; I don't know if it's true."

3

HISTORY AND LITERATURE:
THREE NOVELS

I · Nature and Civilization:
James Fenimore Cooper

THE LITERARY reputation of James Fenimore Cooper has had a various career. In his own day his American contemporaries hailed him as the "American Scott," a designation that irritated Cooper by its implication that he was a derivative writer. No writer takes kindly to such a suggestion, but Cooper's fellow Americans meant it as the highest praise. Proud of being Americans, yet culturally self-conscious of the thinness of the aesthetic achievement of the New World, they meant to do high honor to Cooper by suggesting a comparison with Sir Walter Scott. Americans were, in other words, ambivalent in their bumptious nationalism; Europe was still their standard, whether they rejected it or promised to surpass it. The difficulty Americans have had in understanding the meaning of their national experience in relation to the Old World has proved also to be the theme that has given Cooper's writing enduring worth in our literary tradition.

Yet, before his place in the American tradition was firmly established, Cooper's reputation at first declined to that of being a writer of children's books, a curious fate that also overtook *The Adventures of Huckleberry Finn* and *Moby-Dick*. Like Twain and Melville, Cooper has kept a youthful audience; and the adventures of Natty Bumppo, the hero of the Leatherstocking series, are probably still a part of the reading experience of many young Americans. For that audience *The Last of the Mohicans* and *The Deerslayer* are the important books. Then in the twentieth century, as part of the movement toward defining the roots of our national culture, scholarship rediscovered Cooper, but it was not Cooper as writer of fiction but Cooper as social critic and observer of his times who emerged as important in this reassessment. Emphasis here fell more on Cooper's social criticism in such books as *The American Democrat* (1838) or on the travel books, which incorporated much social commentary, *Notions of the Americans by a Traveling Bachelor* (1828) and *Home as Found* (1838).

Until recently then, we have had two Coopers, one the writer of adventure stories, the romances of the woods, the other the conservative Jeffersonian gentleman troubled by the dangers of an uncouth democracy. Only now have we begun to see that the two are one, that is, that Cooper's social and political attitudes are at the very heart of his fiction and account for both its strength and its weakness. In this contemporary re-evaluation the Leatherstocking series is once again the center of interest, but such novels as *The Last of the Mohicans* seem far less important than *The Pioneers* and *The Prairie*.

The pattern of rise and fall in a writer's reputation may seem to suggest pure caprice on the part of his audience. Robert Frost, talking about poets today, used to ask puckishly, "Whose stock is up? Whose stock is down?"—as if reputation were the consequence of insiders' speculation. But the changing responses to Cooper's writing can better be understood in broader terms. He quickly ceased to be taken as a serious writer because the criteria of judgment changed markedly in America soon after he wrote. Realism, an ambiguous but necessary word for a tendency in writing, provided no categories to take account of Cooper's effects. In 1903 Frank Norris, in *The Responsibilities of the Novelist*, put the realist's case against Cooper: "Cooper, you will say, was certainly American in attitude and choice of subject; none more so. None less so, none less so. As a novelist he is saturated with the romance of the contemporary English storytellers. It is true that his background is American. But his heroes and heroines talk like the characters out of Bulwer in their most vehement moods, while his Indians stalk through all the melodramatic tableaux of Byron, and declaim in the periods of the border nobleman in the pages of Walter Scott." What had once been a comparison in praise had, by the end the nineteenth century, become a term of opprobrium. Literary realism, despite protestations about its giving us the facts of life, derived from literary conventions, but the conventions were those of Balzac and Zola, a commitment to the ordinary and everyday in life and an adherence to plain speech. Mark Twain, part of whose great achievement was to make vernacular speech the stuff of great literature, had made the same point against Cooper in 1895 in an article in the *North American Review*, "Fenimore Cooper's Literary Offenses." The rules governing literary art, said Twain, "require that when a personage talks like an illustrated, gilt-edged, tree-calf, hand-tooled, seven-dollar Friendship's Offering in the beginning of a paragraph, he shall not talk like a Negro minstrel in the end of it. But this rule is flung down and danced upon" by Cooper. Cooper's tales of Indians and pioneers, what Twain called the "broken-twig" school of fiction, so outraged Twain that he parodied them hilariously; they violated his own practice and program for literature. Only children, and not too intelligent children at that, seemed Cooper's proper audience. "Cooper's eye," said Twain, "was splendidly inaccurate."

But there is a kind of accuracy and a dimension of reality that differ from a reality defined by plausibility of detail and adherence to the rhythm of the spoken language. D. H. Lawrence saw this clearly. Discussing the Leatherstocking series, Lawrence wrote: "Now let me put aside my impatience at the unreality of this vision, and accept it as a wish-fulfillment vision, a kind of yearning myth. Because it seems to me that the things in Cooper that make one so savage, when one compares them with actuality, are perhaps, when one considers them as presentations of deep subjective desire, real in their own way, and almost prophetic." The "yearning myth" Lawrence glimpsed beneath the bungled surface of Cooper's fiction was the dream of a new relation between man and man that first required a "cruel sloughing" of the past, to be followed by an emergence into an unencumbered new life. "The Leatherstocking novels create the myth of this new relation. And they go backwards, from old age to golden youth. That is the true myth of America. She starts old, old, wrinkled and writhing in an old skin. And there is a gradual sloughing of the old skin, towards a new youth. It is the myth of America."

Lawrence is making an extraordinary claim for Cooper. He is saying no less than that Cooper somehow touched the quick of experience in America and fashioned in his stories the myth that gives shape and coherence to the meaning of American culture. If, with Norris and Twain, we are so put off by Cooper's stilted language and improbable events that we cannot for the moment suspend our disbelief, we will deny ourselves an awareness of what Lawrence glimpsed and recent critics, especially Henry Nash Smith, have revealed fully to be the reason for Cooper's present importance. James Fenimore Cooper has survived in our literary canon, has been rescued from children and social historians, because his fiction is an im-

aginative embodiment of a pervasive attitude in our culture toward the meaning of life in the New World.

George Santayana once remarked that we are condemned
to live dramatically in a world that is not dramatic. We try to
make sense, as we say, of experience, whether personally as
biography or collectively as history. From the beginning there
were two ways to read the meaning of the American experience. As the first settlers set out from the Old World to the
New, they were both leaving an old home and seeking a new
one. Universally, the voyage or the trip has lent itself to easy
translation into the metaphor of the quest where the physical
journey becomes a symbolic quest for the meaning of it all.
One thinks of the wandering tribes of Israel in the Bible,
Homer's Ulysses, Bunyan's Pilgrim, and Don Quixote. The
metaphor is probably basic to shared human experience, but it
has been especially characteristic of the American version;
from Whitman tramping the open road to Saul Bellow's *The
Adventures of Augie March*, the best of American literature
has been organized around metaphors of setting out and venturing forth into the new and unknown. Until the twentieth
century the metaphor hardly seemed metaphor at all; it conformed so closely to our historical experience that it seemed a
fair description of the American reality.

But the meaning of the journey out of the Old World into
the New always had a certain doubleness to it, an inevitable
ambivalence. One valuation had it that the movement westward into a virgin continent meant the rejection of Europe and
all it represented. In this reading of our collective experience,
Europe stood for the snobbery of social classes, feudalism, rule
by irresponsible aristocrats and kings, the craft of priests, institutional complexity, and social decadence; whereas the New
World stood for the equality of all men, the abolition of social
distinction, freedom, spontaneity, simplicity, and vigor. In
short, Europe stood for the corruption of advanced civilization

and America stood for the beneficence of nature. Yet at the same time, there was another way to read experience. Here, America meant the advance of the best of civilization, choice seed sifted from the Old World for planting in the New, as the Puritans put it, into a raw and savage continent. In this reading the American venture meant the progress of reason, order, enlightenment, and cultivation, an extension of civilization into a wild, untamed, savage continent where law was absent and barbarism posed a constant danger to the achievements of human order. Not only were the terms of evaluation different; they pointed in different directions. For the first the geographical *locus* of value was West, the frontier and, beyond it, the unfallen innocence of an Edenic world; for the second the point of reference was East, ultimately toward Europe and a developed society of urbanity and sophistication.

Such a stark formulation suggests an "either-or" appraisal, and we may ask impatiently, Which was it? But the question is a false one historically and may be a false one humanly. Americans saw the matter of their experience both ways; that is, they affirmed their culture at one and the same time both as a return to the simple harmony of the pastoral ideal as well as an advance in the achievements of high civilization. The late Professor Perry Miller explored this doubleness in the Puritans' conception of the meaning of their "errand into the wilderness," and the same ambivalence permeates American history from the politics of Thomas Jefferson to the historical writing of Frederick Jackson Turner. It even helps to account for the persistent nostalgia of our advanced industrial and technological society in the twentieth century. It is from the field of energy defined by the poles of Nature and Civilization that Cooper's power ultimately derives.

The Leatherstocking series, of which *The Prairie* is the narrative conclusion, was published by Cooper in the years from 1823 to 1841, but the chronology of publication does not fol-

low the chronology of the narrative. If we place the two chro-
nologies side by side, we see what Lawrence meant when he
said that the Leatherstocking series, like the sequence of American historical experience, goes backward in time.

Publication Sequence	Narrative Sequence
The Pioneers (1823)	*The Deerslayer*
The Last of the Mohicans	*The Pathfinder*
(1826)	*The Last of the Mohicans*
The Prairie (1827)	*The Pioneers*
The Pathfinder (1840)	*The Prairie*
The Deerslayer (1841)	

The series is held together by the presence of a central
hero, Natty Bumppo, called according to his age either Deerslayer or Leatherstocking; the period covered is from his youth
in the early eighteenth century to his death on the prairies in
1806. It is important that Cooper first imagined his hero at the
precise moment when his simple code of natural justice ran
athwart the institutionalized code of social justice, a conflict
that defines the essential plot of *The Pioneers*. In that novel
Natty and his Indian friend, Chingachgook, are old and living
on the edge of advancing society, whose central spokesman is
Judge Marmaduke Temple. Natty breaks man-made law, and
Judge Temple, even while recognizing that by the standard of
a higher law Natty is innocent, must, as the standard-bearer of
social order, sentence him to jail. *The Pioneers* closes with
Natty's escape from society and his flight westward into the
setting sun to live out his last days, where we find him in *The
Prairie*.

The *Prairie* is a difficult novel to read, if only because at
first glance its plot seems to make no sense at all. The device of
an abduction by which Cooper transports his socially superior
characters, Inez and Captain Middleton, into the wilderness
runs into the common-sense objection that Abiram White, the

kidnapper, is hardly going to be able to collect a ransom for Inez from her parents if he cannot contact them; every mile his party proceeds farther west makes that increasingly improbable. Only in comparison with this central flaw in the plot do other matters seem less troublesome, such as Cooper's handiness in summoning up trees on the treeless Great Plains and the casual ease with which he disposes of escapes from the Indians. But if in Mark Twain's masterpiece, *The Adventures of Huckleberry Finn*, we have learned not to be bothered by the discrepancy of Huck and Jim floating passively farther and farther into slave territory when they are supposed to be fleeing for Jim's freedom to free territory, perhaps we can learn to allow Cooper the same freedom. Henry Nash Smith has suggested that Cooper "treats the portion of the Plains in which the action takes place as if it were an Elizabethan stage, a neutral space where any character may be brought at a moment's notice without arousing in the audience a desire to have the entrance accounted for." Cooper rather suffers in the comparison, but the suggestion frees us to see what *The Prairie* is really about.

The Prairie is a threnody over the passing of something fine and heroic in American life. From the moment that Leatherstocking appears framed in the setting sun before the startled eyes of Ishmael Bush and his band ("The figure was colossal, the attitude musing and melancholy . . ."), to the calm of his philosophic death at the end, *The Prairie* is about the passing of an ideal natural order before the inevitable advance of society. Despite the open, lonely spaces of the prairie, a considerable number of characters are involved. At one extreme we have the untutored, natural wisdom of Natty Bumppo, and even beyond him the ideal noble savage, Hard Heart; at the other extreme stand the delicate heroine, Inez, and her genteel lover, Captain Middleton. Between we have a remarkable range of social types, from the less socially elevated lovers, Paul Hover and Ellen, to the brutish yet moving figure of the violent outcast, Ishmael. Ishmael is a crucial as well as commanding figure in the book, and the first description of him bears careful scrutiny. By the standards of society, whose finest flower is the refinement of an Inez or a Middleton, Ishmael is animalistic in his powerful movements and savage in the bizarre confusion of his dress. A wanderer, as his name signifies, he has been expelled from society for crimes that began with his violation of the basic institution of ordered society, the rights of property.

As different as they are in all other respects, Ishmael and Natty Bumppo share one important similarity: both reject the law of the "clearings," as Natty calls the area on society's side of the frontier. At their first meeting, in response to Ishmael's rejection of legal property rights by an appeal to nature and higher law, Natty, himself an outcast because he has violated "legal law," can only concur, although Cooper, troubled by the difficulty he has worked himself into, tries to differentiate Natty's position by saying it was somehow drawn from different premises. The problem posed by the agreement between Natty and Ishmael in their mutual rejection of society is touched again and again throughout the story and, in a minor key, by the advice Natty gives to Paul Hover toward the end of the book. He urges Paul to give up the anarchic freedom of "life in the woods" since "different tempers call for different employments." If Paul is to marry Ellen, his place is in society. "Therefore," counsels Natty, "forget anything you may have heard from me, which is nevertheless true, and turn your mind on the ways of the inner country."

In these two encounters, selected from the beginning and the ending of Cooper's tale, we can see clearly the problem that pervades the entire book. Cooper is committed to two conflicting systems of values, one that affirms the untutored wisdom and natural virtue of Natty and the other the manly refinement and civilized code of Middleton. But the two cannot coexist. Although Natty is the bearer of virtues that are in many ways superior to society, or perhaps beyond society, he is fated to vanish before the inexorable advance of civilization, which may be brutal at first in the ax-bearing hands of Ishmael and his sons, but which is good ultimately in the developed state of Inez and Middleton. Schematically *The Prairie*, as all the novels of the Leatherstocking series, is about the inevitable conflict between two species of good. The elegiac note at Natty's death at the end of *The Prairie* is to sound a mournful recognition that one good must give way to the other, even though in the process something heroic and grand is lost.

Roy Harvey Pearce, in a fine essay on the Leatherstocking series some years ago, pointed out that the basic situation was essentially a tragic one. If there is to be sorrow at Natty's passing, it is a sorrow that is to be borne and accepted, not only because it is somehow inevitable, but because the advance of civilized society represents a good of a different kind. To do justice to his theme, Cooper had to do two things. First he had to render Natty Bumppo and make him live in our emotions. The fact that the image of Leatherstocking still survives is a measure of Cooper's success with Natty. His job was relatively simple since it is on the level of straightforward action that Natty lives; his world is, by definition, not complex. Cooper's second job was to render the civilized society that inevitably destroys Leatherstocking's world. Cooper had to create in his fiction an image of an admirably sophisticated world so that we as readers can feel its worth and accept, even while regretting, the justice as well as the inevitability of the passing of Natty's world. It is here that Cooper fails. His civilized men, and especially his civilized heroines, are stock figures, stereotypes drawn from the tradition of the sentimental novel. We are not able to identify with them or believe in them. Further, Cooper fails to render the virtues of civilization in terms appropriate to it. If civilization stands for the order of reason as opposed to Natty's intuition, for a rich, subjective life as opposed to Natty's naïve straightforwardness, for an intense and valuable cultural milieu as opposed to Natty's lean and spare existence, then it had to be presented in its own terms; but Cooper presents the world of civilization as well as Natty's world of nature in terms of action, of pursuit and chase, so that one pole of the dramatic conflict is emotionally absent.

But literature is made up of more than *King Lear* and *The Wings of the Dove*. Cooper's theme was perhaps greater than his art, but a book like *The Prairie* has endured because it represents a flawed attempt to put down in writing an image of intense importance to American culture. Cooper's problem was to establish a dynamic and necessary relationship between nature and civilization, a potentially tragic relationship between the ideal and the real. The problem bristled with difficulties for the writer. Mark Twain produced one great book in the attempt to solve it, and Henry James translated it into an international theme in his complex explorations of the matter of America and Europe. The line of filiation from Cooper extends further to the best of American literature in our own time. It is fair to say that without having read Cooper no reader will catch the full resonance of the lyrical conclusion to Scott Fitzgerald's *The Great Gatsby* or the massive irony of Steinbeck's inversion of the westward movement in *The Grapes of Wrath*. In William Faulkner the relation of civilization to nature becomes a moral drama of man's inevitable fall, especially in "The Bear." The power of that fine long story derives in part from the memory of the American people, even in their cities, of the importance of nature in our historical experience. We still read Cooper today because he was the first of our authors to seize upon the dramatic possibilities of that unfallen western world that stands at the beginning of our national life.

II · The Meaning of History in "Uncle Tom's Cabin"

Uncle Tom's Cabin was first published as a series of installments in the *National Era* of Washington, D. C., an abolitionist journal of slender circulation, called a magazine but actually a newspaper of eight standard-size sheets, edited by an acquaintance of Harriet Beecher Stowe, Gamaliel Bailey. The first public reference to *Uncle Tom's Cabin* was an advertisement in the issue of May 8, 1851, announcing "the publication of a new story by Mrs. H. B. Stowe, the title of which will be 'Uncle Tom's Cabin or, The Man That Was A Thing.' " The first installment appeared in the issue of June 5 but with a change in the subtitle to the one we now have, "Life Among the Lowly."

Before *Uncle Tom's Cabin*, Harriet Beecher Stowe had published only occasional pieces, short stories and sketches, the best of which she collected in *The Mayflower; or, Sketches of Scenes and Characters Among the Descendants of the Pilgrims* (1843). None of them, in theme or in quality, suggest the author of *Uncle Tom's Cabin*, but Harriet's family seems to have thought her something of a genius as a writer and, after the passage of the Fugitive Slave Act in 1850, her sister-in-law wrote "Hattie" saying, "If I could use a pen as you can, I would write something that will make this whole nation feel what an accursed thing slavery is." Harriet's later recollections have her vow on the spot to do so, but it was one thing to decide to write a book against the evils of slavery and another to discover the story by which to do it. In her own account of the process by which her imagination worked, Harriet Beecher Stowe began *Uncle Tom's Cabin* at the end; that is, she fully imagined and wrote out the scene of the death of Uncle Tom, the conclusion of her story, before she knew where to begin in order to prepare for that climax. Only after she had decided to make Uncle Tom a slave in Kentucky and to sell him South, down the river, did she see the rudiments of her plot and only then was she confident enough to write Gamaliel Bailey offering him for publication the story she was about to write. She knew it would be longer than any of her previous little sketches but concluded her letter to Bailey saying that "the thing may extend through three or four numbers. It will be ready in two or three weeks." The numbers finally ran to forty and the two or three weeks stretched to nearly a year, but so began one of the astonishing events in American publishing history.

Uncle Tom's Cabin found an audience from the start. Subscribers to the *National Era* began to write, expressing their delight with the "interest and pathos" of the story. As the number of installments increased, the inevitable happened; Harriet missed an issue in August, again in October, evoking anxious letters from her constant readers. As the novel grew in bulk, there was even the suggestion by the *National Era* that since the story had run so long Mrs. Stowe might stop and conclude the plot briefly, but readers would have none of it. The final installment appeared in the issue of April 1, 1852. Before that time, book publication had been arranged with Jewett and Company of Boston but the publisher had become more and more uneasy with the size of the novel he had on his hands. At one point, he offered to share all income from the book equally with Harriet Beecher Stowe if she would share the publishing costs, an investment of about five hundred dollars on her part. But Harriet and her husband, Calvin Stowe, then a professor at Bowdoin College in Brunswick, Maine, simply had no money even if they had been inclined to take the risk, so Harriet accepted instead the author's customary royalty of 10 percent of the money received from sales. She thereby missed a fortune. No longer was *Uncle Tom's Cabin* available only to the few readers of the abolitionist press. It now had a nation for an audience. Publication date was March 20, 1852. No advance copies were sent out for review, but without newspaper notices the first edition of five thousand copies was gone in two days. By May, fifty thousand sets of the two-volume first edition had been sold. By this time, Jewett had three power presses going twenty-four hours a day, one hundred bookbinders at work, and three mills running to supply the paper. Sales soared to more than three hundred thousand in the first year. In England, because Mrs. Stowe had no copyright there, pirated editions began to appear and from April to December, 1852, according to one authority, twelve different editions appeared; before the public was satisfied, eighteen different London publishers turned out forty different editions and sold about a million and a half copies. At home and abroad, *Uncle Tom's Cabin* was, to put it softly, a success.

Ever since, *Uncle Tom's Cabin* has been one of those novels which is the despair of literary critics and a puzzle for social historians. Its immense, incredible popularity puts a problem to both literary and historical understanding. For the literary critic, the problem is simply how a book so seemingly artless, so lacking in apparent literary talent, was not only an immediate success but has endured. More importantly, if one of the tests of the power of fiction is the way in which a novel provides images that order the confusing reality of life, then *Uncle Tom's Cabin* ranks high. Uncle Tom, little Eva, Simon Legree, Topsy who just growed—these are characters who now form part of the collective experience of the American people. It may be, as one student has observed, that Harriet Beecher Stowe is the one author "everybody *almost* knows." How, though, in literary terms, do we account for that astonishing fact?

The problem seems simpler for the social historian and can be summed up in the anecdote about Lincoln's remark upon meeting Mrs. Stowe: "So this is the little lady who made this big war." But all this proves is that Lincoln was as gracious as he was great. Tolstoi's countess may weep at the play while her coachman freezes on the seat of her carriage in the bitter weather outside, but the tears do not alter the social relationship between nobility and serf; millions, literally, may have cried over *Uncle Tom's Cabin*, but the historian, skeptical of single causes, even more skeptical of the power of emotion in history, hardly dares accept Lincoln's gallantry and say that a novel was *the* cause of our fratricidal, bloody Civil War. Even if the historian allows *Uncle Tom's Cabin* a minor role, even if he accepts it as one of the contributory causes, however small, of the War, what does that say? In what sense does a novel have the power to move a nation to battle?

Mrs. Stowe had a simple answer to questions about the power of *Uncle Tom's Cabin*. She was not the author. God wrote the book. She was simply the medium of His will. Biographers have used Mrs. Stowe's assertion to demonstrate her essential humility, but to be God's amanuensis is hardly to lie low in the dust. The explanation may have come easily and seemed sufficient to a daughter of Lyman Beecher, the great gun of New England Calvinism, but the modern reader is perhaps not so ready to see the finger of God in history or to put a stop to questions by disposing of them with cosmic answers that say everything and therefore nothing. Two tasks face anyone who picks up *Uncle Tom's Cabin* today. The first is obvious: read the book and see it for what it is. That task drives one to a second, to a consideration of the moment in time, the historical context, which provides the terms of the literary action. The modern reader must, in other words, become both literary critic and social historian. That may seem enough, but one must then ask how *Uncle Tom's Cabin* bears upon our own present. Which is another way of saying, "Why read it today?"

In the preface to *The Tragic Muse*, dissatisfied perhaps with his own performance in that novel, Henry James talks at some length about novels, especially Tolstoi's *War and Peace*, which obviously possess great power but a power not amenable to the rules that James considered essential to the art of fiction. Irritated with the success of *War and Peace* that he cannot deny but that he also cannot define, James, in a wonderful phrase, asks what these "loose and baggy monsters" have to do with art. James, in his own fiction, is perhaps the outstanding instance among modern novelists of one wholly committed to self-conscious artistry, careful control of the fictional point of view, economy of form and functional structure. His prescriptions for the art of the novel in his many prefaces to the New York edition of his work are not so much prescriptions as they are rationales for his own preferences. Flaubert rather than Balzac, Turgenev rather than Tolstoi: such are his heroes. They have been the heroes of modern literary criticism, too, following James's lead. The lead is fruitful enough, so long, that is, as one does not forget those loose and baggy monsters that are not to be discovered or understood by it. *Uncle Tom's Cabin* is one and James knew it. In *A Small Boy and Others* (1913), James called Mrs. Stowe's novel "that triumphant work," triumphant, though, because it reached readers of all classes, not triumphant as a work of art. As for literary strategy, "the medium in which books breathe, even as fishes in water, [*Uncle Tom's Cabin*] went gaily roundabout it altogether, as if a fish, a wonderful 'leaping' fish, had simply flown through the air."

The point, simply, is that *Uncle Tom's Cabin* is not to be taken hold of by the fine instruments of James's aesthetic intelligence, the customary tools of contemporary literary criticism. Unless we are to write it off as some miracle of God, as Mrs. Stowe would have it, or some inscrutable phenomenon, some fish out of water, as James would have it, we need to look elsewhere if we are to account for the emotional force that has moved millions and that is indubitably there in the book. The immediate attraction of *Uncle Tom's Cabin* surely lies in Mrs. Stowe's success with the particular, with the host of quickly realized minor characters, the series of set scenes that succeed one another so vividly. But the emotional power of the book derives from the repetitive rhythm of a basic theme that pulses, sometimes strongly, sometimes faintly, throughout the entire action of the book.

The episodic character of *Uncle Tom's Cabin* probably comes from the nature of its publication as a series of installments in the *National Era*, each installment written against a pressing deadline. Remembering, though, the example of Dickens and even Henry James, both of whom wrote under comparable circumstances, one may only say probably. On first reading, however, the appeal of *Uncle Tom's Cabin* lies in the economy with which Mrs. Stowe has caught a considerable gallery of characters. The opening chapter provides as good an example as any. In remarkably few pages, Mrs. Stowe not only gets her plot moving and her main characters before us, but catches in language and gesture two minor characters, the well-intentioned, kindly, but improvident Mr. Shelby and the coarse, uncouth, shrewd slave-trader, Haley. The contrast seems at first all on Mr. Shelby's courteous side. When, extolling Tom, Mr. Shelby describes his Christian piety, Haley answers:

> "Some folks don't believe there is pious niggers, Shelby," said Haley, with a candid flourish of his hand, "but I *do*. I had a fellow, now, in this yer last lot I took to Orleans,—'t was as good as a meetin' now, really, to hear that critter pray; and he was quite gentle and quiet like. He fetched me a good sum, too, for I bought him cheap of a man that was 'bliged to sell out; so I realized six hundred on him. Yes, I consider religion a valeyable thing in a nigger, when it's the genuine article, and no mistake."

Haley (Mrs. Stowe does not dignify him with "Mr.") is brutally direct. In his unfeeling world, the cold calculus of the market measures human worth. But we remember during his speech that Mr. Shelby is another customer " 'bliged to sell out"; more importantly, he accepts Haley's cash nexus as the measure of Tom's religion ("Why, last fall, I let him go to Cincinnati alone, to do business for me, and bring home five hundred dollars.") and his debate with Haley is only whether Haley will value Tom high enough to settle Shelby's entire debt. During that debate, he throws raisins to Eliza's handsome boy, has him dance and mimic, calling him "Jim Crow," unwittingly acting out what Haley names: little Harry is a "fancy article," a pretty package for the pleasure of his master.

Shelby is pained, of course, by what he is doing, troubled by it, but not so he will surrender his own creature comforts. It is Haley who holds up "a glass of wine between his eye and the light," the gesture of one blinded to moral responsibility by sensual indulgence, but Mr. Shelby's posture is morally no better, even if more genteel. Improvidently in debt, he shuffles his responsibility off on another human being, on one who has been a faithful servant. The Haleys of the world exist only by virtue of the Shelbys who look down on them. Haley is the brutal underside of the world whose surface Mr. Shelby adorns, but it is the same world. As Mrs. Stowe says quietly in her contrast of the two: Mr. Shelby "had the appearance of a gentleman." In half a dozen pages, she stirs two characters into vivid life and makes her general theme particular: who can be a gentle man in a system where human beings are only things?

The book is full of such concise vignettes and ranges widely through a considerable gallery of characters from the top to the bottom of society. Each reader will have his favorites. The great triumph of the book is surely Augustine St. Clare, the witty, indecisive, elegant, and tortured master who mocks himself while he mocks his society. Or, Ophelia, the prim, New England moral absolutist who shrinks from the touch of a

Negro. Or, Marie, St. Clare's neurasthenic, petulant wife, denied the love that might have saved her from her all-engrossing love of self. But below these major characters moves a world of sharply realized minor characters: the slave-chaser, Tom Loker, and his ferretlike, shrewd cohort, Marks; the lounging, tobacco-chewing Kentuckians in the tavern; the backstairs world of St. Clare's slaves, a caricature of the social affectations of the master class. Mrs. Stowe's thickly peopled world has more than enough reality in it to absorb us and to allow us to accept the unearthly, idealized, little Eva or to believe in the patient, submissive, suffering, Christlike Uncle Tom.

More importantly, however, as in the scene between Haley and Mr. Shelby, as many individual characters and social types as there are in *Uncle Tom's Cabin*, all enforce and reinforce the essential theme of the novel, that is, simply, the meaning of society's moral failure. Mrs. Stowe early lost touch with what seems to have been the simple design of the book, but she never loses touch with a deeper design, the constant reiteration of what it means to be a moral human being.

The simple design of the book persists until the appearance of Augustine St. Clare who then overwhelms it. At the beginning, we have two plots, two variations on the quest for freedom, two journeys. One is the flight of Eliza and George Harris and little Harry north to earthly happiness and physical freedom; the other is the forced transportation of Tom south to physical degradation and death but to spiritual dignity and ideal freedom at last. In contrapuntal fashion, each journey is played off against the other: George Harris' defiant, agnostic rebellion and Tom's submissive, religious acceptance; or, the cluster of stories of separation and human despair in Chapter XII, "Select Incident of Lawful Trade," with its pathetic climax of Lucy's suicide when she discovers the loss of her child, and the idealized domestic bliss of the Quaker Settlement in Chapter XIII where Eliza and George are finally reunited. The pattern is formal in the mechanical sense only, though, and

Mrs. Stowe soon gives it up. A more important journey underlies the actual journeyings of the novel, a quest for an answer
to whether it is possible to be a moral human being in society.

Part of the power of *Uncle Tom's Cabin* derives from the
fact that, wittingly or not, Mrs. Stowe organized her fiction
around one of the universal motifs in human experience, the
story of a journey that metamorphoses itself into a symbolic
quest, a search for the meaning of life itself. As one stands back
from *Uncle Tom's Cabin* and regards it whole, one sees how
deeply the novel is characterized by movement, how perva-
sively it presents a world of people in constant motion. It is a
world threatened by instability, a world of individuals seeking
a resting place, seeking no less than a home. The only moments
of rest in the novel are tied closely and immediately to home,
and the moments of bliss in the novel, like the Quaker settlement, are domestic.

The tragedy of the Negro is that he has, quite literally, no
home. The pathos of the Negro slave's world lies in this elemental fact. The bare rudiments of human community are not
there for the Negro: husband and wife, mother and child,
again and again are torn one from the other. The Negro's
world is defined by separation and loneliness, a terrible solitude. To a lesser degree—although one must stress the comparative—the same is true also for the world of white men. St.
Clare has lost, by chicanery, his one true love, as we say, and
loses little Eva, too. Even the idealized Quaker family, the
image of ultimate domestic perfection in the book, faces the
constant threat that society will not tolerate it, that the father
will go to jail for living in accordance with his doctrine of
love.

Uncle Tom's Cabin is about slavery but it is about slavery
because the fatal weakness of the slave's condition is the extreme manifestation of the sickness of the general society, a
society breaking up into discrete, atomistic individuals where
human beings, white or black, can find no secure relation one

with another. Mrs. Stowe was more radical than even those in the South who hated her could see. *Uncle Tom's Cabin* suggests no less than the simple and terrible possibility that society has no place in it for love. One can only be a martyr to its power, like Tom, or one can turn one's violent hand against it and by that very act deny the possibility of love, like George Harris, or, as in the compromised and unsatisfactory ending of the novel, one can keep moving on, forsake society, try a new beginning and hope desperately that God's Providence will by some miracle redeem the whole course of human history. It is at this level of the novel that Augustine St. Clare is central and this is why he lingers in the memory of anyone who has really read *Uncle Tom's Cabin*.

St. Clare stands precisely between the poles defined by Tom and George Harris. Incapable of action, like George, unredeemed by faith, like Tom, St. Clare is the mouthpiece for the central dilemma of the book. He sees through the pitiful pretensions of society whether in the Northern or Southern version. Ophelia's prim New England rectitude is as much a product of social conditioning as the young Southerner's hot violence. She hates slavery but she does not love the Negro, and it is perhaps indicative of Mrs. Stowe's empathy with St. Clare that although she has Ophelia finally cry over Topsy, her imagination could not reach to presenting Ophelia and Topsy in Vermont. Not that St. Clare succumbs to the Southern myth that the white man takes patriarchal care of the childish black: slavery is a system of exploitation based upon power and he ridicules the politicians and the ministers who try to gloss that naked, ugly fact with seemly words and soft phrases. What is the nucleus and root of slavery?

Why, because my brother Quashy is ignorant and weak, and I am intelligent and strong,—because I know how, and *can* do it,—therefore, I may steal all he has, keep it, and give him only such and so much as suits my fancy. Whatever is too hard, too dirty, too disagreeable, for me, I may set Quashy to doing. Because I don't like work, Quashy shall work. Because the sun burns me, Quashy shall stay in the sun. Quashy shall earn the money, and I will spend it. Quashy shall lie down in every puddle, that I may walk over dry-shod. Quashy shall do my will, and not his, all the days of his mortal life.

St. Clare sees the full horror of man's tyranny over man, but it is not just white man over black man, it is man over man. The social sanctions differ, but the free laborer of the North is as much the potential victim of fateful economic power as his black brother in the South. With such a vision of the pervasive evil of society, with such a glimpse of general human depravity, St. Clare asks bitterly, "what can a man of honorable and humane feelings do, but shut his eyes all he can, and harden his heart?" Little Eva may not be to our unsentimental modern taste, and we may rightly get irritated with Mrs. Stowe for managing to wring two deathbed scenes out of her, but she presents in overworked and melodramatic terms what St. Clare argues more persuasively: love is literally not of this world. It is St. Clare's corrosive intelligence that lingers and keeps Simon Legree from sliding into the inhuman embodiment of evil that our memory wishfully would like to make him. The horror of Legree's dark mansion and his terrible depravity is that he is the essence of the evil St. Clare sees in the human condition. That is the way of the world. All one can do before it is die and hope for heaven.

Yet, the reader will object that Mrs. Stowe ends her novel on a more hopeful note, with the hope of changing men's hearts and so changing the world. Otherwise, surely, she would not have written *Uncle Tom's Cabin*. The objection is a proper one and to deal with it takes one to the historical context of the novel. If the ending of *Uncle Tom's Cabin* is not, as I think, completely satisfactory, it is because Mrs. Stowe is working with two contradictory attitudes toward the meaning of history, each uneasily in opposition to the other, both of which derive from her religious background in New England Calvinism. One can get at the matter most quickly by reference to the last chapter of the novel, Mrs. Stowe's "Concluding Remarks," where, putting aside the fictional mode, she addresses her reader directly. Having wrung the emotions of her readers with the moral horror of slavery, having insisted that all, Northerners and Southerners, are implicated in the evil, Mrs. Stowe asks rhetorically, "But, what can any individual do?" She answers her question by asserting there is one thing everyone can do: "they can see to it that *they feel right.*" Then, on her final page, Mrs. Stowe presents an apocalyptic vision of a day of wrath, a day of final judgment, "*the day of vengeance*" when Christ shall establish his kingdom on earth, the day when the millennium shall begin. These two moments at the end are the culminations of two attitudes which are at work all through the novel and represent two views of the providential course of history, both of which Mrs. Stowe responds to and both of which she presents in her fiction.

Mrs. Stowe's emphasis on feeling, the emotional logic of the heart against the cold reason of the head, probably accounts for the immediate popular success of *Uncle Tom's Cabin*, and also defines the degree to which the novel acted as a force in the complicated sequence of causes that led to war. The passage of the Fugitive Slave Act, as part of the Compromise of 1850 to placate the South and its fears of an abolitionist conspiracy, embodied one fatal error for the South's cause, and in retrospect it is hard to understand why the South did not see it. After 1850, and because of the Fugitive Slave Act, the North was directly and actively involved in the system of slavery. No longer could it pretend that it had no moral relation with the evil of slavery; the abstract relation, that is, the impersonal relation through an economic market supported largely by the cotton export trade and cotton manufacturing in the Northeast, suddenly became direct and personal. No longer could it be maintained that it was "they," the Southerners, who supported slavery; it was "we," the people of the United States, who did. It did not matter how few actual cases there were in which Federal courts returned escaped slaves to their Southern masters. A few were enough. In Boston, Shadrach, a Negro waiter and escaped slave, was recognized and seized by a Southerner and hustled off to jail; a mob freed him and Boston juries refused to convict its leaders; Northerners were pushed to the position of breaking the law of society in conformity to what they felt to be a higher law of justice. Mrs. Stowe put the complex, legal, and political matter in simple, melodramatic, and moral terms in one of her more sentimental chapters, "In Which It Appears That a Senator Is But a Man," the chapter where Senator Bird, just returned from the state legislature where he argued eloquently and voted for the passage of a Fugitive Slave Act, helps Eliza to escape her pursuers. Great public interests may be involved, "We must put aside our private feelings," as Senator Bird first argues with his wife; yet, faced with an actual, suffering, concrete human being and not an abstract point of law and public policy, the Senator accepts Mrs. Bird's reliance on intuitive feeling, on the dictates of the heart, rather than the reasons of state. Whatever weight one assigns to the various factors that caused the Civil War, war came finally when Americans, North and South, gave up politics and the compromises of reasonable men and moved to arms, emotionally certain of the righteousness of their cause. *Uncle Tom's Cabin* did not create that emotion, but it fed it, and in that limited sense played a part in the coming of Civil War. Any reader of *Uncle Tom's Cabin* could feel, with Mrs. Stowe, that there was something horribly wrong about a society that tolerated slavery, even if he knew as little as Mrs. Stowe what could be done about it.

Furthermore, the depth of Mrs. Stowe's confusion about what could actually be done about slavery can be glimpsed by looking carefully at the pattern of meaning that develops in the dramatic action of the novel around the theme of "feeling" as a guide to moral behavior. The theme is established undramatically at the outset in Mrs. Stowe's "Preface." There she contrasts "the hard and dominant Anglo-Saxon race" with the despised and lowly Negro, suffering under bondage to the white master class, and asserts her intention to "awaken sympathy and feeling for the African race," to extend the "hand of benevolence" with its capacity to reach the heart in accordance with the "development of the great principles of Christian brotherhood." Throughout the action of the novel that follows, the test by which to separate good people from bad people is their capacity to feel emotionally the claim of human brotherhood. Against the force of individual emotional sympathy, however, stands the amoral system of society, the legal relations of slavery, which has its evil way without respect to the moral feelings of the individuals tragically enmeshed in it. So, again in the "Preface," Mrs. Stowe can insist she has no animus against Southerners themselves, only against the system, because "experience has shown her that some of the noblest of minds and hearts are often thus involved." So, at the outset, we have the claims of the individual feeling heart against the determining force of social institutions.

In what follows this prefatory assertion by Mrs. Stowe of what she intends to achieve, we discover a complicated development of the place of feeling in human affairs. A single example will help to get at the matter. When Eliza escapes across the floating ice of the Ohio River, a "poor, heathenish Kentuckian," himself an owner of slaves, helps her to freedom up the opposite bank and directs her to the home of Senator and Mrs. Bird. Mrs. Stowe comments at this point, "So spoke this poor, heathenish Kentuckian, who had not been instructed in his constitutional relations, and consequently was betrayed into acting in a sort of Christianized manner, which, if he had been better situated and more enlightened, he would not have been left to do." At this point, the spontaneous and generous act is defined as one possible only for someone whose natural instincts have not been corrupted by learning or social status. But obviously Mrs. Stowe's case is not that the lower classes are natively wise and good and the upper classes corrupted by class interest and education. Haley is just as crude as the Kentuckian who puts out his hand to Eliza, and Senator and Mrs. Bird who help her on her way are clearly refined and educated members of the upper class. Mrs. Stowe's case is that the "heathenish" Kentuckian was "betrayed" into acting in a Christian manner. Her case throughout the book is that Christian feeling will rescue one from the hardhearted ways of the world, but the chances are greater that one will be open to the emotional claims of such feeling to the degree one is not deeply involved in society. So the bearers of feeling and morality in the novel are little children, Negroes, and women, especially women. "Your little child," as St. Clare says to Ophelia, "is your only true democrat." The Bible is a book by "ignorant and unlearned men" and appeals to the patient nature of the black man and reaches his heart, especially, of course, Uncle Tom's. But it is the woman, above all, who provides the conduit for the flow of feeling and morality into the hard world of men. From Mrs. Shelby at the beginning to Simon Legree at the end, the measure of whose depravity is his rejection of his mother's influence, the examples are myriad. Further, those males who are drawn to morality are clearly feminine in their characters. St. Clare is not only ruled by the memory of his mother, but his manner, his love of finery and perfumed cambric, makes him almost effeminate. As Mrs. Stowe says, his character is "more akin to the softness of women."

It is. But St. Clare asks the awkward question about Mrs. Stowe's compliment: "What can a man of honorable and humane feelings do, but shut his eyes all he can, and harden his heart?" Feeling is simply self-indulgence, the pleasurable *frisson* of self-congratulation, unless one has the faith of an Uncle Tom who leaves justice to heaven. If one wants justice in this world, to see to it that one feels right is an inconclusive act. But there is a woman in the novel who, as a mother guided by her "natural" feelings, does act: Eliza, who will not submit to the cruelty of the world and makes good her impulsive decision to grasp freedom. We tend to remember the stirring manhood of George, Eliza's husband, and his scornful rejection of the hypocrisy of the American democratic faith; George will fight. But at the end of the novel George puts aside his hotheaded anger and gives up the hope of finding freedom in the New World; he will instead emigrate to Africa, to Liberia, and begin the search for justice in the world all over again there. His reason is interesting: "In myself, I confess, I am feeble for this,—full half the blood in my veins is the hot and hasty Saxon; but I have an eloquent preacher of the Gospel ever by my side, in the person of my beautiful wife. When I wander, her gentler spirit ever restores me, and keeps before my eyes the Christian calling and mission of our race."

George's speech seems to emphasize, rather than contradict, the efficacy of the good woman's influence, but it is perhaps equally important to recognize that Eliza's influence also means retreat, escape to another land. Even more important in considering Eliza is the dramatic fact that, as woman, she is unable to achieve her escape. Eliza must become a man to cross over into Canada and into freedom. We cannot say whether Mrs. Stowe was aware of the implications of her decision to put Eliza in the disguise of a man to make good the last step in her escape, but the implications for the meaning of what the woman stands for in *Uncle Tom's Cabin* are immense. The patient, submissive, character, ennobled by feeling, and symbolized most by the good woman, is simply ineffective. Nothing follows but the pleasure of feeling right. This is why "Uncle Tom" remains an epithet, a term of raging scorn, in the mouth of the Negro ever since Mrs. Stowe wrote her book. Many critics have pointed out that Uncle Tom achieves real dignity in his moral superiority at the end of his story, but there is a deeper truth in the fact that he has come to symbolize fawning servility for the Negro who wants his dignity as a man in this world and not as an angel in heaven. It is a truth that points to the inadequacy of Mrs. Stowe's belief, derived as I said from one side of her Protestant upbringing, that salvation depends upon the subjective feeling of the single individual. The result for this world was to leave the world unchanged. So, if *Uncle Tom's Cabin* played some small part in the coming of war, one should remember that this is not the direction in which the book points. Mrs. Stowe's only hope was that men with changed hearts would voluntarily emancipate their slaves, as does George Shelby, or that the Negro would either submit and wait for heaven, like Uncle Tom, or once free would emigrate to Africa.

On this side of Mrs. Stowe's mind, the notion of history is one in which moral progress comes gradually through the conversion of individual men. The line of dynamic force runs from the individual to society. But there is also in the novel, as I have already said, another view of history, one which takes a darker view of the world, which gives up the sentimental hope for gradual moral improvement, and sees the world as locked in sin, beyond the power of man's improvement, to be changed only by the wrath of God. Whereas the stress on man's intuitive feeling undergirds the hope for a gradual upward improvements in the conditions of the world, the stress on man's wickedness and God's sudden judgment implies a cataclysmic break in the sequence of history, a leap across time, in which the outcast, the persecuted, the lowly will come into their own. St. Clare expresses this point of view most directly in the action of the novel and Mrs. Stowe implies it in her own voice at the end, but the notion is most present in Mrs. Stowe's view of the Negro.

From the perspective of our own present, Mrs. Stowe

seems condescending, to say the least, toward the Negro. It is not only that she must make her two lovers, Eliza and George, so white they can easily pass when the need arises, or that her black Negroes usually are there for rollicking, chuckleheaded fun, but that she praises them constantly because they are patient, timid, and unenterprising. Little wonder that so angry a Negro writer as James Baldwin should, today, not be able to see what Mrs. Stowe is saying. What she is saying is that the hard, aggressive, masterful, Anglo-Saxon ruling class is doomed in the sight of God, that America has fallen away from her covenant with God and that the "signs of the times" are that a great convulsion is about to render history. God will chastize those who have not kept His justice on earth. It is the meek who will, literally, inherit the earth. Mrs. Stowe's imagination faltered at the prospect and she could only assert finally a pious trust in a separate nation in Christian Africa that would provide the vanguard of Christ's kingdom of love and equality to come, not just in heaven, but here on this earth. Yet, what a searing judgment even that equivocation was on her America. Trapped in the sinful institutions they had made, her fellow Americans could not save themselves. Only God could do that. Which also may be one of the reasons she thought God had written her book.

After Mrs. Stowe had published *Uncle Tom's Cabin*, she made a triumphant trip to Europe to receive the plaudits of her many admirers there. While in England, she received from the Duchess of Sutherland, a gift, a bracelet whose links were in imitation of the links of a slave's fetters, although in gold rather than coarse iron. There were ten links in all and upon three were inscribed important dates from English history in the slave's struggle for freedom. This was in 1853. In later years,

Harriet Beecher Stowe was able to add her own inscriptions, five more important dates ranging from the Emancipation Proclamation to the passage of the Fourteenth Amendment. Two of the links remained blank. Charles Dudley Warner, who tells the story of the bracelet in his introduction to *Uncle Tom's Cabin* in the collected Writings of Harriet Beecher Stowe, saw a moral in the bracelet: "What will the progress of civilization in America offer for the links nine and ten?"

The question is not a bad one to ask how *Uncle Tom's Cabin* bears upon our own present, why we should read it today. There are less exalted reasons, of course. It is a good story, much better than one might expect, as Edmund Wilson discovered to his slight surprise. Also, it gives us a chance to experience some of the difficulty American society faced in deciding what to do about slavery, a decision that was never made and was left to the brute irrationality of war to determine. But Charles Dudley Warner's question, and perhaps Mrs. Stowe's novel, demands a different sort of answer than these.

One would be presumptuous, indeed, to say that the progress of our civilization has any claim to fill in the last two links in the chain of events whose completion is to signify the triumph of the Negro in his struggle for political, social, and personal dignity. It is tempting to claim some gains as worthy of a place, but a modest guess would be that far greater and more dramatic changes must come before that triumph is realized. What we may gain from reading *Uncle Tom's Cabin*, though, is a small lesson for our own time. Faced with the inertia of institutionalized evil and the selfishness of white men, Harriet Beecher Stowe asked the Negro to be better than the white man. We would be lucky, indeed, if the black man proves more open to compassion and forgiveness than the white man has, but if white men have not yet allowed the Negro his full humanity they had perhaps better not ask him to be more than human. Further, and more importantly, if social justice is to be done here and now, men, black and white, working together, are going to have to make it. We may not achieve it. It may take, as Mrs. Stowe thought, a miracle to save us. But we had better not plan on it.

III · Empiric of the Imagination:
E. W. Howe and "The Story of a Country Town"

HENRY JAMES, in his little book on Hawthorne published in 1879, remarked that Hawthorne was an "empiric" of the imagination. What James meant was that the American writer, at work in a society whose genius was bent toward matters more practical than fiction, "lacked the comfort and inspiration of belonging to a class. The best things come, as a general thing, from the talents that are members of a group. . . . Great things of course have been done by solitary workers; but they have usually been done with double the pains they would have cost if they had been produced in more genial circumstances. The solitary worker loses the profit of example and discussion; he is apt to make awkward experiments; he is in the nature of the case more or less of an empiric."

There is much of James's own predicament as an American writer in what he says of Hawthorne, but the remark points beyond Hawthorne and James himself to a general characteristic of the history of American literature, the presence of the self-taught writer, working alone, discovering for himself the demands of his craft. At least half the meaning of the national experience of the American people has been the notion that America has meant a new beginning, a fresh start, unencumbered by tradition and the past. Nowhere is the notion more discernible than in the careers of our novelists and poets. Cooper, Hawthorne, Melville, Whitman, Mark Twain, Emily Dickinson, Dreiser, Thomas Wolfe: each begins anew, largely innocent of the advantages of a literary tradition, unaware of belonging to a "class" of writers. Only in retrospect do we see that the tradition of the new is, paradoxically, *the* American tradition. It may account for the curious fact that so many American writers are remembered for a single book rather than a sustained body of work. In any event, it is in this tradition of the solitary imagination, striking out in new directions on its own, that one must begin an assessment of the importance of Edgar W. Howe's one important novel, *The Story of a Country Town.*

Howe wrote *The Story of a Country Town,* as he tells us in his preface, entirely at night after "a hard day's work as editor and publisher of a small evening newspaper." The newspaper was the Atchison, Kansas, *Daily Globe.* In addition to being editor and publisher, Howe wrote a regular daily column for the paper, "Globe Sights," which has won him a small place in the history of American journalism as one of our earliest "columnists." Howe ran the *Globe* from 1877 to 1911, when he gave it up to begin *E. W. Howe's Monthly* (1911–1933), which drew H. L. Mencken's praise as one of the "most curious" as well as one of the "most entertaining" of American periodicals. But it was during the late evening hours of 1882, weary from the day's newspaper work, that Howe wrote *The Story of a Country Town.* It alone has earned him a place in the history of American literature.

Forty-five years later, in 1927, in a foreword for a new edition of the novel, Howe, although he was uncertain about the time of original composition, remembered with a printer's professional memory that after seven or eight publishers had rejected *The Story of a Country Town* he decided to print it himself with "a new font of minion [type] purchased for the purpose" and ran the book "four pages at a time, on a medium Gordon job press." The first edition of two thousand copies appeared under the imprint of Howe and Company, Atchison, Kansas, in the fall of 1883. Howe sent a copy to a friend, an actor, who in turn passed it on to H. G. Crickmore of the New York *World* who, Howe remembered, "was really the horse editor, with strong disposition toward books and plays." Crickmore wrote the first public notice of the book. Howe also sent copies to Mark Twain and William Dean Howells, both of whom he admired as writers; both responded handsomely, praising the novel, and publishers immediately sought the book they had once rejected. Howe accepted the first offer, which came to him from James R. Osgood. The novel was a success. Within two years it was reprinted twenty-five times; a little more than a half-century later, according to *Publishers' Weekly*, it had been "printed in a hundred editions by six different publishers." By 1927, the plates were so badly worn that a new set, by then a third, had to be made, and Howe mistakenly took the opportunity to revise *The Story*, mainly cutting those pages that contained sardonic comments on the self-delusion of farmers and organized agrarian protest movements, thus depriving the novel of some of its contemporary flavor.

The Story of a Country Town was Howe's only good novel. When Howe sent one of his privately printed copies of *The Story of a Country Town* to Mark Twain, Twain responded in a rambling letter in which he remarked, at one point, "You may have caught the only fish there was in your pond." Twain was right. Afterward—*The Mystery of the Locks* (1885), *A Moonlight Boy* (1886), *A Man Story* (1887) —Howe's writing was, as one critic put it softly, "less than mediocre." In an excellent essay on Howe, Sylvia Bowman has suggested that *The Story of a Country Town* was Howe's only successful novel "because he related experiences and problems from which he had himself suffered." In this view, the act of writing the novel was therapeutic, a form of Freudian catharsis, unlike the Aristotelian, in which the intense emotion that is purged is that of the author, not that of the audience. Miss Bowman marshals convincing evidence for her case. The blind and irrational jealousy of the fictional Jo Erring had its source in the facts of Howe's own life. Late in life, in his autobiography, *Plain People*, Howe said, "There is more of the author in Jo Erring than in any other portion of the novel," and Howe's youngest son remembered his father as "the most wretchedly unhappy man I ever knew." In his youth, Howe had many romantic affairs: in one city he went with four girls at the same time; in another, he fell in love within a week with the sister of the proprietor of his hotel; in still another, he had an affair he later could not describe because it would not meet "the approval of editor or publisher." Yet, publicly, in magazine articles as well as in Jo Erring's story, Howe made inordinate demands on the purity and unblemished reputation of women. Without knowing all one would have to know to determine its origins in Howe's emotional life, Jo Erring's self-destructive jealousy seems to have had its roots somewhere deep in Howe's own personality.

Before writing *The Story of a Country Town*, Howe had also acted out in his private life the awful failure of communication between man and woman which pervades the novel. The inability of Jo and Mateel to reach each other, which is foreshadowed in the silence of Jo's own parents and paralleled in the bleak reserve of Reverend Westlock's marriage, had a biographical parallel as well. After Howe and his wife moved to Atchison in 1877, Howe lived in a cottage in the yard and refused to speak to his wife, who lived in the main house. Divorce followed soon. Further, just as Jo's jealousy and the silent war between the sexes had their origins in Howe's personal experience, so too the story of the dour, driven Reverend

Westlock and unwanted Ned, the narrator of the story, derives from Howe's relationship with his father. Howe's father preached the same harsh religion as Reverend Westlock, rarely spoke to his children, and left his family after a scandalous affair with his wife's widowed sister, not to return until after his wife's death. Yet Howe's childhood did not keep him from becoming as stern and unrelenting a father as his own. He was a forbidding and angry man, and his children feared his black moods and violent ways.

The Story of a Country Town seems to present an illuminating instance of the way in which a writer, drawing upon his intense interior life, projects different aspects of his personality onto different characters and, by arraying these characters one against the other, makes objective drama out of the subjective divisions within his own self. Yet such a perspective on the novel is frustrating in its very fascination because, as I have already said, one cannot know all one needs to know to have a clear view of the matter. Howe's neurotic life and the act of sublimation which led to the creation of the novel may make *The Story of a Country Town* far more interesting a document for the modern reader than it could have been for Howe's contemporaries, but it fails to say why the novel achieved its importance in the first place. It puts the author, rather than the book, at the center of one's field of vision, and it is the book finally with which one must deal. As William Dean Howells wrote in the review which firmly put *The Story of a Country Town* in the way of a public, "It is with the novel, and not with the novelist, that we have to do at present."

Before clinical psychology provided a further dimension of interest to Howe's work, *The Story of a Country Town* had achieved a secure place in its own right, and why it did is a matter of literary history and not psychology. Apart from its probable relation to the author's personality, the novel is important for two reasons. First, it is the earliest expression in our fiction of disenchantment with the agrarian ideal of the simplicity and virtues of rural life and the noble farmer, living in pastoral harmony with a fructifying and beneficent Nature. Second, and closely related to the first, *The Story of a Country Town* stands at the beginning of the literary movement called "realism" in American literature, with its programmatic acceptance of the daily life of ordinary people as the proper subject for fiction. If not a total success as a novel, *The Story of a Country Town* remains important because it marks important new directions in our cultural history.

The Story of a Country Town begins, "Ours was the prairie district out West, where we had gone to grow up with the country," and the irony persists throughout the novel. The *Union of States* newspaper which Reverend Westlock buys refers to the neighborhood it serves as "the garden spot of the world," and Ned discovers that all western papers say the same of their own little worlds. But the world of Fairview and Twin Mounds is a joyless, grim, repellent world of dissatisfied and emotionally starved people. The women are pale and unhappy; the men overworked and frustrated; the children deprived of play and driven to their tasks. A mood of gray, damp gloom pervades the novel from beginning to end.

In 1883, *The Story of a Country Town* was a subversive novel. Since Jefferson had written, in a famous passage in *Notes on the State of Virginia* (1781–1785), that, "Those who labor in the earth are the chosen people of God, if ever He had a chosen people, whose breasts He has made His peculiar deposit for substantial and genuine virtue," it had been a major article of the American faith that there was something especially admirable about the farmer and a life lived close to nature. As settlers moved into the great valley of the Mississippi, the valley was transformed from wilderness to garden and became, in the imagination of the American people, "the garden of the world," with all the Edenic connotations of that phrase. In 1851, Representative George W. Julian of Indiana argued that "the life of a farmer is peculiarly favorable to virtue; and both individuals and communities are generally happy in proportion as they are virtuous." Julian went on to sing with the "poets and philosophers in all ages" of the "pleasures and virtues of rural life." Ten years after Howe published his story, the great American historian, Frederick Jackson Turner was to find that the movement from East to West, away from Europe to the western frontier, embodied the meaning of the "really American" part of our experience, and as late as 1921 Senator Capper still argued that the American farm was "the nursery of a genuine freeborn citizenship which is the strength of the Republic."

Henry Nash Smith, in *Virgin Land: The American West as Symbol and Myth,* has shown how the image of the agricultural society of the interior of the American continent became, by the nineteenth century, "a collective representation, a poetic idea," which defined the promise of American life. "The master symbol of the garden embraced a cluster of metaphors expressing fecundity, growth, increase, and blissful labor in the earth, all centering about the heroic figure of the idealized frontier farmer." The young man told to go West went not only in pursuit of the main chance but in the hope of realizing the ideal society of America's dream for itself, the good society of a simple and noble breed of men living in unsophisticated innocence and happiness.

The dream becomes nightmare in *The Story of a Country Town.* In the world of Howe's novel, the tramp of civilization westward is "dusty." Those who settle in Fairview are simply "too poor and too tired" to do otherwise. Young Ned Westlock, observing the "miserable and discontented" people, the "surly and rough" men, the "pale and fretful" women, decides the world they have left behind "must have been a very poor one that such a lot of people left it, and considered their condition bettered." Later, looking back on his childhood, Ned finds in his memory only the image of the spreading shadows of the cold, gray church and "walls damp and moldy because the bright sun and the free air of heaven had deserted them as a curse."

Yet in the world of Twin Mounds where every man "had reason to feel humiliated that he had not accomplished more," Ned, as he grows older, notices that "most of [the men] were as conceited as though there was nothing left in the world worthy of their attention. Their small business affairs, their quarrels over the Bible, and an occasional term in the town council, or a mention for the legislature or a county office, satisfied them, and they were as content as men who really amounted to something." The final damnation of the village is that these incipient Babbitts do not even see their miserable and straitened lives for what they are. The cynical Lytle Biggs, selling charters for the Farmer's Alliance and rural magazines which pander to the self-delusion of the people, tells Ned that the agrarian ideal is, simply, a fraud.

The Story of a Country Town marks the moment when the myth of the garden in America gave way to the wasteland of broken dreams. After Edgar W. Howe came other American writers: Joseph Kirkland, Hamlin Garland, Edgar Lee Masters, Zona Gale, Sherwood Anderson, and Sinclair Lewis. They deepened, amplified, and finally made a tradition in American letters of what Howe, writing alone out of his own bitter experience, had first put down.

When Osgood and Company published *The Story of a Country Town*, William Dean Howells, who had already recieved a copy of the first edition from Howe, took advantage of the chance to review the book in the form of an "open letter" to *The Century Magazine*. Howells greeted Howe publicly as one who bore "witness" to the "prevalence of realism in the artistic atmosphere." Howells was a generous man, and he extended the same open hand to many young writers, especially to those who seemed fellow-workers in the field of realism. Without stopping to define the term, even admitting "the name is not particularly good," Howells claimed realism to be "almost the only literary movement of our time that has vitality in it" and asserted that the importance of *The Story of a Country Town* derived from its place in the developing tradition of literary realism. Every critic of Edgar W. Howe has said the same thing since. One must be candid and admit that difficulties face anyone who continues to say so.

The first difficulty lies in deciding what it means to say a novel is "realistic." Howells, in his review of *The Story of a Country Town*, seems to have in mind some notion of representativeness: "It is simply what it calls itself, the story of a country town in the West, which has so many features in common with country towns everywhere, that whoever has lived in one must recognize the grim truth of the picture." The test here would be to compare the novel with a survey of the characteristics of all western country towns in 1883. It is doubtful if Howells had such a tiresome task in mind, especially since the logical conclusion of such an attitude would be to eliminate fiction. If the best art is that which takes us closest to reality, then the wisest course surely would be to take the next step: to ignore art, and confront reality directly. Implicit in Howells' brief statement there is another test, but it turns out no less treacherous than the first: the reader will recognize the "grim truth" of the fictional picture, especially if he has lived in a country town. But one of the features of Howe's picture is the simple fact that those who do live in such towns do not recognize the reality of their existence, so either his picture is false or Howells' criterion is useless.

What Howells seems probably to have in mind is the notion that the reader is able to believe in the world which Howe presents, to accept it as if it were real. This is a matter of Howe's art and not a matter of comparing his art with something outside the novel or inquiring into the responses of his readers. So Howells can say that "the art is feeblest in the direction of Agnes, who is probably true to life, but seems rather more than the rest to have come out of books." The test here is not whether "patient" Agnes Deming, with "the magic of a woman's touch," is true to life, but whether Howe's art can stir into fictional life the inert, pasteboard figure out of the sentimental novel from which Agnes derives. That test brings us back to Howe's book.

To the modern eye, *The Story of a Country Town* is cluttered with trappings "out of books": the tolling of foreboding church bells; the wild, dark stormy night of murder; the deserted wife with the inevitable light in the window, whose sinful husband returns in the dead of winter a moment too late; the wandering sea captain who discovers his long-lost child. Even the names of the characters seem unfortunate: Jo Erring, who makes a fatal error in demanding so outrageously much of love; Clinton Bragg, the posturing and swaggering braggart; Lytle Biggs, the little man who talks so big. The Reverend Goode Shepherd would seem to require no comment, but for the pleasant fact that the minister who succeeded Edgar W. Howe's father in real life actually was named "Shepherd"; which only proves that to copy reality is not a sure way to believable fiction.

Yet, even to a critical modern eye, *The Story of a Country Town* endures despite these obtrusive, awkward features. It does because the novel is more "realistic" than Howells allowed himself to see. At the beginning of realism as a literary convention, Howe, crudely to be sure, anticipated the two directions in which realism inevitably had to go: one was toward naturalism, the other toward the psychological novel.

William Dean Howells seems to have been constitutionally disposed toward happy endings and poetic justice. Even while recognizing the "grim" and "intolerably sad" world of Howe's fiction, Howells had to soften the harshness a bit: the "gloom, one feels, is a temporary but necessary condition, out of which the next generation is sure to emerge." There is little in the novel to support such a hopeful theory of progress. Although Howells wished not to accept the unrelieved gloom of the book as final, he saw clearly what *The Story of a Country Town* was about: "It is not in the presentation of individuals, however, but rather in the realization of a whole order of things, that the strength of the book lies." Howe's title pointed to the strength of the book. The novel was the story of a counry town, a story of the environment which produced the many individuals whose particular stories otherwise seem so tangentially related. The subject of the novel, one would like to say its "hero," is the collective environment itself, the country town.

The point needs stressing because Mark Twain, at least, could not see it. In his letter to Howe, Twain wrote, "Next time, I wish you'd leave out Biggs, or anybody else whose diversions interrupt the story. *Nothing* should ever be allowed to break the speed of a story." Twain goes on in the next paragraph to talk of Mateel and Jo; he is using "story" in the conventional sense of plot and action. Howe is not. What holds the novel together, what joins the multitude of plots, is the shaping force of the environment itself. In such a reading, Chapters 16 and 21, which otherwise advance the "action" of the novel not at all, are central, and Lytle Biggs and Big Adam belong in the novel as appropriate minor expressions of the major theme: the way in which the environment of the country town makes each individual in it a function of its force.

Realism is a matter of literary technique; naturalism is a matter of theme. The theme of the naturalist in fiction is that man is determined by forces beyond his control. The force may be biological (there is a suggestion of this in Mateel, whose ineffectiveness is derived constitutionally from her father), sexual (as in the collapse of Reverend Westlock's stern Puritan will), or environmental (Big Adam, who anticipates Sherwood Anderson's "grotesques" in *Winesburg, Ohio,* is the most colorful instance). There may be no necessary connection between realistic technique and naturalistic theme, but historically the line of filiation is direct. The usual account of the history of American literature begins naturalism with Dreiser's *Sister Carrie* (1900), but the history of the imagination refuses to follow the numbers of the years. Howe's bold leap can be understood better, perhaps, if one looks all the way forward to John Dos Passos' triumphant tour de force, *USA,* in which the technique of the novel about society itself, and not the individuals in it who are but puppets of its power, achieved its formal end.

If realism, in one direction, led to "the whole order of things," as Howells put it, in which the individual became increasingly insignificant, in another it led curiously to the subjective, interior world of the individual. Captivated by the successful positivism of science, arbiters of literary taste in the nineteenth century began to insist that the writer of fiction not "make up" his stories, but write about things as they are, things that are real. The demand that the writer be faithful to experienced fact had the paradoxical effect of driving the writer in upon himself. His response to reality is his only avenue to how things really are, and the path led inward to subjective response as well as outward to objective fact. In the former direction the strange result is the denial of reality except as it affects individual consciousness. In the career of a writer greater than any mentioned so far, James Joyce, the development is clearly marked: from the solid slices of Dublin life in *Dubliners* to the night-long dream of H. C. Earwicker in *Finnegans Wake.* In our time, the tendency seems to have run its logical course, and the writer has become his own hero.

To invoke James Joyce is to impose a terrible handicap on Edgar W. Howe, but in *The Story of a Country Town* he stumbled on the problem implicit in a simpleminded theory of realism, although he failed to manage it effectively. If Howe had not deserted the task he set himself of telling *The Story of a Country Town* through the developing consciousness of Ned Westlock, he might have been a major figure in our literary tradition rather than the minor one he is. But one must remember that Howe had almost no useful example before him. For us, Henry James's insistence on the dramatic importance of point of view and Mark Twain's creation of Huck Finn have intervened, and we can see more clearly than Howe what he had to do. He boldly begins with Ned and asserts that what is important is what is remembered. Ned makes no claim for the truth of his memory; he invites us in the first chapter to accept it as false and distorted. But at that very moment we hear two "Neds" speaking; one the young boy who was there, the other the older man looking back on that young boy. Innocently, one suspects, Howe worked himself immediately into a difficult technical problem. He soon gave it up. Sometimes Ned speaks as if he were innocent of what is to come; at other times, he is clearly speaking from some vantage point beyond the end of the action of the novel itself; sometimes Howe's authorial voice intrudes. The point of view becomes multiple and confused.

Closely related to this central technical flaw in the novel is Howe's inability to dramatize the substance of the action. Jo Erring tells Ned how his mother feels; Reverend Westlock leaves a letter to describe his internal torment; Barker must tell his story to Agnes and Ned and Mrs. Westlock; Jo explains to Ned at great length what his trouble is. We are never inside these characters, sharing vicariously in their lives; we are always being told, not shown, what the matter is. One wishes Howe were a better writer, that he were part of a literary tradition which might have helped him solve his narrative problems, but to wish that is to forget that the "tradition" which solved those problems came after Howe, not before him.

It would be unjust, even unfair, to Edgar W. Howe to say that *The Story of a Country Town* is a great or major novel. It is not. But it is an important novel for reasons which make it interesting and still worth reading. Suddenly, and for one time only, Howe produced a novel which dates a major shift in American literary consciousness. The secret of his single success may lie hidden in the irrecoverable depths of Howe's psychic life, but the meaning of the success lies in the fact that *The Story of a Country Town* gave voice to the bitter frustrations of reality which had no place in the official ideals of American culture. In trying to present a new and different version of how things really are, Howe found himself involved with problems of style and form which were to perplex other and better writers than he. Only long after the fact can one see that literary tradition is not something which is simply there to be used. It is created by writers like Howe, working alone, stumbling and making false starts, empirics of the imagination.

JAMES GOULD COZZENS: THE CONDITION OF MODERN MAN

THE COVER of James Gould Cozzens' novel, *By Love Possessed*, bears an emblem: an old French gilt clock, precisely at the hour of three, adorned by a pastoral scene in which a cupid is about to loose his arrow at the heart of a young shepherd peeping through the vegetation at a largely undraped sleeping nymph. This clock appears in the novel, on the first and last pages, and embodies figuratively what the novel presents dramatically in the pages that lie between. *By Love Possessed*, as all of Cozzens' mature work, is about the condition of man, and in the world of James Gould Cozzens man's condition is limited. One limit is set by time, the moment in which man has his being. It is precisely three o'clock. The other limit is set by man's nature, divided between reason and passion. The shepherd is about to fall victim to the blind instincts of the heart. The burden of Cozzens' fiction is that man must recognize and accept his condition and still bear the responsibility of action. So in the final sentence of *By Love Possessed*, the hero quietly says, "I'm here." Here I am now, at this moment in all of its contingencies, not in some irrecoverable past or in some wished for future; as I am, in all my humanity, a living mixture of weakness and strength, not in some ideal state of being. To act in the full awareness of the irony of the conditions within which he must act is, for Cozzens, the dignity of man.

If this is Cozzens' theme—and it is, I think, present in all the major novels—then he may now have found his own moment in time; until now Cozzens has been neglected, but there are signs that this neglect is about to end. History has finally prepared for him an audience that can share his angle of vision. Until it did, Cozzens went his solitary way, writing fine novels, pursuing his own sense of what life is about, undeterred by the almost total absence of recognition. Beginning in 1924 with *Confusion*, a bad first novel he would like to forget, Cozzens has now written an even dozen novels. He found his major theme by the thirties and in 1948 won the Pulitzer prize with *Guard of Honor*. The many-volumed *Literary History of the United States* which, as a co-operative venture in scholarship, undertook to do for our generation the definitive job on our literature, also appeared in 1948. Hardly a figure, however minor, fails to be noticed, even if only in the copious bibliography. Not a line is given James Gould Cozzens. This is not so strange as it might first seem to one who admires Cozzens. Literary fashions are not purely literary; they indicate states of mind, and the American mind was not in a state to appreciate Cozzens. It is true that Cozzens' style has had something to do with his failure to gain attention; he has none of the flair, the verbal pungency, which immediately attracts. But, of course, style and subject matter are finally one, and the fault seems to be that we were not prepared to see what the matter was. Now perhaps we can.

In *Ask Me Tomorrow*, a novel which draws closely on Cozzens' personal experience, the hero, a young writer named Francis Ellery, watches a hotel ballroom full of people and thinks that "he would like to write about it, if only he could grasp the dramatic inner meaning that lies in the simultaneous occurrence of diverse things." If *Ask Me Tomorrow* is somewhat autobiographical, it is so only as a portrait of the artist as a young man, because Cozzens can do what young Francis Ellery wishes he could do. The characteristic situation of Cozzens' best work is a brief and thickly-peopled moment in time in which a wide variety of characters and incidents are united by a single dramatic inner meaning. *Ask Me Tomorrow* itself covers only a few days in the life of Francis Ellery; the action of *The Last Adam* takes one month; *Men and Brethren* less than twenty-four hours; *The Just and the Unjust* begins at 10:40 on a Tuesday morning and ends just after midnight on Friday; *Guard of Honor* occupies about three days; and *By Love Possessed* precisely forty-nine hours. The strict ordering of time, the compression of action into a narrow frame, is not simply the virtuosity of a skilled storyteller, although one must admire that too. By thoroughly exploring a limited segment of human experience in all its ramifications, Cozzens means to make us appreciate more fully the complexity of moral action. Human right or wrong for Cozzens never exists outside the tangled web of time. And, as Francis Ellery sees, diverse things happen simultaneously. A typical Cozzens novel involves a wide range of characters and a multitude of actions. The numerous subplots function together not only to intensify the dramatic inner meaning common to them all, but to show that no action takes place in isolation. Each action is irrevocably conditioned by all the others. To consider a course of action as if it were self-contained, to act as if one's will were free, is, for Cozzens, to act naïvely, to ignore the teachings of experience.

Cozzens' work is defined not only by these technical devices, the compression of dramatic time and the interpenetration of various actions, but also by certain pervading themes, the need for experience and the discrepancy between the ideal and the actual. The Cozzens hero is generally an older man or, at least, one being schooled into the wisdom of maturity. The hero of *By Love Possessed* wonders at one point if the full status of an adult is given to anyone under forty. Not by James Gould Cozzens. Colonel Ross, the old judge on wartime duty in *Guard of Honor,* puts the matter succinctly:

> Colonel Ross was not sure whether today's different attitude came from being twenty years wiser or just twenty years older. He had, of course, more knowledge of what happens in the long run, of complicated effects from simple causes, of one thing stubbornly leading to another. Experience had been busy that much longer rooting out the vestiges of youth's dear and heady hope that thistles can somehow be made to bear figs and that the end will at last justify any means that might have seemed dubious when the decision to resort to them was so wisely made. Unfortunately, when you got to your end, you found all the means to it inherent there. In short, the first exhilaration of hewing to the line waned when you had to clean up that mess of chips. The new prudence, the sagacious long-term view would save a man from many mistakes. It was a pity that the counsels of wisdom always and so obviously recommend the course to which an old man's lower spirits and failing forces inclined him anyway.

Colonel Ross's skeptical acquiescence to the stubborn facts of life is, in *Guard of Honor,* the mark of his wisdom and maturity. Cozzens measures all his heroes by the same rule. Julius Penrose, the philosophical, crippled lawyer of *By Love Possessed,* puts the code bluntly. "As a wise old man once said to me: Boy, never try to piss up the wind. Principle must sometimes be shelved. Let us face the fact. In this life we cannot do everything we might like to do, nor have for ourselves everything we might like to have." But Julius Penrose points to the paradox in such a view of life. Man is not to lapse into a sullen fatalism because he cannot do all he wants to do; he must stir himself to do what he can. "The paradox is that once fact's assented to, accepted, and we stop directing our effort where effort is wasted, we usually can do quite a number of things, to a faint heart, impossible." To learn the art of the possible is to be mature in Cozzens' world, and it requires a long schooling in the facts of life. Colonel Ross in his novel says, "If you did not know where the limits were, how did you know that you weren't working outside them? If you were working outside them you must be working in vain." To learn where the limits are and to learn to accept them is to attain the full status of adulthood. This is present as a theme in all of Cozzens' later work, and it is at the center of one of the best, *The Just and the Unjust.*

Cozzens does a bold thing at the start of *The Just and the Unjust.* This novel is about Abner Coates, a young assistant district attorney, and the action centers largely about a trial for murder which Abner Coates helps prosecute. The novel begins at the opening of the trial in a high-ceilinged, semicircular courtroom where the acoustics give a spectator little chance of hearing anything intelligible. Abner Coates is aware that, involuntarily, he is an actor in a drama and that "his audience was finding the performance, of which he was part, a poor show compared to what true drama, the art of the theater or the motion picture, had taught them to expect. Art would not take all day Monday to get a jury. Art never dreamed of asking its patrons to sit hour after hour over an impossible-to-hear lawyer's colloquy, with no action." Cozzens' point, of course, the point of all his novels, is that life is not dramatic; it is not filled with stirring climaxes or crucial moments. Life is the slow process of adjustment to half-seen facts and complicated decisions. Here, in *The Just and the Unjust,* he boldly invites the reader to contrast life with art. But his invitation is art. Cozzens deliberately sets himself dramatically unpromising material and then, tongue in cheek, suggests that art would never deal with such material. There is a danger here, certainly, the danger of the mimetic fallacy, to write undramatically about the undramatic. In *The Just and the Unjust* Cozzens may seem to run close to the line, but only the reader lulled into taking Cozzens at face value will miss the artful way in which *The Just and the Unjust* is put together. Although the murder trial is the subject of the book, the theme of the book is Abner's initiation into the facts of life. His love affair, his involvement in politics, the minor actions which involve a fatal automobile accident and the voyeurism of a perverted high school teacher, all work toward this single theme. *The Just and the Unjust* is a novel about the formation of a young man. Abner Coates is made to face life as it is and to accept the responsibilities of maturity, to discard his youthful protest against the distance between the way things should be and the way things are. As a quiet study of the fruits of maturity, the novel embraces a comprehensive hierarchy of ages: one of the defense attorneys is a young man in his twenties; Abner Coates is thirty-one; the district attorney is in his forties; the patient, tired and finally effective political boss is in his fifties; and Abner's father, Judge Coates, manfully bearing up under the adversity of a stroke, is in his sixties. These men represent an ascending scale of practical wisdom, so that the final words of the novel are fittingly left to Abner's elderly father. He tells his son, "We just want you to do the impossible," which is simply to get up and face life every day and do what needs to be done.

The epigraph to *The Just and the Unjust* is a quotation from Lord Hardwicke: "Certainty is the Mother of Repose; therefore the Law aims at Certainty." The novel then ironically demonstrates there can be no certainty in anything man has a hand in by dramatizing the distance between Olympian justice and its human embodiment. For Cozzens, to accept the facts of experience is to accept the discrepancy between what is and what should be; with this as a theme, he focuses his novels on those areas of modern life where the ideal is presumed to govern. The heroes of his later work are always professional men: a doctor in *The Last Adam*, a minister in *Men and Brethren*, a lawyer in *The Just and the Unjust*, a judge who doubles as a military man in *Guard of Honor,* and a lawyer again in *By Love Possessed.* Cozzens turns to the professions for his heroes because of the contrast implicit between the ideal code of the profession and the actuality which pervades it. He can measure the difference between what should be and what is most economically in those areas clearly defined by a professional standard. If, considering Cozzens as a novelist of professions, one immediately thinks of Sinclair Lewis, one must as immediately recognize a difference. Although Cozzens takes infinite care with the authentic details which command belief (Zechariah Chafee, reviewing *The Just and the Unjust* in the *Harvard Law Review,* thought it should be required reading for every young lawyer), he is not interested in the profession as such. He is sympathetic with his professional heroes because they, of all people, are aware of the discrepancy between their professions and their actions and strive, fully conscious of the irony of their predicament, to realize a goal they know is ideal.

Cozzens published his first novel while a Harvard sophomore. Later, in a dictionary of American authors, he wrote, "My first novel was written when I was nineteen, and that, and the next, and the next, were about what you would expect." Passing the same judgment on himself that he does on his characters, he said, "I have the advantage of being older now." Today, on the flyleaf of his other novels, those first novels (*Confusion, Michael Scarlett* and *Cockpit*) are never listed. Because, as Cozzens wrote a Princeton undergraduate, "I began my career with the (I know now) fantastic accident of happening on three successive publishers who lacked judgment and so accepted for publication three novels written before I had taught myself to write or had any idea of what novels should do. Most novelists of course write such first books but they remain manuscripts." One may accept Cozzens' painful sense of the inadequacy of his youthful work, yet the first, *Confusion,* strikes the very note he was to explore successfully in his mature fiction: the necessity for experience, the adjustment of the ideal to the actual. The story itself, full of preposterous Russian counts and sophomoric philosophizing, is about the defeat of innocence when exposed to the confusion of actual life. Cozzens inverts the Jamesian situation: the innocent young girl is a European, and America is the world of experience. But to think of Henry James is to weight the novel too much; its worth now is that it states at the outset the typical Cozzens situation although it fails to realize it in novelistic terms. Late in the novel, the young heroine comes to realize that life is not ideal. "There ought to be some sort of moral beauty," she says, "which isn't marred by the ridiculous or the clumsy or the inane. And you just don't find it. Each one of us has irradicable meannesses and flaws. And then things happen in such a way. Life isn't an abstract thing, it's the concrete lives of millions of human beings. When you build on life you build on a sort of quicksand."

Cozzens' developed position is an acceptance of this judgment. In Cozzens' world one does build on quicksand and one must continue to do so fully aware that he stands on shifting ground where the ideal is marred by the ridiculous and violated by the meanness of us all. Read by itself, *Confusion* might be taken as an adolescent protest that this is so; the weakness of the novel is that the reader is not sure how to take the meaning. (In *Cockpit* youth quite ingeniously triumphs over the shrewd adult world.) But by the time he had taught himself to write, Cozzens not only would avoid such infelicities as "irradicable," he would have learned how to project his own sense of life so that the reader, caught up in the fiction, must assent to its imaginative reality. No artist develops in a simple linear fashion, getting better and better, exploring his theme more deeply and more intelligently in each successive novel, but Cozzens comes close. With only slight variations from the straight line, Cozzens has steadily strengthened his grasp.

By Love Possessed is the story of forty-nine hours in the

life of Arthur Winner, a tall, spare, balding, fifty-four-year-old lawyer. Early in the action, a young judge, enmeshed in his own problems, asks Arthur Winner, "Could you ever have changed what's going to happen? You know this much: Whatever happens, happens because a lot of other things have happened already. When it gets to where you come in—well, it's bound to be pretty late in the day. . . . Freedom, I read at college, is the knowledge of necessity." Arthur Winner recognizes the emotion behind the query, the dissatisfaction with the kinds of victory to be won in life. "Might all of them be forms of defeat: givings-up; compromises; assents to the second best; abandonments of hope, in the face of ascertained fact that what was to be, was to be?" With a remarkable economy, every action of the book tests this question. Some characters in the novel evade the question; some escape into alcoholism or to the institutionalized comfort of the church; some lapse into a brutalized cynicism to hide from the question. But Cozzens leads the reader to an inevitable acceptance of Arthur Winner's answer at the end: "Victory is not in reaching certainties or solving mysteries; victory is in making do with uncertainties, in supporting mysteries." But if this is the answer, the conclusion is not fatalistic. Man is not excused because this is so; he cannot resign his responsibility; he cannot quit because he knows that the end of man is defeat. Stoically, using what resources of reason and strength of will he has, man must continue to seek the order which the conditions of life and man's nature will not allow. The irony is there in the hero's very name: Winner. There are no winners in Cozzens' world; the only victory is to recognize and accept that fact.

By Love Possessed was a Book-of-the-Month-Club selection; Hollywood, in its fondness for the resounding sum, bought it for $100,000; Time magazine has even enshrined Cozzens in its pantheon of modern heroes by putting him on the cover. This sudden rush of acceptance—and one hopes that Cozzens is as immune to good fortune as to bad—raises a question. Why now? Why not before? Cozzens is aware that he has not been in fashion. Once, when invited to lecture at Princeton University on the novel, he declined, writing that he had observed "that novelists are not very interesting when they air their views about the novel. As well as grieving the judicious by glimpses they generally give of that coxcomb and jackass seldom far to seek in anyone with a creative faculty, those I've heard or read were never long in indicating that they don't know a damn thing about their 'art'—and that's the case, I think." In a second letter, he put emphatically his sense of his own separateness:

> Not to mince it, current critical opinion and I greatly disagree about what's good. As part of his professional job I think a novelist should examine all contemporary novels that attract attention. I do this; and I then take care to observe what critics say of them. Too often for it to be mere chance or minor difference in taste, I'm flabbergasted to find the consensus discovering Profound Feeling, Deep Insight, Moving Symbolism, and Living Characters where I saw deplorable sentimentality, cheap and childish thinking, silly pretentiousness, and preposterous people. Here, clearly, someone's wrong; and at that I'm satisfied to leave it. Like so many of those who are really self centered, absorbed altogether in what they are doing, I haven't even the weakest urge to show others their errors, argue them into agreement, prove I'm right. This makes the obvious part both of prudence and of common civility easy for me—I just shut up, stay at home, and attend to my work.

In one of the early as well as one of the few essays on Cozzens, the late Bernard De Voto, writing from the "Editor's Easy Chair" of *Harper's* magazine, tried to answer why Cozzens had not received the critical acclaim due him; his answer may also contain the reason why acclaim has come to Cozzens now. In his usual muscular fashion, De Voto used Cozzens to cudgel modern criticism. Critics shy away from Cozzens, De

Voto thought, because "he is a writer. His novels are written. . . . So they leave criticism practically nothing to do. They are not born of a cause but of a fine novelist's feeling for the lives of people and for their destiny. . . . They contain no fog of confused thinking on which, as on a screen, criticism can project its diagrams of meanings which the novelist did not know were there. There is in them no mass of unshaped emotion, the novelist's emotion or the characters', from which criticism can dredge up significance that becomes portentous as the critic calls our attention, and the novelist's, to it. Worse still, they are written with such justness that criticism cannot get a toe-hold to tell him and us how they should have been written. Worst of all, the novelist's ego has been disciplined out of them, so criticism cannot chant its dirge about the dilemmas of the artist in our time."

Now despite much of the nonsense here, the notion that the better a writer is the less criticism has to say about him, despite this wrong-headedness, De Voto has two shrewd things to say about Cozzens' career. First, Cozzens' books are not "born of a cause"; they are not the product of any social or political movement. Second, Cozzens has not gone with the literary fashions of the time, the novel of elaborate symbolical structure, or the novel of sensitive introspection. If this is true, Cozzens has stood apart from some sizable movements in our literature. He has gone his own way which is not the way of the novel of social protest or of the psychological novel; nor has he followed the dominant mode of modern fiction, the method of symbolism.

Yet, if one goes back to the early work, one discovers that Cozzens worked successfully in the modes which now seem so alien to him. *Son of Perdition,* Cozzens' fourth novel and the one he likes to consider his real beginning, is interesting for two reasons: it marks the tentative discovery of the way Cozzens will organize his major novels while, at the same time, it wavers between two ways of handling the story. *Son of Perdi-*

tion takes place in little less than a day at Dosfuegos, Cuba, the sea terminal of the United Sugar Company. Early, then, Cozzens is working toward the tight unity he will exploit better later. Cozzens had already written one novel, *Cockpit*, about the sugar industry, but he does not make special use of his knowledge of its operations; *Son of Perdition* does not qualify as the novel of a profession. But in this early novel (although it was his fourth book, he was still only twenty-six), Cozzens is already exploring the problem of the limits of human action, the moral complexity arising from man's limitations as man. At one point in the novel Cozzens compares the clean efficiency of the machine with the muddled quality of humanity. He notes "the machine's inhuman beauty, the reason and might of the machine, confounded so inevitably by the rooted folly, the poor stubborn pride of man." But Cozzens is not arguing the program of the Italian Futurists; man's nature is not susceptible to the perfect rationality of the machine. Man is constantly the victim of his own rooted folly.

Son of Perdition has, even if as tendencies, the characteristics of Cozzens' best manner. It fails only in one, the interpenetration of the various levels of action. The novel is sharply divided between the Americans who have descended on Cuba with the United Sugar Company and the natives of Cuba. Although there is little functional relationship between them, Cozzens comes close to something brilliant in the way he juxtaposes the two societies. Two characters dominate the American group: the chief of United Sugar, Joel B. Stellow, and a drifter and troublemaker, Oliver Findley. Given their own world, they exist simply as strikingly different types. But by counter-poising them against the superstition of the natives, Cozzens surrounds Stellow and Findley with the suggestions of the symbolic roles of God and the Devil. Here Cozzens is having the best of both worlds without committing himself to either. In two subsequent novels, *S.S. San Pedro* and *Castaway*, both short books, Cozzens pursues what, for want of a more precise term, one might call the "symbolic." In actual order of chronology, *The Last Adam* falls between these two books and suggests how Cozzens was hesitantly finding his way. But before he found it, Cozzens proved he could write one of the most successful psychological novels of our contemporary fiction. *Castaway* is worlds removed from Cozzens' later work; a nightmare inversion of the Robinson Crusoe myth, it belongs to the world of Kafka. The hero, Mr. Lecky, is locked in a department store over a long weekend. With everything that modern society has to offer in the way of material goods, he is paralyzed by fear, either pursued by a madman or haunted by his own madness. Whichever, the point is clear enough: with all the material resources of the modern world, man has not the spiritual resources to sustain himself. In American literature, one must go back to Melville's "Bartleby the Scrivener," to discover another piece of fiction with the same surrealistic power. One can understand, given the critical position that Mr. De Voto bewails, that so good a critic as Stanley Edgar Hyman can think *Castaway* Cozzens' best book as well as one of the most neglected novels in recent years because Cozzens presents here, in all its psychological horror, the alienation and aloneness of modern man.

The danger, however, in drawing a sharp contrast between the stages of Cozzens' career is that one will miss in the later work the subtle way in which Cozzens has domesticated his symbolism. In *By Love Possessed*, the setting and the weather, so natural in themselves, gradually add a dimension of meaning to the novel and so, by definition, function symbolically. As the action progresses, a dark storm gathers, just as fate gradually encloses Arthur Winner. At the orgastic climax of the tender love affair between the hero and his wife, the storm breaks. The next day we learn that a bolt of lightning had at the same moment riven a great sheltering tree at Ponemah, Arthur Winner's summer house. With that news one recognizes that the idyllic security of childhood so carefully associated in the early pages of the novel with Ponemah, is not to be sustained in the adult world in which love is only fleetingly realized amidst the storms of experience. Ponemah is, in Arthur Winner's world, not only the garden of his first wife, it is *the* Garden, the world of innocence before man's fall into time and the corruption of his human estate. One need only read Cozzens' first novel, *Confusion*, in which there figures a place of retreat from the world also called Po-ne-mah, to realize what Cozzens means when he says that when he grew older he taught himself what a novel should do. It should project the world of myth and symbol in the common experience of the characters' daily lives. So when the final revelation of Arthur Winner's own character comes in a scene in the garden, the inevitable snake is believably there.

Cozzens' increasing insistence on the actual as he develops his technique is, of course, a function of his subject matter, an insistence on the here and now. So one suspects that it has never been a matter of style; it is the image of the world which the style presents and of which it is itself a part. Cozzens' central theme, that man must do what he can with the facts as they are, that one must accept the world as given, runs counter to the mood of much recent American history. Rebellion against society, which Cozzens thinks is callow, characterized the fiction of the twenties; the reformation of society, which Cozzens thinks is naïve, characterized the fiction of the thirties. Despite Bernard De Voto, Cozzens' fiction may be born of a cause, a personal cause, the cause of a skeptical conservative who does not think too much can be done with the way things are. Outside of his fiction, Cozzens has said, "I am more or less illiberal, and strongly antipathetic to all political or artistic movements. I was brought up an Episcopalian, and where I live the landed gentry are Republican." The tone is a little shrill here, but it suggests a personal position behind the fictional world which helps one understand why Cozzens remained out of fashion despite his superior skills as a novelist. One need not be a member of the landed gentry or a Republican, of course, to appreciate

Cozzens' view of the condition of man. Happily, Cozzens is a novelist, not an apologist. But it is probably true that more Americans can more readily share Cozzens' view now than ever before. Since the Second World War, high aspirations and heady ideals have come to seem somewhat embarrassing, if not a little absurd, to many Americans. So the acceptance of Cozzens today may be as much a function of the intellectual climate as was his neglect before.

If history has caught up with Cozzens, it is because, in a more important sense, history has caught up with the American people. With a remarkable prescience, Tocqueville remarked in the early nineteenth century that because of the social conditions of the country Americans "owe nothing to any man; they expect nothing from any man; they acquire the habit of always considering themselves as standing alone, and they are apt to imagine that their whole destiny is in their own hands." The cast of mind Tocqueville perceived led on one side to the Horatio Alger legend and the myth of the self-made man in the hands of the apologists for our great capitalists. On the other, it led to great literature and the creation of a characteristic American hero, the solitary, self-propellant man, heroically alone. He is the character demanded by Emerson and given us most richly by Thoreau in *Walden*, the new man who realizes his character by taking his way not to man but from man. Since 1783 when Crevecoeur asked his famous question, "What is this new man, this American?" down to Henry James's hero Christopher Newman, named after the discoverer who gave this new man a new world in which to act, Americans have tended to think of themselves as beginning history over again, making a fresh new start. The westering experience of the American people dramatized in their daily lives the notion that the archetypal American was he who moved away from society, out of civilization, and began anew. He is Natty Bumppo and Huck Finn. R. W. B. Lewis has explored with brilliance the cultural dialogue that took place around and about this heroic figure and has named him the American Adam.

The image of the American as a new man was not without its paradoxes, of course, and Hawthorne and Melville have alerted us to them. But the chief irony in such a dramatization of American history was that the moral Nature of the Transcendentalists and the Jeffersonians was also the physical one of coal, iron and oil, the raw materials of a vast complex industrial civilization in which man's direction is to man, not away from man. Henry Adams made this irony the central fact in *The Education* and saw that "the new American [was] the child of incalculable coal-power, chemical power, electric power, and radiating energy." Emerson could innocently write that history was but the lengthened shadow of a man, but when Adams returned from England to the new industrial America that had won the Civil War he "found his energies exhausted in the effort to see his own length. The new Americans, of whom he was to be one, must, whether they were fit or unfit, create a world of their own," but it was to be the world we now live in, the world of complex structures, interdependence and organization, not the world of freedom from social forces and escape from history.

Richard Blackmur once said in conversation that James Gould Cozzens was the only contemporary writer who had taken the organization of modern society for his theme. Because Cozzens does not write about the man in the gray flannel suit many readers will miss the fact that Cozzens is a contemporary writer in the deepest sense of the term. His subject is the limited world in which man is enmeshed in a congeries of forces which radiates far beyond his personal control. Cozzens' heroes are professional men, themselves an instance of a specialized society, and his subjects are various; but his theme is the complex world in which man, in his already limited estate, is further limited. In *Guard of Honor*, seemingly about the special state of war, Cozzens asks if war is really so different: "No. Not if you could face the too-little-faced fact that war really brought you nothing that peace, mere living, couldn't eventually bring." Mere living can be a heroic enterprise in Cozzens' fiction because it involves man in a historical and social web that he can neither control nor renounce. All he can do is the impossible, live in it and accept it with skeptical and ironic good sense.

Henry Adams wrote that the "old-fashioned logical drama required unity and sense; the actual drama is a pointless puzzle, without even an intrigue." Adams is describing the modern world; Cozzens' heroes live in it. The point is not that Cozzens may have read Adams (although their mutual admiration of Pascal suggests an intellectual affinity) but that both are reacting imaginatively to the conditions of modern man. The view of human nature present in Cozzens' fiction is not modern; it has roots certainly in the seventeenth century, echoes of which sound throughout Cozzens' pages. But it is a view of man, however traditional, which has a special significance for modern man. Divided between reason and passion, called to act in a world he cannot control, he may be the new man, the new hero, that the conditions of modern life demand. If so, James Gould Cozzens has presented him richly for our contemplation.

THE CULTURE OF FREEDOM

PART III

THE CULTURE OF FREEDOM

1

SELF AND SOCIETY

I · Benjamin Franklin: The Making of an American Character

BENJAMIN FRANKLIN bulks large in our national consciousness, sharing room with Washington and Jefferson and Lincoln. Yet it is hard to say precisely what it means to name Franklin one of our cultural heroes. He was, as one book about him has it, "many-sided." The sheer variety of his character has made it possible to praise him and damn him with equal vigor. At home, such dissimilar Yankees as the laconic Calvin Coolidge and the passionate Theodore Parker could each find reason to admire him. Abroad, David Hume could say that he was "the first great man of letters" for whom Europe was "beholden" to America. Yet D. H. Lawrence, brought up, he tells us, in the industrial wastelands of midland England on the pious saws of "Poor Richard," could only "utter a long, loud curse" against "this dry, moral, utilitarian little democrat."

Part of the difficulty in comprehending Franklin's meaning is due to the opposites he seems to have contained with complete serenity within his own personality. He was an eminently reasonable man who maintained a deep skepticism about the power of reason. He was a model of industriousness who, preaching the gospel of hard work, kept his shop only until it kept him and retired at forty-two. He was a cautious and prudent man who was a revolutionist. And, to name only one more seeming contradiction, he was one who had a keen eye for his own advantage and personal advancement who spent nearly all his adult life in the service of others. Small wonder that there have been various interpretations of so various a character.

The problem may seem no problem at all. Today, when we all know that the position of the observer determines the shape of reality, we observe the observer. If Franklin, seeing to it that the streets of Philadelphia are well lit and swept clean at a moderate price, that no fires rage, does not appeal to D. H. Lawrence, we tend not to think of Franklin. We think of Lawrence; we remember his atavistic urge to explore the dark and passionate underside of life and move on. Franklin contained in his own character so many divergent aspects that each observer can make the mistake of seeing one aspect as all and celebrate or despise Franklin accordingly. Mr. I. Bernard Cohen, who has written so well on so much of Franklin, has remarked that "an account of Franklin . . . is apt to be a personal testament of the commentator concerning the America he most admires." Or contemns.

Yet there still remains the obstinate fact that Franklin could mean so many things to so many men, that he was so many-sided, that he did contain opposites, that he was, in other words, so many different characters. One suspects that here is the single most important thing about Franklin. Rather than spend our energies trying to find some consistency in this protean, many-sided figure, trying to resolve who Franklin truly was, we might perhaps better accept his variety itself as our major problem and try to understand that. To insist on the importance of the question, "Who was Benjamin Franklin?" may finally be more conclusive than to agree upon an answer.

The place to begin to ask the question is with the *Memoirs,* with the *Autobiography* as we have come to call them, and the place to begin there is with the history of the text. Fascinating in and of itself, the history of the text gives us an initial lead into the question of the elusiveness of Franklin's personality.

The *Autobiography* was written in four parts. The first part, addressed by Franklin to his son, William, was begun during some few weeks in July and August, 1771, while Franklin was visiting with his friend, Jonathan Shipley, the Bishop of St. Asaph, in Hampshire, England. Franklin was then sixty-five years old. As he wrote the first part he also carefully made a list of topics he would subsequently treat. Somehow the manuscript and list fell into the hands of one Abel James who eleven years later wrote Franklin, returning to him the list of topics but not the first part of the manuscript, urging him to take up his story once again. This was in 1782, or possibly early in January, 1783. Franklin was in France as one of the peace commissioners. He wrote the second part in France in 1784, after the achievement of peace, indicating the beginning and the ending of this short second part in the manuscript itself.

In 1785, Franklin returned to America, promising to work on the manuscript during the voyage. Instead he wrote three of his utilitarian essays: on navigation, on how to avoid smoky streetlamp chimneys, and on his famous stove. He did not return to his life's story until 1788. Then, after retiring from the presidency of the state of Pennsylvania in the spring, Franklin, quite sick, made his will and put his house in order before turning again to his own history. This was in August, 1788. Franklin was eighty-three years old, in pain, and preparing for death. The third part is the longest part of the autobiography, less interesting than the first two, and for many years was thought to conclude the manuscript.

In 1789, Franklin has his grandson, Benjamin Franklin Bache, make two fair copies of Parts I, II and III in order to send them to friends abroad, Benjamin Vaughan in England and M. le Veillard in France. Then, sometime before his death in April, 1790, Franklin added the last and fourth part, some seven and one-half manuscript pages, which was not included, naturally, in the fair copies sent abroad. For the rest, Mr. Max Farrand, our authority on the history of the text:

> After [Franklin's] death, the publication of the autobiography was eagerly awaited, as its existence was widely known, but for nearly thirty years the reading public had to content itself with French translations of the first and second parts, which were again translated from the French into other languages, and even retranslated into English. When the authorized English publication finally appeared in 1818, it was not taken from the original manuscript but from a copy, as was the preceding French version of the first part. The copy, furthermore, did not include the fourth and last part, which also reached the public in a French translation in 1828.
>
> . . . the complete autobiography was not printed in English from the original manuscript until 1868, nearly eighty years after Franklin's death.

The story is, as I have said, interesting in and of itself. The tangled history of one of our most important texts has its own fascination, but it also provides us the first clue to our question. Surely it must strike any reader of the *Autobiography* as curious that a character who speaks so openly should at the same time seem so difficult to define. But the history of the text points the way to an answer. All we need do is ask why Franklin wrote his memoirs.

When the Quaker, Abel James, wrote Franklin, returning his list of topics and asking "kind, humane, and benevolent Ben Franklin" to continue his life's story, "a work which would be useful and entertaining not only to a few but to millions,"

Franklin sent the letter on to his friend, Benjamin Vaughan, asking for advice. Vaughan concurred. He too urged Franklin to publish the history of his life because he could think of no "more efficacious advertisement" of America than Franklin's history. "All that has happened to you," he reminded Franklin, "is also connected with the detail of the manners and situation of a rising people." Franklin included James's and Vaughan's letters in his manuscript to explain why he resumed his story. What had gone before had been written for his family; "what follows," he said in his "Memo," "was written . . . in compliance with the advice contained in these letters, and accordingly intended for the public. The affairs of the Revolution occasioned the interruption."

The point is obvious enough. When Franklin resumed his story, he did so in full self-consciousness that he was offering himself to the world as a representative type, the American. Intended for the public now, his story was to be an example for young Americans, as Abel James would have it, and an advertisement to the world, as Benjamin Vaughan would have it. We had just concluded a successful revolution; the eyes of all the world were upon us. Just as America had succeeded in creating itself a nation, Franklin set out to show how the American went about creating his own character. As Benjamin Vaughan said, Franklin's life would "give a noble rule and example of self-education" because of Franklin's "discovery that the thing is in many a man's private power." So what follows is no longer the simple annals of Franklin's life for the benefit of his son. Benjamin Franklin plays his proper role. He becomes "The American."

How well he filled the part that his public urged him to play, we can see by observing what he immediately proceeds to provide. In the pages that follow James's and Vaughan's letters, Franklin quickly treats four matters: the establishment of a lending library, that is, the means for satisfying the need for self-education; the importance of frugality and industriousness in one's calling; the social utility of religion; and, of course, the thirteen rules for ordering one's life. Here, in a neat package, were all the materials that went into the making of the self-made man. This is how one goes about making a success of one's self. If the sentiments of our Declaration were to provide prompt notes for European revolutions, then Franklin, as the American Democrat, acted them out. Family, class, religious orthodoxy, higher education: all these were secondary to character and common sense. The thing was in many a man's private power.

If we look back now at the first part, the opening section addressed by Franklin to his son, William, we can see a difference and a similarity. The difference is, of course, in the easy and personal tone, the more familiar manner, appropriate to a communication with one's son. It is in these early pages that Franklin talks more openly about his many *errata*, his "frequent intrigues with low women," and displays that rather cool and calculating attitude toward his wife. Rather plain dealing, one might think, at least one who did not know that William was a bastard son.

But the similarity between the two parts is more important. The message is the same, although addressed to a son, rather than to the world: how to go about making a success. "From the poverty and obscurity in which I was born and in which I passed my earliest years," writes the father to the son, "I have raised myself to a state of affluence and some degree of celebrity in the world." A son, especially, must have found that "some" hard to take. But the career is not simply anecdotal: "my posterity will perhaps be desirous of learning the means, which I employed, and which, thanks to Providence, so well succeeded with me. They may also deem them fit to be imitated." The story is exemplary, although how the example was to affect a son who was, in 1771, about forty years old and already Royal Governor of New Jersey is another matter.

The story has remained exemplary because it is the success

story to beat all success stories: the runaway apprentice printer who rose to dine with kings; the penniless boy, walking down Market Street with two large rolls under his arms, who was to sit in Independence Hall and help create a new nation. But notice that the story does not deal with the success itself. That is presumed, of course, but the *Autobiography* never gets to the later and more important years because the *Autobiography* is not about success. It is about the formation of the character that makes success possible. The subject of the *Autobiography* is the making of a character. Having lifted himself by his own bootstraps, Franklin described it that way: "I have raised myself." We were not to find the pat phrase until the early nineteenth century when the age of the common man made the style more common: "the self-made man." The character was for life, of course, and not for fiction where we usually expect to encounter the made-up, but that should not prevent us from looking a little more closely at the act of creation. We can look in two ways: first, by standing outside the *Autobiography* and assessing it by what we know from elsewhere; second, by reading the *Autobiography* itself more closely.

A good place to begin is with those years in France around the end of the Revolution. It is so delicious an episode in plain Ben's life. More importantly—as Franklin said, one can always find a principle to justify one's inclinations—it is in these very years at Passy that Franklin, in response to James's and Vaughan's letters, wrote those self-conscious pages of the second part of the *Autobiography*. Just as he wrote the lines, he played them. As Carl Van Doren has written, "the French were looking for a hero who should combine the reason and wit of Voltaire with the primitive virtues celebrated by Rousseau. . . . [Franklin] denied them nothing." This is the period of the simple Quaker dress, the fur cap and the spectacles. France went wild in its adulation and Franklin knew why. "Think how this must appear," he wrote a friend, "among the powdered heads of Paris."

But he was also moving with equal ease in that world, the world of the powdered heads of Paris, one of the most cosmopolitan, most preciously civilized societies in history. Although he was no Quaker, Franklin was willing to allow the French to think so. They called him *"le bon Quackeur."* The irony was unintentional, a matter of translation. But at the same time that he was filling the role of the simple backwoods democrat, the innocent abroad, he was also playing cavalier in the brilliant salon of Madame Helvétius, the widow of the French philosopher. Madame Helvétius is supposed to have been so beautiful that Fontenelle, the great popularizer of Newton, who lived to be one hundred years old, was said to have paid her the most famous compliment of the age: "Ah, madame, if I were only eighty again!" Madame Helvétius was sixty when Franklin knew her and the classic anecdote of their acquaintance is that Madame Helvétius is said to have reproached him for not coming to see her, for putting off his long anticipated visit. Franklin replied, "Madame, I am waiting until the nights are longer." There was also Madame Brillon, not a widow, who once wrote to Franklin, "People have the audacity to criticize my pleasant habit of sitting on your knee, and yours of always asking me for what I always refuse."

Some, discovering this side of Franklin, have written him off simply as a rather lively old lecher. Abigail Adams, good New England lady that she was, was thoroughly shocked. She set Madame Helvétius down as a "very bad woman." But Franklin, despite his public style, was not so provincial. He appealed to Madame Brillon that he had spent so many days with her that surely she could spend one night with him. She mockingly called him a sophist. He then appealed to her charity and argued that it was in the design of Providence that she grant him his wish. If somehow a son of the Puritans, Franklin had grown far beyond the reach of their sermonizing. Thomas Hooker had thought, "It's a grievous thing to the loose person, he cannot have his pleasures but he must have his guilt and gall with them." But Franklin wrote Madame Brillon, "Reflect how many of our duties [Providence] has ordained naturally to be pleasures; and that it has had the goodness besides, to give the name of sin to several of them so that we might enjoy them the more."

All this is delightful enough, and for more one need only turn to Carl Van Doren's biography from which I have taken these anecdotes, but what it points to is as important as it is entertaining. It points to Franklin's great capacity to respond to the situation in which he found himself and to play the expected role, to prepare a face to meet the faces that he met. He could, in turn, be the homespun, rustic philosopher or the mocking cavalier, the witty sophist. He knew what was expected of him.

The discovery should not surprise any reader of the *Autobiography*. Throughout it, Franklin insists always on the distinction between appearance and reality, between what he is and what he seems to be.

> In order to secure my credit and character as a tradesman, I took care not only to be in *reality* industrious and frugal, but to avoid all *appearances* of the contrary. I dressed plain and was seen at no places of idle diversion. I never went out a fishing or shooting; a book, indeed, sometimes debauched me from my work, but that was seldom, snug, and gave no scandal; and to show that I was not above my business, I sometimes brought home the paper I purchased at the stores, thro' the streets on a wheelbarrow. Thus being esteemed an industrious, thriving young man, and paying duly for what I bought, the merchants who imported stationery solicited my custom; others proposed supplying me with books, and I went on swimmingly.

Now, with this famous passage, one must be careful. However industrious and frugal Franklin may in fact have been, he knew that for the business of social success virtue counts for nothing without its public dress. In Franklin's world there has to be someone in the woods to hear the tree fall. Private virtue might bring one to stand before the King of kings, but if one wants to sit down and sup with the kings of this world, then one must help them see one's merit. There are always in this world, as Franklin pointed out, "a number of rich merchants, nobility, states, and princes who have need of honest instruments for the management of their affairs, and such being so rare [I] have endeavoured to convince young persons, that no qualities are so likely to make a poor man's fortune as those of probity and integrity."

Yet if one wants to secure one's credit in the world by means of one's character, then the character must be of a piece. There can be no false gesture; the part must be played well. When Franklin drew up his list of virtues they contained, he tells us, only twelve. But a Quaker friend "kindly" informed him that he was generally thought proud and overbearing and rather insolent; he proved it by examples. So Franklin added humility to his list; but, having risen in the world and content with the degree of celebrity he had achieved, he could not bring himself to be humble. "I cannot boast of much success in acquiring the *reality* of this virtue, but I had a good deal with regard to the *appearance* of it."

He repeats, at this point, what he had already written in the first part of his story. He forswears all "positive assertion." He drops from his vocabulary such words as "certainly" and "undoubtedly" and adopts a tentative manner. He remembers how he learned to speak softly, to put forward his opinions, not dogmatically, but by saying, " 'I imagine' a thing to be so or so, or 'It so appears to me at present.' " As he had put it to his son earlier, he discovered that Socratic method, "was charmed with it, adopted it, dropped my abrupt contradiction and positive argumentation, and put on the humble enquirer." For good reason: "this habit . . . has been of great advantage to me."

What saves all this in the *Autobiography* from being merely repellent is Franklin's self-awareness, his good humor in telling us about the part he is playing, the public clothes he is putting on to hide what his public will not openly buy. "In reality," he writes, drawing again the distinction from appearance, "there is perhaps no one of our natural passions so hard to subdue as *pride;* disguise it, struggle with it, beat it down, stifle it, mortify it as much as one pleases, it is still alive and will every now and then peep out and show itself. You will see it perhaps often in this history. For even if I could conceive that I had completely overcome it, I should probably be proud of my humility." Here, despite the difference in tone, Franklin speaks like that other and contrasting son of the Puritans, Jonathan Edwards, on the nature of true virtue. Man, if he could achieve virtue, would inevitably be proud of the achievement and so, at the moment of success, fall back into sin.

The difference is, of course, in the tone. The insight is the same but Franklin's skeptical and untroubled self-acceptance is far removed from Edwards' troubled and searching self-doubt. Franklin enjoys the game. Mocking himself, he quietly lures us, in his Yankee deadpan manner, with the very bait he has just described. After having told us that he early learned to "put on the humble enquirer" and to affect a self-depreciating pose, he quotes in his support the line from Alexander Pope, "To speak, though sure, with seeming diffidence." Pope, Franklin immediately goes on to say, "might have joined with this line that which he has coupled with another, I think less properly, 'For want of modesty is want of sense.'"

If you ask why *less properly*, I must repeat the lines,

> Immodest words admit of *no defence,*
> *For* want of modesty is want of sense.

Now is not the "want of sense" (where a man is so unfortunate as to want it) some apology for his "want of modesty"? and would not the lines stand more justly thus?

> Immodest words admit *but* this defense
> That want of modesty is want of sense.

This, however, I should submit to better judgements.

Having been so bold as to correct a couplet of the literary giant of the age, Franklin quietly retreats and defers to the judgment of those better able to say than he. Having just described the humble part he has decided to play, he immediately acts it out. If we get the point, we chuckle with him; if we miss the point, that only proves its worth.

But one of the functions of laughter is to dispel uneasiness and in Franklin's case the joke is not enough. Our uneasiness comes back when we stop to remember that he is, as his friends asked him to, writing his story as an efficacious advertisement. We must always ask whether Franklin's disarming candor in recounting how things went on so swimmingly may not be yet another role, still another part he is playing. Actually, even with Yale's sumptuous edition of Franklin's papers, we know little about Franklin's personal life in the early years, except through his own account. The little we do know suggests that his way to wealth and success was not the smooth and open path he would have us believe. This leads us, then, if we cannot answer finally the question who Franklin was, to a different question. What does it mean to say that a character so changeable, so elusive, somehow represents American culture? What is there in Franklin's style that makes him, as we say, characteristic?

At the outset in colonial America, with men like John Winthrop, there was always the assumption that one would be called to one's appropriate station in life and labor in it for one's own good and the good of society. Magistrates would be magistrates and printers would be printers. But in the world in which Franklin moved, the magistrates, like Governor Keith of Pennsylvania who sends Franklin off on a wild-goose chase to England, prove to be frauds while the plain, leather-aproned set went quietly about the work of making society possible at all, creating the institutions—the militia, the fire companies, the libraries, the hospitals, the public utilities—that made society habitable. The notion that underlay an orderly, hierarchical society failed to make sense of such a world. It proved impossible to keep people in their place.

One need only consider in retrospect how swiftly Franklin moved upward through the various levels of society to see the openness, the fluidity of his world. Simply because he is a young man with some books, Governor Burnet of New York asks to see him. While in New Jersey on a job printing money he meets and makes friends with all the leaders of that provincial society. In England, at the coffeehouses, he chats wtih Mandeville and meets the great Dr. Henry Pemberton who was seeing the third edition of Newton's *Principia* through the press. As Franklin said, diligent in his calling, he raised himself by some degree.

The Protestant doctrine of calling, of industriousness in the world, contained dynamite for the orderly, hierarchical, social structure it was originally meant to support. The unintended consequence showed itself within two generations. Those who were abstemious, frugal, and hardworking made a success in the world. They rose. And society, rather than the static and closed order in which, in Winthrop's words, "some must be rich some poor, some high and eminent in power and dignitie; others meane and in subieccion," turned out to be dynamic, fluid and open.

If there is much of our national character implicit in Franklin's career, it is because, early in our history, he represents a response to the rapid social change that has remained about the only constant in American society. He was the self-made man, the jack-of-all-trades. He taught thirteen rules to sure success and purveyed do-it-yourself kits for those who, like himself, constituted a "rising" people. Franklin stands most clearly as an exemplary American because his life's story is a witness to the uncertainties about social status that have characterized our society, a society caught up in the constant process of change. The question, "Who was Benjamin Franklin?" is a critical question to ask of Franklin because it is the question to which Franklin himself is constantly seeking an answer. In a society in which there are no outward, easily discernible marks of social status, the question always is, as we put it in the title of reference works that are supposed to provide the answer, "Who's Who?"

Along with the uncertainties generated by rapid social mobility, there is another aspect to the difficulty we have in placing Franklin, an aspect that is more complex and harder to state, but just as important and equally characteristic. It takes us back again to the Puritans. In Puritan religious thought there was originally a dynamic equipoise between two opposite thrusts, the tension between an inward, mystical, personal experience of God's grace and the demands for an outward, sober, socially responsible ethic, the tension between faith and works, between the essence of religion and its outward show. Tremendous energy went into sustaining these polarities in the early years, but as the original piety waned, itself undermined by the worldly success that benefited from the doctrine of calling, the synthesis split in two and resulted in the eighteenth century in Jonathan Edwards and Benjamin Franklin, similar in so many ways, yet so radically unlike.

Franklin, making his own world as he makes his way through it, pragmatically rejects the old conundrum whether man does good works because he is saved, or is saved because he does good works. "Vicious actions are not hurtful because they are forbidden, but forbidden because they are hurtful," he decides, and then in an added phrase calmly throws out the God-centered universe of his forebears, "the nature of man alone considered."

Content with his success, blandly sure it must be in the design of Providence that printers hobnob with kings, Franklin simply passes by the problem of the relation between reality and appearance. In this world, appearance is sufficient. Humanely skeptical that the essence can ever be caught, Franklin decided to leave the question to be answered in the next world, if there proved to be one. For this world, a "tolerable character" was enough and he "valued it properly." The result was a commonsense utilitarianism which sometimes verges toward sheer crassness. But it worked. For this world, what others think of you is what is important. If Franklin, viewed from the perspective of Max Weber and students of the Protestant ethic, can seem to be the representative, *par excellence*, of the character who internalizes the imperatives of his society and steers his own course unaided through the world, from a slightly different perspective he also turns out to be the other-directed character David Riesman has described, constantly attuned to the expectations of those around him, responding swiftly to the changing situations that demand he play different roles.

We admire, I think, the lusty good sense of the man who triumphs in the world that he accepts, yet at the same time we are uneasy with the man who wears so many masks that we are never sure who is there behind them. Yet it is this, this very difficulty of deciding whether we admire Franklin or suspect him, that makes his character an archetype for our national experience. There are great advantages to be had in belonging to a culture without clearly defined classes, without an establishment, but there is, along with the advantages, a certain strain, a necessary uneasiness. In an open and pluralistic society we have difficulty "placing" people, as we say. Think how often in our kind of society when we meet someone for the first time how our second or third question is apt to be, "What do you do?" Never, "Who are you?" The social role is enough, but in our more reflective moments we realize not so, and in our most reflective moments we realize it will never do for our own selves. We may be able to, but we do not want to go through life as a doctor, lawyer, or Indian chief. We want to be ourselves, as we say. And at the beginning of our national experience, Benjamin Franklin not only puts the question that still troubles us in our kind of society, "Who's Who?" He also raises the question that lies at the heart of the trouble: "Who am I?"

II · John F. Kennedy:
The Meaning of Courage

THE BACK COVER of the memorial edition of *Profiles in Courage* shows John F. Kennedy, with that infectious grin, finger pointing, arm about to be thrust out, standing with the seal of the President of the United States before him and the draped flag of the United States behind. The energy, the youth, the shining confidence, the zest to engage in debate leap out of the picture. They leap out of a background of solid black. John F. Kennedy is dead.

To sit now with the image of the living man in one's hands, it is still hard to believe he is not still living, dead before he was forty-seven years old. But out of the blackness of death Kennedy still lives, larger than life, in the memories and the emotions and the minds of his fellow Americans. After death, the real Kennedy is now the symbolic Kennedy, the figure about whom has clustered the yearnings, the ideals, and the aspirations Americans have for themselves and their country. That symbolic Kennedy also stands between the reader and Kennedy's book. We know what happened, and we cannot undo that knowledge. We read *Profiles in Courage* now with a different eye. The present changes the meaning of the past. We can get the record straight, as historians like to put it, but the

meaning of that straightened record is inextricably involved in
the meaning we also try each day to discern in the confusion of
the living present. The memory of John F. Kennedy is part of
that present.

In 1955, Harper and Brothers published *Profiles in Courage*
when John F. Kennedy was "Jack" Kennedy, the junior senator from the state of Massachusetts. If Kennedy had not gone
on to be President of the United States, further, if he had not
been assassinated in Dallas, Texas, before he had the chance to
act out in office the passion he brought to the presidency,
surely *Profiles in Courage* would simply be one of those intelligent and interesting books which we might remember, perhaps, but not remember with such intensity of feeling. But the
career was brutally cut short in one of those acts of violence
which are as much a part of American culture as the hopefulness and the idealism of the young man who fell in Dallas. He
fell before his performance allowed the historian to measure his
deeds against his words. That is why *Profiles in Courage* is now
an important book. We seek a sense of the man in order to
understand the deep emotional response to the memory of the
man. We seek some light to penetrate the blackness.

The point is important and may be told by an anecdote.
The emotional legacy left by Kennedy is intense in the United
States, but it is yet deeper and even more fervent in western
Europe. An American abroad, especially a professor of American history who has to talk again and again, in England, in
Belgium, in France, in Italy, stands astonished before the living
legend of Kennedy outside the United States. It is almost as if
our friends wanted desperately to think the highest and best of
America. Perversely, being an intellectual, one tries to redress
the balance, and suggest that legend outruns fact, that Kennedy
did not achieve enough in office to warrant the extravagant
estimation of him which one finds everywhere. Precisely this
happened at a conference on American history at the Catholic
University of Louvain in Belgium. At that conference, young

Europeans constantly invoked Kennedy as their benchmark for excellence, and the American professors there found themselves in the awkward position of seeming rather cool, rather distant from the emotion Kennedy's name aroused.

One American historian there quite properly pointed out that historians did not measure a man as president by what he said before he became president, or by what he said or did after he was president, but by what he did, and not by what he said, while he was president. By that standard, he did not see how it was possible to rank Kennedy very high, and, provocatively, he went on to say he did not understand, could not comprehend, the passionate veneration of Kennedy's memory. Emotions flared, as always when profane hands are laid upon the sacred, and in the vigorous discussion which followed there was much talk of the Kennedy "style." Finally, in exasperation, a young man at the back of the room rose to his feet and, like young men everywhere, castigated the cold, bloodless skepticism of his elders. He concluded with a rejection of the very word, "style." For him, it smacked too much of high fashion, of clothes put on and as easily taken off, too much of the image-making one associates with the commercial calculus of Madison Avenue and the meretricious world of advertising. He pleaded instead for the importance of Kennedy's "spirit," that ineffable sense the young like himself had caught from Kennedy which made it possible for them once again to believe in politics and ideals and a better world.

The young man was right, and the historian would do well to remember it. Much of the importance of John F. Kennedy for the present moment is not what he did or did not accomplish in office, but what he represented, and still represents, to the American imagination. It is from this perspective that one turns today to look at *Profiles in Courage*. What does it tell us of the man we have lost?

Profiles in Courage consists of eight vignettes, eight "profiles" of men who sat in the United States Senate and by their various actions at crucial moments in American political history displayed courage, the strength to resist political pressure, and to take a lonely stand on their own sense of what was right. The eight profiles are bracketed by a first chapter, "Courage and Politics," and a last chapter, "The Meaning of Courage." Himself a senator, Kennedy was obviously exploring his own sense of what it meant to occupy that high office. Beyond the fact that Kennedy's eight heroes were all senators of the United States, no region or party or moment in time includes them. They come not only from different parties in our national history, but from the North and the South, the East and the West. But whatever their party and whatever their section, each of Kennedy's eight senators at a crucial moment chooses an unpopular course and acts in the light of what he conceives to be the higher interest of the nation as a whole, against party, against section, even against the will of his constituents. It is this intrinsic personal quality which establishes the common nature which all eight share. Otherwise, in temperament, in the kind of political decision each confronts, in results, there is only diversity. Some stand for principle, some for compromise, some are vindicated and maintained in office, some are vilified and rejected, but all display what John F. Kennedy calls political courage.

One may say two things about Kennedy's eight acts of political courage. The first is simple. Each decision Kennedy describes is a decision to further the national good, not the good of the individual senator, not the good of his region, not the good of his party, not even the good as seen by the misguided people who make up the nation he somehow wishes to serve. Each senator has the courage to stand by his own sense of what is right and just, to stand by his own sense of what best serves the national interest. Kennedy was, in other words, a passionate nationalist. He placed the collective good of the United States before any other interest. Further, he did not believe that those other interests automatically added up to the national interest. The national interest, the good of the whole people, transcended particular interests and often came in direct conflict with them. It is this side of Kennedy which lies behind those now famous words from his inaugural, "Ask not what your country can do for you; ask what you can do for your country."

The second thing one may say about Kennedy's eight acts of political courage is that Kennedy believed that leaders should lead. To put it another way, he reveals himself in *Profiles in Courage* to be, perhaps surprisingly, an elitist. Not an elitist in the sense that he believed in an elite based on wealth or class or family or education, but in the sense that he believed the members of the United States Senate, and by implication other elected officers, did constitute a political elite and should recognize that fact and accept the burden of personal decision which goes with it. Like Thoreau, Kennedy believed in the majority of one. However complex the calculus of political action, at the end one had to live by one's own convictions. One must finally march to the beat of one's own drum.

But there is no arrogance about Kennedy's insistence that each man must follow his own convictions, no suggestion that any of his heroes, or any man, has a pipeline to ultimate truth and wisdom to justify the rightness of his personal and private judgment. Kennedy had a clear sense of the clouded complexity of political action. His first chapter on "Courage and Politics" is a good primer on the kinds of pressures brought to bear upon a senator. When he came to the Senate, Kennedy tells us, the first piece of advice he received was, "The way to get along is to go along." For Kennedy there was wisdom and not just crass opportunism in that bit of advice. Senators, he knew, are human beings and social animals; inevitably, they wish to have the esteem of their colleagues; they like to be "liked." Further, on some issues they must go along, they must learn to compromise on some matters to achieve others more important. As Kennedy put it, "their intellects tell them that a fair or poor bill is better than no bill at all, and that only through the give-and-take of compromise will any bill receive the successive approval of the Senate, the House, the President and the nation." But, he immediately went on to say, "the question is how we will compromise and with whom."

Senators, naturally enough, wish to get re-elected. Office is their life. They may wish to, but not many will act as did that congressman from California who told an importunate voter in his district to "take two running jumps and go to hell." Senators have constituents and one respectable theory of democratic politics is that the representative is there, as the name implies, to represent his constituents and to represent their interests. It may be difficult to separate the voice of economic pressure groups (who, to complicate the matter further, are also a chief source for campaign funds) from the voice of the people, but that difficulty does not negate the fact of the real and tremendous pressure brought to bear upon a man in office by the will of those who put him in that office. So, the senator stands at the center of a great number of forces which pull this way and that: the esteem of his colleagues, his desire to remain in office, the discipline of his party, the real virtue of compromise on some issues, and the pressure of his own constituents. All these play upon the individual politician and they erode the meaning, as well as the practicality, of independence.

But Kennedy's eight heroes are men who did resist such pressures, who did stand for their independence, who did place their own judgment before and above all else. Now, the easy way to admire these eight men would have been to admire their courage because they were right. But the remarkable thing about Kennedy's book is that he does not take that easy and sentimental way out. He does not admire these men because they were right. Quite the opposite. He admires them because, right or wrong, they had the guts to stick by their own sense of what was right or wrong. Courage is his subject. It is courage, not wisdom, he extolls. At one point, describing the opposition of the liberal but isolationist senator, George W. Norris of Nebraska, to the internationalism of Woodrow Wilson, Kennedy remarks, "It is not now important whether Norris was right or wrong. What is now important is the courage he displayed in support of his convictions." The remark is characteristic and variations on it appear throughout Kennedy's book. What is one to make of it? To take a cruel example, are we to admire the bestial act of political assassination simply because the assassin had the courage to do the deed? What standard does Kennedy's admiration of courage provide?

His chosen heroes have, of course, their own standards, most of them estimable to most men. Edmund G. Ross of Kansas, during Reconstruction, deserts the radical wing of the Republican party in its attempt to impeach the President of the United States, Andrew Johnson. Senator Ross was no friend of the South, and no friend of Andrew Johnson, but in the Senate, against incredible pressure from all sides, he refused to give the vote which would have provided the two-thirds majority necessary to convict. He did so out of his commitment to the doctrine of the separation of powers in the American Constitution, out of his belief that if Johnson were to be removed from the presidency on such weak charges that the executive office would become a plaything at the whim of Congress, and that this would unbalance the system established in the Constitution by the founding fathers.

Robert Alonzo Taft, "Mr. Republican," the conservative senator from the state of Ohio, gratuitously went out of his way to attack the legality of the Nuremberg trials which condemned the perpetrators of Nazi atrocities. There was no necessity, no occasion which demanded that Taft speak out. Doing so, he weakened his chance to become his party's candidate for the presidency of the United States, the one great ambition of his political life. But the *ex post facto* nature of the laws under which Nazi criminals were tried offended Taft's high regard for the decorum of legal procedure and his primary commitment to the rule of law, even in cases where he despised those the law protected.

Young John Quincy Adams, another junior senator from Massachusetts, outraged New England and defied the Federalist party which had sent him to the Senate, by siding with Thomas Jefferson, the enemy of his own father, in support of Jefferson's continental expansionism, which weakened the political hegemony of New England, and in support of Jefferson's embargo against trade with England, which destroyed New England's commerce and its prosperity. Adams did so, not just because his vision went beyond New England's regional interests, but because he had been taught by his father, President John Adams, the old Puritan doctrine that "the magistrate is the servant not . . . of the people, but of his God." Adams acted in obedience to a higher law, confident as only an Adams could be that he knew God's will, and disdained, as he put it later when he was president himself, to be "palsied by the will of [his] constituents."

The integrity of the political system embodied in the Constitution, respect for the rule of law, belief in the supremacy of a law higher than the wishes of a transient majority: all these are, as I have said, estimable grounds on which to base one's actions, grounds on which many Americans may comfortably stand. Kennedy clearly shares respect for many of the motives which gave his lonely heroes the courage to act. But not all. He recognizes that Taft's commitment to legal procedure could frustrate justice in the higher sense Adams had in view, and says of Taft, as he had of George W. Norris, "we are not concerned today with the question of whether Taft was right or wrong." We are concerned, insisted Kennedy, with "Taft's unhesitating courage in standing against the flow of public

opinion for a cause he believed to be right." To insist again, it
is not the wisdom or the rightness of an action which is Kennedy's subject. It is the courage to act.

One may understand the appeal of Kennedy's insistence on
the importance of individual action, and the courage to take
that action, by remembering the time in which he wrote. Kennedy published *Profiles in Courage* in 1955. The decade of the
1950's already seems a long time ago. That was the decade of
the "silent generation," the decade of the great success of
books like David Riesman's *The Lonely Crowd* and William
Whyte's *The Organization Man.* Today, as students take to the
streets of the United States, it is hard to recall that the dominant
fear of observers of the American scene in the 1950's was that
American youth had opted for security and comfort, for adaptation to the system, for conformity, and had turned their
backs on the ancient tradition of independence and dissent.
Mass society and mass conformity were the themes of serious
as well as journalistic critiques of the quality of American culture. The American, it was said, had changed from the inner-
directed man who looked to himself and had become the other-
directed man, sensitively attuned to the expectations of those
around him. He was the faceless man in the crowd. That was
the mood of the time, as quickly as that mood has changed in
so few years. Kennedy's appeal, the appeal which is the subject
of *Profiles in Courage,* was against this mood, this mood of
acquiescence and cynicism. He held up an older ideal, the ideal
of resistance to the mood of the mass man.

The context is important. The immediate moment in which
Kennedy wrote goes far to explain much of his appeal. He
spoke for the confident belief that one man counted, that one
man could change the course of events, that one man could

have an effect, if only one had the courage of one's convictions. This is the message of *Profiles in Courage*, a message which John F. Kennedy dramatized in his own person, in his lean and eager presence and rapid and clipped speech, a message he later summed up as the "New Frontier." Kennedy's appeal, especially to the young, was that the world was still an open and plastic world, open to change and renewal, if only one had the courage to resist the tyrannous weight of mass conformity.

But there is a curious conclusion to the celebration of resistance, the celebration of the courage to stand, as Kennedy said of Taft, against the flow of public opinion. There is, at least, when that celebration becomes the celebration of an act simply because it shows the courage to be different. To put it another way, the man who takes a course because it is opposite to the popular mood is as much a creature of the crowd as the man who chooses to follow the crowd. He just marches in a different direction. But the way the crowd is going still determines his direction. To state it more precisely, although more ponderously, he becomes a negative function of the crowd. If a man resists the dominant mood simply because it is the dominant mood, then he is indistinguishable, except for strategy, from the man who goes along simply to go along. We can no more admire the one than the other. Which brings us back to the critical question, the question Kennedy himself finally had to come to at the end of his book, what standard do we have to measure the meaning of courage. Why is courage in and of itself an admirable quality?

If Kennedy appealed to an older tradition of independence and self-reliance, he did not, however, share the assumptions which had once provided support for that position. When, for example, Thomas Jefferson defended the rights of the minority, he did so in the trust that the truth is great and will prevail, in the trust that reason would finally manifest itself in conflicts among men. Or, for another example, when Ralph Waldo Emerson wrote the sentence every schoolboy knows, "Trust thy-self: every heart vibrates to that iron string," he wrote in the assurance that "to believe your own thought, to believe that what is true for you in your private heart is true for all men." Emerson's assurance depended on the trust that all men share a common nature, that beneath the crust of convention and cir-cumstance, if men had the courage to break through that crust, all men would discover the same truths.

There is none of this in Kennedy, none of the sanguine as-surance in the rationality of man or in the moral order of the universe. Yet, stripped of the old supports which bolstered the courage to be one's self, Kennedy still affirmed that courage. For his eight senators, he thought that the situation which es-pecially demanded courage of each of them was the desire to serve the national interest, but he was even skeptical of that large abstraction. He quotes John Adams to the effect that it is not true "that any people ever existed who love the public bet-ter than themselves." To what, then, does one turn to affirm one's admiration of those who have the courage of their own convictions?

Kennedy's answer was simple. It was not because his sena-tors " 'loved the public better than themselves.' On the con-trary it was precisely because they did *love themselves*—be-cause each one's need to maintain his own respect for himself was more important to him than his popularity with others—because his desire to win or maintain a reputation for integrity or courage was stronger than his desire to remain in office—be-cause his conscience, his personal standard of ethics, his integ-rity or morality, call it what you will—was stronger than the pressures of public disapproval—because his faith that *his* course was the best one . . . outweighed his fear of public re-prisal."

"It was precisely because they did *love themselves*." As an older book has it, "Love thy neighbor as thyself." But that wise counsel means that one must love one's self before one can begin to know how to love one's neighbor. Charity begins at home. The bedrock of Kennedy's admiration of courage is the glimpse he has of the simple fact that if one does not act out of self-love, out of one's necessity to please one's self, then what follows can only be self-hatred and impotence and disgust. What is primary is the necessity to be one's self, and to take delight in that act of being. Whether one is right or wrong, whether action leads to success or failure, such considerations are secondary. They are not essential. What is essential is the primacy of the self and the courage to be that self.

Norman Mailer, in a famous article, once hailed Kennedy as the "existentialist" in politics, although later Mailer thought that Kennedy had let him down. The epithet is fashionable, but still useful. Kennedy, at bottom, insisted that the beginning of everything else was the courage to accept what one was and act on that self-acceptance, that love of self which finally makes it possible to love others. One will not do violence to others because that would violate one's own self. It is this image of Kennedy which somehow reached the young, which still lives in the spirit of Kennedy. As the young put it today, "Do your own thing." Don't get seduced by comfort or raped by power. Love yourself enough to be what you are, whatever that may be. If you don't do your own thing, if you start doing someone else's thing, then you become alienated from your own self. The rest is ashes.

One can put the position in more seemly language, perhaps, but it is this sense of the courage of the single individual to be what he is that lies at the heart of John F. Kennedy's book, *Profiles in Courage*. Perhaps, as I said at the start, it is the blackness of death, that ultimate negation of the self, which makes this quality in Kennedy seem so strong to us today. We might not have seen it in 1955. But despite all the trappings of glamor, despite the wealth, the Harvard education, the handsome wife, despite the presidency, the sweet smell of success itself, the quality that emerges most is the spirit of a lonely man, yet finding courage to be the man he was alone with. In a sentence I much admire, the late Joseph Schumpeter once wrote that the mark of a civilized man is his ability to stand unflinchingly for the relative validity of his beliefs. It took a civilized man to write *Profiles in Courage*.

2

SOME REFLECTIONS
ON FREEDOM

IF WE HAD no problems in our present world, we would have no need for the history of our past. If ever we reached that utopia which in our fainter moments we sometimes long for, in which all conflict was put behind us, we would have no questions to ask of history because we would have no need for knowledge to prepare us for action that must be taken in our own present. This does not mean that history can ever yield us a moment in the past identical to our own and, thus, give us pat answers, or that our interest in the past is simply utilitarian; but it does mean that there can be no history, properly speaking, without questions; and questions are always given to us in the present tense.

A lack of problems is, in itself, hardly a problem for us today—quite the opposite. "The proper work of mankind," wrote Dante, is "intellectual growth." But he went on to say that "since individual men find that they grow in prudence and wisdom when they sit quietly, it is evident that mankind, too, is most free and easy to carry on its work when it enjoys the quiet and tranquility of peace." We may feel so sharply the inability to sit free and easy in our world that we may think that we must put off our proper work until we can labor at it in peace. No thought could be more dangerous. If we do not now think what we are doing, we may in the future discover that we are in a world we never meant to make. Further, the world we mean to make is a world of freedom and liberty; and beneath all the material panoply of power, our struggle today is at bottom a struggle about ideas, especially the ideas of freedom and liberty. We want, as a famous pamphlet has it, a world in which "the free development of each is the condition for the free development of all." But these words, to which we might quickly and willingly assent, are from *The Communist Manifesto;* and we are, humanly, outraged that those who seem to us the powers of darkness should claim the same bright ideals we do ourselves. "It is necessary," writes Mortimer Adler in his introduction to *The Idea of Freedom,* for men "to understand the opinions they oppose, if not perfectly, at least well enough to join issue and be in communication as well as in opposition." If we fail to understand the opinions we oppose, we may fall into the effortless luxury of dismissing them as hypocrisy or mere propaganda; worse, we may fail to understand ourselves. We may fail at our own proper work, which is, simply, to think what we are doing.

With its scholarly detachment and colorless prose, no book might seem more remote from our present passionate concerns than Mr. Adler's compendious volume. *The Idea of Freedom* is a formidable book (nearly 700 pages) and is, although Mr. Adler's name appears on the title page, the product of some years of work by the staff of the Institute for Philosophical Research (a second page carefully lists the thirty-three other persons who had a hand in its making). At first, the anonymous style might seem simply an institutional fault, but Mr. Adler tells us that he and his collaborators deliberately sought a neutral tone in order to achieve some measure of objectivity. For *The Idea of Freedom* is not philosophical. It does not aim to say the truth about freedom: it aims only to say the truth about what men have said about freedom. Its purpose is to survey and order analytically all that men have thought on the subject of freedom in the past twenty-five centuries of Western thought, abstracting all statements from their historical setting and treating them all as if in a dialogue going on at the present moment. *The Idea of Freedom* takes no sides. It hopes only to make the subject of freedom clear so men who disagree will know what they disagree about. If we mean to think about the value of freedom, Mr. Adler's spacious survey provides a good place to start.

One immediate value of *The Idea of Freedom* is the rich sense it gives of the variety of meanings men have attributed to freedom. So loosely woven a net has caught some strange fish. Spinoza, for example, in the *Theologico-Political Treatise*, argued that man is free only to follow reason and, since the state is the embodiment of reason, citizens "are obliged to fulfill the commands of the sovereign power, however absurd these may be, else they will be public enemies, and will act against reason which urges the preservation of the state as the primary duty." Freedom, then, becomes the duty to obey. At the opposite pole, the anarchist Bakunin could say flatly that "citizens are slaves as long as they obey the official representatives of the law, the leaders which are imposed upon them by the state— even if these leaders were confirmed by universal suffrage." In these two instances, Spinoza and Bakunin are obviously talking about two different things. For Spinoza, freedom is the freedom to be something, to live in relation to a law higher than one's actual self, in his case, reason; for Bakunin, freedom is freedom from something, in his case, freedom from all external restraint. Can it be said, then, that when men are using different sense of the same word that they are talking about the same thing? Are there only particular freedoms, no such general thing as Freedom? Must we always use the word in the plural?

Mr. Adler thinks not. The whole method of *The Idea of Freedom* is platonic, to classify particular, distinguishable notions about freedom with the intention of framing a general and superior definition which includes them all and in terms of which fruitful controversy might then proceed. Mr. Adler proposes three concepts of freedom, "no more, no less," that will subsume all that has been said on the subject. These are circumstantial freedom, acquired freedom and natural freedom. One who believes that freedom is circumstantial thinks that man is free to the degree that circumstances permit, and to effect man's freedom pays attention to the conditions in which man lives. Acquired freedom, on the other hand, depends on a change or a development within man himself by which he achieves a state of mind or character that differentiates him from other men without regard to circumstance, as in the argument that the wise slave in a dungeon is freer than the passion-ridden tyrant on a throne. The third category, natural freedom, includes those, especially the Thomists, who believe that all men always have inherently the ability to be free, however unfavorable the circumstances or however short one may fall of acquiring the requisite wisdom or virtue. Any one thinker may include more than one of these categories in his own view of freedom, of course, and within any one category there is still considerable room for difference. For example, in the case of circumstantial freedom, some may argue that men need only be freed from constraining circumstances, while others might insist that man must be afforded circumstances which encourage his freedom. The former might seek considerable restriction on the sphere of social action, while the latter might argue for the responsibility of society to provide auspicious circumstances; but both would agree that freedom depends on circumstances, however conceived.

The Idea of Freedom ends with an attempt to define Freedom, with the capital letter, to provide a statement about freedom that will include the three partial categories, just as each of those, in turn, includes its own varieties. The "general understanding" of freedom arrived at is: "*A man who is able* (A) under favorable circumstances, to act as he wishes for his own individual good as he sees it, or (B) through acquired virtue or wisdom, to will or live as he ought in conformity to the moral law or an ideal befitting human nature, or (C) by a power inherent in human nature, to change his own character creatively by deciding for himself what he shall do or become, is *free in the sense that he* has in himself the ability or power whereby he can make what he does his own action and what he achieves his property." Much as in the Whiggish writings of John Locke, the word "property" here carries a large meaning: "what a free man does is *his own act,* what he becomes is of *his own making,* and what he achieves is *proper to himself,* i.e., his property, his own. . . ." A skeptic might observe that only one who is also the co-author of *The Capitalist Manifesto* would construe what is proper to one's self as property, but even the generous will realize that so large a definition involves us inevitably in a further consideration of the ideas which establish it (as, in this instance, say, Richard Schlatter's admirable and succinct *Private Property: The History of an Idea*).

More troublesome than the prospect of the infinite regression of defining the ideas that define the single idea of freedom is the obstinate, practical objection that a general verbal solution may satisfy philosophers, but will hardly quiet the passions of the partisans for one version rather than another, even if they can be brought to agree that the general statement includes their differences. One may finish *The Idea of Freedom* with the quiet luxury of forgiving all by understanding all. Not so after reading Professor Sir Isaiah Berlin's *Two Concepts of Liberty.*

Professor Berlin's short pamphlet deals only with political

thought, and there only with two central and opposed meanings of the idea of liberty. Where *The Idea of Freedom* is cool and anonymous, *Two Concepts of Liberty* is pungent and personal; where Mr. Adler and his associates hope to do no more than to help man to think, Professor Berlin is man thinking. Further, the contrast is not merely one of style or intention. Where *The Idea of Freedom* is unhistorical, even anti-historical, *Two Concepts of Liberty* is deeply historical and argues implicitly against an academic tolerance of what might seem, when abstracted from the realities of history, a slender difference in definition.

Professor Berlin offers two concepts of liberty, "negative" and "positive." The negative sense is involved in answer to the question, "What is the area within which a subject—a person or a group of persons—is or should be left to do or be what he wants to do or be, without interference by other persons?" The positive sense comes in answer to the question, "What, or who, is the source of control or interference, that can determine someone to do, or be, one thing rather than another?" The two concepts are distinguished negatively and positively in the sense that one version of liberty is *freedom from* control, the other *freedom to* do or be something. Both, clearly, are special instances of circumstantial and acquired freedom, and Mr. Adler, too, gives each a chapter in his work.

Professor Berlin thinks men generally use the word "freedom" in its negative sense: "I am normally said to be free to the degree to which no human being interferes with my activity. Political liberty in this sense is simply the area within which a man can do what he wants." The emphasis on human interference is important; as Helvétius put it, "it is not lack of freedom not to fly like an eagle or swim like a whale." Professor Berlin does not confuse power with liberty. When Richard H. Tawney argues that freedom to dine at the Ritz is not freedom unless one has the money, the lack of economic power is a lack of freedom only on the assumption of a particular social and economic theory about the nature of poverty. If poverty is the result of personal inability or moral failure, then the lack of economic power is no infringement on liberty; but if poverty is the result of human actions which have arranged society to the profit of some and the loss of others, then it is. "The criterion of oppression," says Professor Berlin, "is the part that I believe to be played by other human beings, directly or indirectly, in frustrating my wishes. By being free in this sense I mean not being interfered with by others. The wider the area of non-interference the wider my freedom."

The negative concept of freedom is, of course, the view of classical liberalism, of men like Locke and John Stuart Mill in England and Benjamin Constant and Tocqueville in France. As with such liberals, the argument quickly becomes where the line can be drawn, what the area of noninterference can be. This may involve considerable haggling, but the negative concept of liberty always means liberty *from*, an absence of interference at some point. The positive concept of liberty, on the other hand, derives "from the wish of the individual to be his own master. I wish my life and decisions to depend on myself, not on external forces of whatever kind. I wish to be the instrument of my own, not of other men's, acts of will. I wish to be a subject, not an object; to be moved by reasons, by conscious purposes which are my own." The freedom which consists in being one's own master and the freedom which consists in not being prevented by other men from choosing as one does may "seem concepts at no great logical distance from each other—no more than negative or positive ways of saying the same thing." But Professor Berlin's whole point is that two concepts have developed historically in sharply divergent directions.

The notion of being one's own master leads, by sleight of hand, to a division within the self. One is master of himself to the degree that he achieves his "true" or "higher" self, conforms, as Spinoza would have it, to the demands of reason, or, as others would have it, to some entity larger than one's individual self, the party, the church, the nation, or the race. "This entity is then identified as being the 'true' self which, by imposing its collective, or 'organic,' single will upon its recalcitrant 'members,' achieves its own, and, therefore, their 'higher' freedom." At this point, one has come far from the simpler negative goal of liberty; one can ignore the actual wishes of men and bully or torture them in behalf of their "true" selves, in the name of what they "really" wish. Professor Berlin leaves it clear what he thinks of this "monstrous impersonation" in the name of liberty.

One might, of course, make as great a logical monster of the negative concept of liberty. To Professor Berlin's defining question, "What is the area within which a person is or should be left to do or be what he wants to be?" one might ask, in turn, "What he *may* want to do, or what he *really* wants to do?" One could then start down the same twisting road that leads to an identification of the protesting, empirical self with the tyrannical, "higher" self. But Professor Berlin is content to observe that, although logically this may be so, historically the positive school of liberty has lent itself more readily to this "splitting of the personality."

When Professor Berlin wrote his brilliant essay on Tolstoy's philosophy of history, *The Hedgehog and the Fox,* he took his title from an ambiguous old saying that while the fox knows many things, the hedgehog knows one thing. In *Two Concepts of Liberty,* Professor Berlin openly joins the foxes of history: "If, as I believe, the ends of men are many, and not all of them are in principle compatible with one another, then the possibility of conflict—and of tragedy—can never be wholly eliminated from human life, either personal or social." It is this pluralistic view of human existence that lies behind the high value put on freedom; if men "had assurance that in some perfect state, realizable by men on earth, no ends pursued by them would ever be in conflict, the necessity and the agony of choice would disappear, and with it the central importance of the freedom to choose." It is, further, because of the firm belief that the ends of life are many that one "must establish a society in which there must be some frontiers of freedom which nobody should ever be permitted to cross."

Here is the crux of the matter. Formerly, it was not so difficult to believe in freedom, however difficult it always has been to establish it in practice, because, formerly, men seem to have been able to believe in some absolute order—natural law, the revealed will of God, the dictates of reason—which supported and justified their ideal of freedom. We, today, seem to have lost any sense of a shared standard to measure our actions by, and, much like Professor Berlin, generally argue for freedom on the grounds of the sheer necessity of pluralism. But since we cannot have freedom in everything, we feel the pinch, the need for some rule to justify ourselves to ourselves (certainly not to the authority we hold in contempt) when we assert our freedom. In formulating his own rule, Professor Berlin suggests that whatever names we give to the rules which draw the frontiers of freedom, "what these rules or commandments will have in common is that they are accepted so widely, and are grounded so deeply in the actual nature of men as they have developed through history, as to be, by now, an essential part of what we mean by being a normal human being."

There are certain objections to be made to this formulation. First, it is elliptical to the extreme. Professor Berlin quickly goes on to make clear his belief that liberty has little to hope for from the rule of majorities: "Democracy as such is logically uncommitted to it, and historically has failed to protect it." Then "accepted so widely" by whom? Some civilized and thoughtful elite that will tell the majority where the boundaries of their freedom lie? Obviously, the word "normal" here implies some normative value, not a statistical observation. Then are we not once again in the hands of Professor Berlin's hated positive school, appealing to our wiser, better selves against our actual, base selves? Even the accent, presumably to escape the idealists, on the "actual nature of men" has lurking behind it somewhere a finalist evolutionary view of development in which man achieves in history what constitutes the essence of being human. Here again we are well down the road which in the rest of his essay Professor Berlin so eloquently urges us to keep our feet from. The attempt to draw the frontiers of the negative concept of liberty seems to involve us finally, and perhaps necessarily, in some kind of positive concept. It is, of course, hardly to Professor Berlin's discredit that he cannot finally untangle the knot that has resisted the fingers of so many before him. What is to his credit is that, with controlled eloquence, he has given us a lucid and passionate statement on the nature of liberty that will surely become one of the classics of the literature on freedom.

To the intellectual analysis of Mr. Adler and the historical grasp of Professor Berlin, Christian Bay, in *The Structure of Freedom*, adds considerable sociological and psychological detail to our understanding of the complex conditions of human freedom. But, after that added modern sophistication, *The Structure of Freedom* comes to the same ultimate problem: "The chief difficulty in [the] approach toward the maximization of freedom is the lack of consensus about the priorities between human rights." In speaking of "human" rights rather than "natural" rights, Mr. Bay attempts to circumvent the same problem Professor Berlin does in speaking of the "actual nature of men." Mr. Bay's solution has the advantage over Professor Berlin's of being more explicit, but the disadvantage of being not very useful. Human rights, he claims, "correspond to objective requirements pertaining to certain universal human needs and can therefore be claimed as valid, potentially at least, in all cultures that permit and encourage an expanding individual freedom." Mr. Bay rejects the problem of the universality of human needs by asserting that "the great men of various cultures have exhibited so much similarity in values that one must assume that there are either universal human propensities or universal cultural elements, or more likely both." But his next sentence abandons the argument: "But even if this had not been the case, the standards each of us has should be absolute for each of us." But freedom is still left inside a vicious circle. We may have to have the will to believe in the truth of our beliefs, but the will of some dissident individual will hardly find a way in a culture that has not chosen to permit and encourage individual freedom.

In *The Structure of Freedom*, Mr. Bay puts freedom of expression second after freedom from coercion as the most desirable of freedoms because, after one is left alive, freedom of expression is instrumentally necessary to arrive at the determination of any other freedoms that a society might wish to establish as human rights. But this sensible, practical justification will work only in a society that has already agreed that decision should be reached by discussion. So, when Mr. Bay admits that "general priorities between freedoms must ultimately be decided by majorities, however, since these are questions of value," it is difficult to reconcile the remark with the notion that certain freedoms, having "become more generally recognized as more basic than others," can be extended as "rights" to all citizens, "regardless of majority opinion." The reconciliation can be made only on Mr. Bay's self-admitted "optimistic assumptions" that "majority decisions will be enlightened and humanistic."

Mr. Bay's assumptions lay bare the heart of the matter. The definition of freedom not only involves us in the definition of other values, as Mr. Adler makes us aware. It finally involves us in a definition of man himself. "The conception of freedom," Professor Berlin writes, "directly derives from the view that is taken of what constitutes a self, a person, a man. Enough manipulation with the definition of man, and freedom can be made to mean whatever the manipulator wishes."

Some years ago in a book that received little attention, *The*

Tower and the Abyss, Erich Kahler faced this problem squarely. Mr. Kahler called his book, "An Inquiry into the Transformation of the Individual." His statement of the problem and his conclusion will be disheartening to anyone who believes in the ultimate reality of the individual self, a belief on which all claims for freedom for the individual must finally rest. Without drawing directly on Emile Durkheim's studies, Mr. Kahler makes much the same analysis of modern society. Modern society is losing its sense of shared values because of the enormous growth of "collectives," that is, groups brought together by the increasing rationalization of all areas of social life, especially, but not only, the productive. Man's relation to other men becomes increasingly a matter of his function in society. The result, to use Durkheim's famous phrase, is "anomie," the loss of a common conscience, the destruction of community. But if the increase in rationalization in modern life and the corresponding growth of collective groups threaten the security, perhaps even the identity, of the individual by cutting him loose from any sense of shared life, Mr. Kahler's "possible utopia," the emergence of a way of life in a community, "an entity in itself, apart from the individuals" who compose it, threatens to submerge the individual completely in some abstract entity called "Man," not much different from Rousseau's general will, where the empirical individual is finally lost sight of. Mr. Kahler does not blink at his own logic; he decides that our concern for the concrete individual person is now a thing of the past. He forces us to consider the drastic possibility that history is at one of its great turning points and that our old assumptions about the nature of the individual and the meaning of freedom may no longer make sense.

Our problem is to decide whether the individual has any rights at all over against the society in which he lives and moves. Recently we have discovered society to be so real that the individual seems to become but a shadow of its will. If our relativistic anthropologists are wholly right, then one is an individual to the degree that he embodies the imperatives of his culture, much as in the eighteenth century one was an individual to the degree that he approximated the norm of reason. Although we might shrink from it, there is, in this view, no sense in talking about an individual's rights.

The notion of cultural determinism goes far back in Western thought, but, relatively, the modern discovery of society can properly be dated from Robert Owen's *A New View of Society*, which grew out of Owen's experience of building an entire town to run his mills at New Lanark. Despite the logical difficulties he quickly fell into, Owen realized sooner than most how society is literally its own creation, how it can make itself, how men can make other men in their own image of what men should be. What is revealing in Owen's case is not that he had his idea, but how he came to it. He came to it by the technological accident of having to create a community, the whole settlement of New Lanark. We do right to deplore Owen's naïve rejection of the past and his crude insistence on practical experience, but he provides a valuable clue to the social source of much of our concern about the meaning of individual freedom. John Stuart Mill, in his review of Tocqueville's *Democracy in America*, made the shrewd remark that the mere presence of machines in the environment makes men contemptuous of tradition. There, triumphantly before them, stands an instance, a working instance, of man's capacity to mold the world to his wishes. To transfer the rationalization and organization implicit in the machine, or in that larger machine, the factory, to human affairs is not a long or a hard step: to reduce each person to a functional part of a successful and rational whole. If this is at all true, then modern society may tend to favor the notion that man may blueprint his human relations as well as his productive capacity. Without having read the closeted philosophers of "positive" liberty, whom, interestingly enough, Professor Berlin constantly calls "technicians," modern man may become just as contemptuous as they of the need for variety and spontaneity in life, of the need for, in a word, freedom.

To suggest a social source for the threat to freedom today is to suggest that the problem is not simply one of a cold war or of competing ideologies. It is a problem arising out of the conditions of modern life under which we all now live. On the other hand, it is not to insist on a crass materialism. "It may be," writes Professor Berlin, "that without the pressure of social forces, political ideas are stillborn: what is certain is that these forces, unless they clothe themselves in ideas, remain blind and undirected." That is our proper work, to keep the eyes of our minds open. Books are not our only resource, but they can help. The study of the history of freedom, or of any of our ideals, may not provide us with the contentment of a final answer, but it may lead us to that admirable maturity described by the late Professor Joseph Schumpeter: "To realize the relative validity of one's convictions, and yet stand for them unflinchingly, is what distinguishes a civilized man from a barbarian."

3

FREDERICK GRIMKE:
THE DYNAMICS OF FREEDOM

WHEN, IN 1834, George Bancroft remarked on the need for a
book which described the nature of American democracy, a
correspondent replied that "no dependence can be placed upon
any treatise that has yet appeared which professes to discuss
[the business of government]. You must draw upon your own
resources, you must think,—and think alone." The opinion was
widely shared. Orestes Brownson thought no American had
produced a "work on politics of the slightest scientific value."
George Sidney Camp, in the preface to his little book, *Democracy* (1841), dwelt at length on the anomaly that "in a democratic country, where self-government has been successfully
exercised by the people for nearly three quarters of a century"
there was no literature on democracy to which one might refer
"the young democratic disciple." The result was that Americans "journey on, living in the rich experience and practical
enjoyment of democratic freedom, but in entire and reckless
indifference to its abstract principles." Camp accounted for the
anomaly by observing, with mild wit, that the "chief specula-

tors" of the day were "in merchandise and real estate." Having won independence, with a continent to conquer and a nation to make, Americans were content "with the practical results" of their political system, hardly inclined to "patient study of its abstract nature." We have been "all action," said Camp. "There has been no room for the thinker; he has been jostled to one side."

Historians have agreed. The single high moment in American political thought remains the Revolutionary and Constitutional period, but even there the brilliance of a John Adams or an Alexander Hamilton, a Thomas Jefferson or a James Madison spent itself on shaping institutions rather than making books. State papers, occasional essays and letters were their form, not the architectonics of speculative theory. Once the challenge of revolution had passed and the need for a national government had been met, the intelligence of Americans turned to fields other than political theory. Even the terrible crisis of a Civil War brought forth blood, not political imagination. After the founding of the republic, American political thought seems, as Herbert Croly put it, a career in "intellectual lethargy." The result is that we have turned to outsiders, especially Tocqueville, for critical perspective on our practice.

Yet, there is an exception to test the rule. There was at least one American, Frederick Grimke, who decided to step aside from the practical affairs of everyday life and devote himself to an analysis of the underlying principles of American democratic practice. The result was *Considerations Upon the Nature and Tendency of Free Institutions* which appeared in two editions in the author's lifetime, in 1848 and 1856, and in a third, in 1871, after his death. The three editions are, however, no measure of the book's contemporary fame, only of the author's tenacity. *The Nature and Tendency of Free Institutions* received only passing comment upon publication and has been largely lost to sight since. But, if one of the tests of American scholarship is its responsibility to the sources of our common life, then Grimke's book deserves to be restored to its proper place. It is a penetrating analysis of the theory and institutions of American democracy. It fairly deserves comparison with Tocqueville's justly famous work, *Democracy in America*, and is in certain ways superior. It is, in any event, the single best book written by an American in the nineteenth century on the meaning of our political way of life.

We know frustratingly little about Frederick Grimke. What hints we have might recommend themselves to the intuition of, say, Henry James for whom a gesture or a phrase could, under the pressure of his imagination, reveal the significance of an entire life; further, the collective story of the Grimké family deserves the rich imagination of a William Faulkner. Restricted, though, by the pressure of fact, the historian of Frederick Grimke has little to say.

Born September 1, 1791, into the famous Grimké family of Charleston, South Carolina, Frederick Grimké was one of fourteen children of John Faucheraud Grimké and brother of Thomas Smith Grimké and Sarah and Angelina Grimké. Grimke's father, a jurist and legal historian, author of *The Public Laws of the State of South Carolina* (1790), had gone as a young man to England to study at Eton and then Trinity College, Cambridge (A.B., 1774), after which he studied law in the Middle Temple in London. A young American abroad as the Revolutionary crisis threatened, the father was active in representing the colonial cause in England. The outbreak of the Revolution interrupted his studies and brought him home. He fought in the Continental Army, rising to the rank of lieutenant-colonel, served in the state House of Representatives under the Articles of Confederation, and was a member of the state convention that ratified the Federal Constitution, which he supported. His chief work lay, however, in the law, and as the *Dictionary of American Biography* puts it, "he did his best work as a legal compiler in the period of legal reform following the revolution."

Thomas Smith Grimké, Frederick's older brother, a graduate of Yale (A.B., 1807), a lawyer, was an important figure in the ferment of reform in the early nineteenth century. Deeply religious (he had originally intended to become a minister) and strongly nationalistic (as a state senator he opposed South Carolina on the tariff and upheld the federal government during the nullification controversy in 1832), Thomas Smith Grimké was actively involved in a wide variety of reform movements, from plans to simplify spelling and support of utilitarian education, which he thought appropriate to a democratic society, to the temperance movement and the peace crusade. But it is Frederick's sisters, Sarah and Angelina, who are best known to history because of their place in the abolitionist movement and the crusade for women's rights.

The two movements were intertwined in the minds of the Grimké sisters from the start. Sarah, the elder, regretted she had not been born a man so she could become a lawyer; her life-long devotion to the ideal of equality for her own sex was inextricably involved with her struggle on behalf of the Negro for freedom from the repressive forces of society. At first, Sarah was the leader. Restive under the institutional forms of her inherited Episcopalianism, Sarah was converted to the Quaker faith after exposure to the Society of Friends on a trip to Philadelphia. Angelina followed her lead, but the social conservatism of the Philadelphia Friends satisfied neither.

The turning-point of their lives, and the point at which Angelina seems to have gone beyond her older sister and assumed the dominant role, came in 1835 when Angelina wrote a letter to William Lloyd Garrison, urging him to continue his good work, a letter which Garrison published in *The Liberator* (September 19, 1835). Sarah disapproved, as did the conservative Friends of the Philadelphia meeting, but there was no turning back for Angelina, and the next year she published her *Appeal to the Christian Women of the South,* a pamphlet which asked the women of the South to use their moral influence to destroy the terrible iniquity of slavery. Written by a Southern woman, the *Appeal* had an obvious attraction for Northern abolitionists; in the South it was publicly burned and Angelina was threatened with prison if she were ever to return to her native city and state. Sarah overcame her initial reluctance and followed the course of her younger sister; in 1836, she wrote an *Epistle to the Clergy of the Southern States.*

The Grimké sisters were now identified with the cause of radical abolitionism. After first addressing audiences composed only of women, both achieved great notoriety, at a time when women were supposed to be seen and not heard, as the first women to deliver speeches before a mixed audience. The need to defend their own right to speak made them inevitable leaders in the cause for women's rights as well as opponents of slavery. After Angelina married Theodore Weld in 1838, Sarah lived with her, partly to help her sister who was frail and in chronically poor health.

Most of what one can discover about Frederick Grimke is through his letters to Sarah which still survive. Frederick followed his older brother, Thomas Smith Grimké, to Yale where he roomed in his senior year with Samuel F. B. Morse, the painter and inventor, and became a member of Phi Beta Kappa and senior orator of the Class of 1810. He returned to Charleston where he studied and practiced law, and about the time of the death of his father in 1819 moved to Ohio, first to Columbus, then to Chillicothe. The reason for choosing Ohio remains obscure, but it seems that he was a "protégé" of Thomas Worthington (1773–1827), "The Father of Ohio Statehood." In any event, he quickly impressed those he met. "He has been in the state about eighteen months," wrote a young friend in the Governor's office, "and has received the distinguished appointment of President Judge of the Court of C.[ommon] Pleas—He is a man of fine talents." Grimke's first position on the bench as a judge in the Court of Common Pleas was by appointment to fill a vacancy, but in 1830 he was elected by the General Assembly to a regular appointment as presiding judge. In 1836, he was elected to the Supreme Court of Ohio, a position which he held until 1842 when he resigned to devote himself to study and writing, the major result of which six years later was *The Nature and Tendency of Free Institutions*.

Thus far the record. The rest of what one may say about Frederick Grimke is largely a matter of inference and speculation. It is clear that his life struck others as modest and retiring. The author of a notice of *The Nature and Tendency of Free Institutions* in the *Southern Quarterly Review* wrote, "Mr. Grimke . . . has long been known in the South as a gentleman, at once of great ability and modesty; of an ability which would justify his claim upon general attention, yet of a modesty that shrinks from notice altogether." Grimke's style of life, as a bachelor living in hotels, further suggests a certain withdrawal from the social life about him, and when, in *The Nature and Tendency of Free Institutions*, he describes the virtuous life of the judge he sounds as if he were elevating his own inclinations to the level of principle. It is not expected, he wrote, that the judge "will mingle in all the gayety and frivolity of fashionable life. He is thus placed out of the way of temptation more than other men and is insensibly beguiled into a train of conduct the most favorable for the practice of both public and private virtue."

Yet beneath Grimke's outward modesty, one may detect considerable ambition. That ambition is implicit in the "Preface to the Second Edition" of *The Nature and Tendency of Free Institutions* where he attacks the "vitiated taste for reading" which spurned knowledge for books which were "of a superficial or of an exciting character." The result was not only "to enfeeble the understanding and even to pervert the moral faculties," wrote Grimke, but "the mischief extends it-self to the few who are possessed by a noble ambition. Their efforts are chilled by the mental dyspepsia which prevails around them when they stand in need of being powerfully braced by a healthful and invigorating influence."

Whether out of personal coldness or dissatisfaction with the "mental dyspepsia" of Chillicothe, Ohio, Grimke turned in upon himself, withdrew from political and social life, and in his ambition set himself the task of educating his contemporaries to understand the nature of their own society. But he did not do so sourly. He obviously enjoyed his hotel life. He wrote Sarah on April 22, 1857, after a new hotel had been built in Chillicothe after the great fire, "I am boarding in a hotel as formerly. You know Dr. Johnson told Boswell that a tavern was 'the home of human felicity.' " Or, again, in response to some "fine things" Sarah had said of him in one of her letters, Grimke wrote that she had caused him to remember "the senti-ment of Michael Angelo, who on being asked why he had never married, replied that his profession was his wife, and his productions his children."

If Grimke appeared cold to most people, he had an ambi-tion and a passion he revealed at least to his sister, Sarah. He kept a book of "maxims" and once filled a whole letter to her with sixty of them. Maxim "50" read, "Some persons have an appearance of reserve which is mistaken for coldness. Exactly the reverse is the case. Instead of too little, they have an excess of passion. The intensity of their feelings makes them use con-stant efforts to restrain them, and this to commonplace folks, gives them the appearance of coldness." Sarah must have rec-ognized the character because she scored the margin beside this particular maxim. Nor did Grimke surrender the pride and am-bition which led him to devote himself to a lonely life of writ-ing. His contemporaries may have refused to recognize his worth but Grimke was willing to let the future judge. When he died in 1863, *The Nature and Tendency of Free Institutions* was virtually forgotten, but in his will Grimke set money aside for a final edition of his work with the instruction that a copy "be presented to the Congressional Libraries of the United States and the Confederate States, to each of the States, and to the chief Universities in each."

Further, if Grimke felt stifled in the intellectual atmosphere of his time and place, he did not surrender to it. However provincial the details of his outward life, Grimke's inner life was intellectually rich and cosmopolitan. He was alert to the best contemporary European thought of his time and kept a considerable library of books, many of which he ordered directly from Paris. His letters to Sarah are full of suggestions for her reading. He had lavish praise for Comte's *Positive Philosophy* ("The French mind has thrown off no greater work") and urged Sarah to "make an absolute *study*" of Harriet Martineau's translation, especially the last three books. When he was only up to volume fourteen of a French edition of Sismondi's *History of France* in thirty volumes, he recommended the work warmly to Sarah; when she complained she did not have time to read so much, he lectured her on what one could get through if one only put aside four hours a day for reading. At the same time, Grimke was alert to the thought and writing of his own country. He recognized the value of Robert Baird's *Religion in America* (1844), yet criticized it justly as being far from a "philosophical" work; "it is altogether a work of detail." He listened to lectures by the Transcendentalist, Theodore Parker, and wrote Sarah that Parker's "distinction between the Reason and the Understanding is borrowed from Coleridge, who borrowed from the German School. But it is without any foundation."

The Nature and Tendency of Free Institutions bears sufficient witness to the breadth of Grimke's reading; one need not multiply examples from his letters to his sister. The point is simply that Grimke, living in a small town in the Old Northwest when the region was barely out of the frontier state, brought a range of reference and comparative study to bear upon his analysis of American political institutions which is admirable and which may still stand as an example to students of American life. Writing to Sarah about the poor state of medical knowledge, Grimke insisted, "Individual cases prove nothing." He carried the same attitude to his study of American political institutions, and studied the practices of the ancient republics and contemporary Europe as well as the constitutions of the several states in order to make his study a "philosophical" work and not merely the work of "detail" he thought Baird's book on religion to be.

Yet, among all the subjects and through all the reading Frederick Grimke wrote about to Sarah, there was one topic he refused to confront: Negro slavery. Grimke accepted slavery on the basis of a belief in the racial inferiority of the Negro. His sisters did not agree with him and reticence on the subject was not mutual; it lay on Frederick's side alone. In a long letter after Sarah had obviously responded to a re-reading of *The Nature and Tendency of Free Institutions* when it appeared in a second edition, Grimke wrote: "I feel very much concerned to think that my chapter on slavery has given you so much trouble. You adopted the true sentiment on reading it in the first edition. You remarked, 'I differ with you, but I admire a mind *which is true to its own convictions.*' You probably do not recollect that you have not written me a single letter during the last twelve months which has not contained something on the subject. The golden rule you laid down in 1850, is I believe the most reasonable, the most natural, and the most just which can be adopted."

Grimke's reluctance to write to Sarah about Negro slavery can be understood in many ways. First, simple tact: he had said all he had to say in *The Nature and Tendency of Free Institutions* and there was no reason to exacerbate the feelings of a sister for whom he obviously cared deeply. Second—a generalization of the first—his "convictions" were markedly different from those of the world of his sisters and Theodore Weld. Grimke did not believe in the power of moral persuasion; he was skeptical of plans to reform the world and suspicious of the personal motivations of reformers themselves. He would approach these matters obliquely, but he never confronted Sarah with them directly. For example, he wrote Sarah, "The picture drawn by Victor Considérant, in 'Destinée Sociale' is very flattering, and delightful to look upon; but this fair exterior all vanishes at the touch of experience. The extreme feebleness of our condition, the imperfection of our faculties, and our dependence for enjoyment, on events which we can in no way control, naturally, and necessarily, produce this effect. And as this is the case, we must submit to the disadvantages, which are a law of our being, and not endeavor to exaggerate them by any artificial plan of life." Grimke did not believe, as did the Transcendentalists whom he criticized in the person of Theodore Parker, that man had access through intuition to the truth. He was a skeptical man who insisted upon the hard facts of daily experience. He knew he shared little of the fervent hopefulness which had led his sisters by the route of the inner light to a millennial dream of a world governed by love and justice.

These two reasons, Grimke's tact and his desire not to challenge further the assumptions of his sister's life, are probably sufficient to account for his decision to avoid slavery and the Negro in his letters to Sarah. But there is a possible third reason. There was another brother among the Grimké children, Henry, and Frederick Grimke may have known what his sisters were finally to discover only after his death: there was, through Henry, a Negro line of descent in the Grimke family.

Henry appears fleetingly in Frederick Grimke's letters. Although Frederick was not a wealthy man, he advanced loans to his brother which went unpaid. "Poor fellow," Frederick wrote Sarah after Henry's death, "it is only surprising that he should have lived so long, for as nothing contributes so much to longevity as the love of life, so nothing contributes so much to shorten it, as a distaste, and a disgust for life. In his letters to me, two or three years ago, he was fond of ruminating on death, as an effectual relief from all unhappiness. I thought I had diverted his mind from this melancholy mood, but his late letters to you show that he had again returned to it. To defects which never injured any human being but himself, he joined many virtues. To his faults then we will be 'a little blind; and to his virtues very kind.' "

How much Frederick knew of the "faults" of his death-obsessed brother, one can not know; Sarah and Angelina discovered the truth only by chance after the Civil War. In any event, in addition to a distinguished line of white descent, the aristocratic Grimké family had a line of black descent, no less distinguished. Henry, in addition to a family by his white wife, had by Nancy Weston, a family slave, three sons, Archibald Henry, Francis James and John Grimké. In his will, Henry provided that his Negro sons should be freed and left them under the guardianship of their white half-brother, E. Montague Grimké. But five years later, their white brother tried to sell them into slavery, which led, in the flat understatement of Francis J. Grimké years later, "to some complications." To escape slavery, Francis J. Grimké ran off and became the valet of an officer in the Confederate Army. After two years, on a visit to Charleston where the officer he served was stationed at a fort in the harbor, he was arrested and thrown into jail for some months. While Francis was recuperating after jail in the home of his slave mother, E. Montague Grimké, fearful that Francis would run off again, sold him to another Confederate officer whom he served as body servant until the end of the Civil War.

After the war Francis J. Grimké and his brother, Archibald Henry, went North to school. Their brother, John, stayed behind in South Carolina with their mother. Francis and Archibald came finally to Lincoln University in Pennsylvania where a faculty member, impressed with their ability, wrote about them to Samuel Shellabarger, the congressman from Ohio, who in turn wrote a story about the Grimké boys for the press. Angelina Grimké happened upon Shellabarger's account in a Boston newspaper and, bravely, wrote to Francis and Archibald to discover whether they were freed slaves who took her family's name or were actually her relatives. When they discovered that the boys were indeed their nephews, Angelina and Sarah visited them, acknowledged them, and assisted them in their further education.

Sarah and Angelina made their discovery after Frederick's death, so the rest may be quickly told. Francis J. Grimké went to Princeton Theological Seminary, became pastor of the Fifteenth Street Presbyterian Church in Washington, D.C., and trustee of Howard University. Archibald Henry Grimké went to Harvard Law School, practiced law in Boston, wrote biographies of William Lloyd Garrison and Charles Sumner, and was active in Massachusetts politics. In 1894, President Cleveland appointed him Consul to Santo Domingo. Both brothers were unremitting throughout their lives in the struggle for full citizenship and rights for the Negro, and both sided with W. E. B. Du Bois in the struggle against the leadership of Booker T. Washington which led to the schism in the Negro movement in 1906 and to the founding of the N.A.A.C.P. in 1909.

For Frederick Grimke, the ultimate irony in the story is that his own relatives provided living proof of the inadequacy of his belief that the Negro was incapable of seizing the advantages of freedom which, except for the Negro, he understood so well.

Since Grimke's title declares that his book will be a consideration of institutions in a free society, a convenient place to begin is with his analysis of how the departments of government, institutions narrowly conceived, do function. To do so is, however, only convenient, because Grimke conceives of institutions in a much wider sense. He sees particular institutions as the expression of the general structure of society which calls them into being. He is a sociologist of politics. His sociology, in turn, implicates him in a consideration of the social dynamics of history and an ultimate justification of free institutions which involves no less than a theory of human nature. He is, finally, a philosopher of politics. The three levels of analysis are not discrete, of course; they interpenetrate each other on nearly every page he writes, but one may separate them in order to grasp clearly what Frederick Grimke called "the dynamics of freedom."

The Political Institutions of Freedom

From the beginning, there have been in American political thought two, implicitly antithetical views of the nature of a proper constitution and the security it provides against arbitrary power. The first places emphasis on the form of government created by a constitution, on the institutional arrangement of the departments of government; responsible government is to be achieved by setting up a government in which power is distributed carefully among the various parts in order to check undue power by any one particular branch in the whole, finely articulated, self-regulating system. In this view, checks against arbitrary or irresponsible power are institutionalized within the government which the constitution creates. In the American experience, it is the view one normally associates with the term, "checks and balances."

The second view puts emphasis not so much on the organization of the departments of government created by the constitution but on the creation of government itself, the process by which governments are made, and unmade, and insists that the true check on the power of government, on any one or all of the particular branches of government, lies always in the power of the people outside the doors of the government. In this view, the measure of a good constitution is not simply the form of government but the effectiveness of the process by which the people out of government are constantly able to discipline government by exercising the inalienable power which ultimately sanctions all governments. In the American experience, it is the view one normally associates with the term, "constituent power."

The remarkable thing about Grimke's analysis of how in the United States the institutions of government actually function is his clear recognition of the centrality of the constituent power principle. Although he devotes an individual chapter to each of the three major departments of government, the executive, the judiciary, and the legislature, and has interesting comments on each, his major point in each of these chapters is that the separation of powers in the frame of the American constitution works not because power is distributed within the government but because all branches of the government are, directly or indirectly, responsible to the will of the majority of the people outside the doors of government. To drive his point home, he devotes a further chapter to the question "Is the American Government a Balanced One?" His answer is that if one thinks in the traditional terms of a balanced constitution "in which the principal checks to power reside within the government, the American government is not a balanced one." But it is balanced in "a still higher sense" in that restraint upon government derives from the surveillance of the people who are outside the government and who control each of the powers parcelled out within the government only for the practical purpose of making more effective the various functions of government.

Early in his book, Grimke remarks that "all the mechanical contrivances for balancing government are falling from our

hands and can only be superseded by the engine of knowledge." What Grimke means by "knowledge" will, ultimately,
take us to a consideration of his conception of the nature of
man, the assumptions which lie at the base of his politics, but
for the moment what is important is his observation that in a
society where the people choose their rulers it is artificial and
finally useless to pit power against power within the government since all power is, and should be, he insists, the servant of
the people. Sovereignty, for Grimke, is a function of society,
not a function of government.

The importance Grimke attaches to the responsibility of
government to the people shows clearly in his discussion of the
legislature and his logical preference for a unicameral rather
than a bicameral system within the states. He accepts the division of the Federal government into a Senate and House since
the national government was not meant to be, to use his favorite term, a "consolidated" government but a federation of
states. But in the states, since the people elect both houses of
the legislature by roughly the same qualifications, he points to
the obvious fact that the check does not lie between the two
but between each and its responsibility to the people. He admits that tradition may sanction the continuing existence of the
division of the legislature into two branches, but he argues that
in a democratic society the true check lies not in that division
but in the fact that both branches are the creatures of a sovereign people. Likewise, in his discussion of the executive power,
Grimke makes a virtue of a weak president on the ground that
he will be more responsive to the will of the people.

The most interesting instance of Grimke's belief "that once
a nation has entered upon the task of self government it is
bound to encounter all the perils which are incident to it" and
of his confidence that these "perils" are "the means provided
for preserving the integrity of the system" is to be found in his
treatment of the judiciary and his rejection of the notion that
the judiciary should be free from popular control. An inde-

pendent judiciary, so important to the view that government should be controlled by the separation of powers and a system of checks and balances, represented the major obstacle to Grimke's reliance on the power of the people to control and make government responsible.

Grimke opens his chapter on the judiciary by disposing of the authority of Montesquieu who argued that the judicial branch was powerless. Anyone familiar with the thought of Grimke's time will recognize the boldness of the strategy and how free Grimke was, in rejecting Montesquieu, from accepted clichés about American political institutions. At least since Hamilton's use of the authority of Montesquieu in Federalist No. 78, those who wished to insist upon life tenure for judges and their independence from the vagaries of popular democracy had constantly invoked the authority of "the celebrated Montesquieu." Hamilton's use of Montesquieu was ingenious, if not ingenuous. What Hamilton wished to do in Federalist No. 78 was to convince the people of the state of New York that the organ of government closest to their will was that organ furthest removed from them in their electoral capacity, namely, the court. He did so by arguing that the court was responsible to the will of the constituent people as embodied in the Constitution and, in putting a negative to an act of the legislature, that the court was simply being responsible to the people over and above the heads of their agents, their directly elected representatives. To lend authority to his position, Hamilton added a footnote: "The celebrated Montesquieu, speaking of them, says: 'Of the three powers [the executive, the legislature and the judiciary], the judiciary is next to nothing.' "

Grimke calmly sets Montesquieu, and Hamilton, aside by saying that in a monarchy where the king is sovereign and where the judges are appointed by the king this might be true, but in a democratic republic where the people are sovereign the judiciary "seems to possess a disproportionate share of power." If power is to be responsible to a free people, it must be responsible to the will of that people, so Grimke endorses the application of the principle of constituent power to all branches of government "indiscriminately" by arguing for limited tenure in the appointment of judges. Grimke argues that a judge, whether appointed or elected, should hold office for a sufficient number of years to enable him to master the intricacies of his role in government, but not so long as to be insensitive to "the healthful influence of those opinions and feelings which grow up in the progress of every improving society." What Grimke obviously fears is a lag or a gap between the demands of the society and the attitudes of judges protected in their opinions by life tenure. The reason for his fear is the recognition, derived probably from his own experience on the bench, that the court is a legislative as well as a judicial body; that, as a later age would put it, judges make law.

Grimke repudiates the notion that the court simply applies the law to particular cases, the idea "commonly entertained," as he puts it, that "it is simply invested with the power of expounding the law." But, he points out, the "power of expounding comprehends a great deal and reaches much further than is generally imagined." Both the argument that the court is controlled by previous decisions and the argument that the court simply applies general principles to particular cases leave wide latitude for the particular judge. As much as Grimke admires the principle of *stare decisis* because it represent adherence to the accumulated experience of men, he observes that any particular case may easily be arraigned under contradictory precedents. Or, if the court applies general principles, then the question is simply "principles determined by whom?" Inevitably, he argues, the judicial power is also a legislative power and dangerous precisely because the legislative function it performs "is a fact entirely hidden from the great majority of the community."

Grimke's handling of the judicial power represents his total commitment to the faith that the true "regulative principle" in society is to be found in "public opinion." At this point he confronts the question which Jefferson dismissed in his lighter moments with the suggestion that the nation should have a revolution every generation. Grimke solves the essential problem of how the people outside the doors of government are to make their will felt upon those who exercise power inside government by understanding what few in his time had yet come to recognize, the necessary place of the party in American politics.

Today it seems an unaccountable lapse in the general wisdom of the Founding Fathers that they paid no attention to the one institution that would make representative government actually work, namely, the party system. In the first generation, opposition to those in power, "the government," was understood only as the work of a "faction," a self-interested and disgruntled minority. The Federalists, during the Alien and Sedition crisis, came close to identifying opposition to governmental policy with treason, and Jefferson was not being simply politic in his famous first inaugural when he assumed that all Americans comprised one great party. The notion persisted into the age of Jackson. As *The United States Magazine and Democratic Review*, the organ of the Jacksonian Democratic party, put it in its first issue, "there does not exist in the people, with reference to its great masses, that irreconcilable hostility of opinions and leading principles which would be the natural inference from the violence of the party warfare in which we are perpetually engaged," and assumed that all Americans would range themselves under "the broad and bright folds of our democratic banner" once Democrats had led them to understand the issues "rightly." Neither did Grimke think there were "irreconcilable" divisions among the American people, but almost alone in his time he saw and defined the necessary function of party. Not even Martin Van Buren, one of the great builders of party organization, quite grasped the heart of the matter, as is clear from his *Inquiry into the Origins and Course of Political Parties in the United States* (1867).

What Grimke clearly saw was the necessity of party organization in a society committed to control by the people over the government. Unless some agency emerged to give institutional form to the amorphous shape of public opinion, then the principle of constituent power would fall victim to two opposite and undesirable extremes, either the sterility of an ideal incapable of practical implementation, or the violence of a revolutionary destruction of existing government whenever it proved irresponsible to the will of the people. "Popular parties," Grimke recognized, "are not only the natural result of elective government but, what is of much more consequence, they are absolutely necessary to uphold and preserve it." Grimke's point is that political institutions in a society where power resides in the people require a different kind of control than they do in a non-representative government. "In the artificial forms of government," he goes on to say, "a system of checks and balances is devised . . . to maintain each department in its proper place; but such an expedient would be futile and powerless where government means vastly more than the rule of the persons who fill the various public offices." Since the essence of free political institutions is to confer power upon the people, Grimke observes, "We want something more, therefore, than a scheme of checks and balances within the government. . . . We must contrive some machinery equally extensive for the purpose of controlling them." The development of the institution of the political party provided the necessary "machinery" and, Grimke concludes, "popular parties very naturally, not to say necessarily, take the place of that curious system of checks and balances which are well enough adapted to a close aristocracy or pure monarchy, but which play only a subordinate part in representative government."

For Grimke the "distinguishing feature" of American political institutions was "that we may vary the paraphernalia of government as much as we please, but it still obstinately persists in every one of its departments to be a government based upon the popular will." The power of the "popular will" was not only the distinguishing feature of American government, it was its distinguishing virtue, and Grimke wished his fellow countrymen to recognize that fact and its inevitable corollary, the necessity of party organization to provide an institutional voice for the popular will and to bring it to bear upon each and every office of government. He recognized that "the prevailing spirit of party" with its "eternal din and confusion" had led "zealous and patriotic individuals" to wish to do away with party politics. But he reminded such individuals that the "passions and fierce disputes" of party politics were "the only means in a society, not enlightened above what it falls to the lot of humanity to be, by which any signal change in the public policy of the state or the condition of the people can be obtained."

At this point, Grimke obviously faces the problem of defining the nature of public opinion to which political parties are to give voice, but before turning to his discussion of that problem, one must first consider one further check upon the power of government which bulks large in Grimke's discussion of the institutional arrangement of government, namely, the dual system of political authority which divides power between the national government and the several states. Although Grimke explicitly repudiates the arguments of John Taylor and demolishes John C. Calhoun's doctrine of nullification, he defends the autonomous power of the individual state to secede from the Union in order to defend its particular interest.

Grimke's defense of the right of a state, as a last resort, to secede from the Union is to protect slavery. He is not, however, an apologist for slavery, nor a defender of the South in the reactionary style of a George Fitzhugh. Grimke can see no reasonable solution to the problem created by the South's "peculiar institution" and uneasily accepts it as a given fact of life, a necessity imposed, however unfortunately, upon society. In this respect, he is probably more characteristic of the general run of Americans, North and South, than benevolent abolitionists like his two sisters, on the one hand, or aggressive feudalists like Fitzhugh, on the other. Grimke's grudging acquiescence to slavery as an institution results from his inability, or his unwillingness, to extend to the Negro his conception of the nature of man and of the consequences of freedom. He excludes the black man on the basis of a dubious theory of race. But, again, Grimke probably spoke for the majority of Americans in his time who celebrated freedom for themselves and denied it to the Negro.

The most that can be said for Grimke is that he was unable to imagine the extension of freedom to the slave. But at least he was candid. Although slavery and the Negro appear nowhere in the two chapters that deal with nullification and secession, in the midst of his discussion of classes in the United States Grimke says, "But if one only knew how to deal with so difficult and delicate a subject" as Negro slavery, "if one only had the ability requisite to remove the institution without leaving worse consequences behind, there can be no doubt that it would be better that all the occupations of society should be filled by a free population exclusively." Lacking that ability, Grimke did not indulge in the cant that slavery was a good thing or that the South was better for it. "The men of the South," he wrote, "cannot reasonably contend that the institution of slavery is a benefit 'per se,'" and he scouted the notion, so dear to Fitzhugh, that the prevalence of "novel and startling doctrines in religion, morals and politics" in the North argued for a better ordered society in the South. Grimke found slavery itself repugnant, but accepted the conservative, pragmatic argument that the consequences of emancipation "in communities where the slaves are very numerous and of a race entirely distinct" from their masters were worse than the institution itself.

Since the Negro and slavery do not arise in Grimke's discussion of the place of the state in the federal system of national government, one might argue, as some have done for John C. Calhoun, that he was simply extending to its logical conclusion the classical liberal position of the protection of all minority interests against the intrusion of the power of the state and the tyranny of the majority. Yet, in the face of Grimke's acceptance elsewhere of equality and the will of the people, this seems unlikely and is made even more unlikely by the history of the text. The entire second chapter in Book IV on the right of a state to withdraw from the federal union, to secede, was added to the second edition of *The Nature and Tendency of Free Institutions*. In the first chapter of that book, on the "veto power" of the state to set aside obnoxious legislation by the national government, Grimke had, certainly to his own satisfaction, destroyed Calhoun's doctrine of nullification. Since at the same time he had, however reluctantly, accepted the necessity of the institution of slavery, he must have realized that he had left the slave South in an awkward position with no way to defend itself. So, confident of his own reading of the Constitution, Grimke added to the second edition the second chapter which argues for acceptance of the right of secession. The end he had in view, however, was the preservation of the Union.

Grimke begins his discussion of the "veto power" of the individual state with a review of the dual system of government in the federal system whereby the individual citizen is subject to two sets of laws, those of the particular state and those of the national government. "It is the independent character of these two classes of government," he says, "which has caused some eminent minds in America to doubt whether the judicial power of the union extends to the determination of the validity of the state laws when they conflict with the federal constitution. It has been supposed that there could be no arbiter in this case and that the states, nay each of them separately, must necessarily possess a veto upon the decisions of the national tribunal." He then directly confronts the notion put forward by John Taylor and John C. Calhoun that when a single state challenged the constitutionality of a law Congress was required to call a constitutional convention to determine the issue. Grimke scouts this proposition on two practical grounds: first, that it is clearly contrary to the amendment process laid down in the Constitution itself; second, and more important it would constitute a retrogressive step and destroy the achievement of a system of government where the laws act upon individuals and not upon groups, however defined. But Grimke's two reasons are only historical and practical. He cuts deeper into the issue by turning the doctrine of nullification back upon itself.

If any one state may summon a convention because it challenges the usurpation by the federal government of a power the state thinks is reserved to it, then, Grimke points out, logically any other state may do the same if it believes a state is exercising a power which is delegated to the national government. The practical conclusion would be, says Grimke, that "if a state has the right to veto a law of the federal government because it is not a delegated power, for the same reason will the federal government have a right to veto a law of a state because it does not fall within the reserved powers." And he pointedly asks the South if it believes that such laws as the exclusion of free men of color, as in North and South Carolina and Louisiana, would survive the veto power of a northern state. The ingenious strategy of Taylor and Calhoun was, Grimke insisted, "a two-edged sword." Further, Grimke thought, Calhoun's argument in his *Discourse Upon the Constitution* was woven out of a "sophism." The fact that the Constitution was ratified by the several states no more meant that the national government could be undone by the act of a single state than a government created by individual citizens could be undone by the will of a single individual.

At this point Grimke faced the fact that he had denied the southern states any legal or political argument within the American system of government. So, inevitably, he confronted the ultimate and last resort, the right of secession, when a state thought its particular interests violated by the national government. Grimke affirms the right of secession, but arrives at his goal by a curious route. The heart of Grimke's argument is that, contrary to Taylor and Calhoun, the act of secession is not an assertion of the sovereignty of the state, but quite the opposite, "an unequivocal admission that the sovereignty does not reside in the state seceding." Since the federal union is a cession of power by the states singly to the states jointly, to use Grimke's formulation, there is no possible recourse to nullification by the single state. There is only withdrawal, which is the obverse of the exercise of sovereignty. "In the case of secession, instead of the constitution and laws being removed out of the way of the discontented state, the state itself removes out of the way." Grimke puts the matter this way to drive home the point at issue, that the individual state must defer to the sovereignty of the federal government so long as it remains in the union. The consequence was that "each state for itself, and for itself only, may withdraw from the union." A league of states against the sovereign power of the federal government would be an act of rebellion. Grimke wished to isolate the single state, force it to recognize that in the act of secession it was implicitly admitting it was not the seat of sovereign power, while he still defended its right to depart if it saw fit.

The conclusion of Grimke's argument for the right of secession was the hope that recognition of the right was the surest way to see that the right was not used. The individual state would instantly recognize the enormous disadvantages of "standing alone in the midst of a firm and compact league" and so defer secession until it was the last remaining option; at the same time, "open recognition of the right to secede will render it disgraceful to embark in any scheme of concerted resistance

to the laws while the state continues a member of the Union."
In the North, a frank avowal of the right of secession would
impose caution and restraint upon the national government.
"The public councils would be marked by more reflection
when a moral agency was substituted in the place of brute
force."

With that sentence, Grimke reveals the heart of his trust,
the belief that the solution of the problems which threatened to
rend the nation North and South lay in calm considerations by
reasonable men concerning the advantages and disadvantages of
the Union. He drastically underestimated the emotional appeal
of an emergent southern nationalism or the mystique of the
Union which Lincoln was to dramatize. His own cool rationality could lead him, at the end of his chapter on secession, to
envisage the time "when the same causes which led to the formation of the present Union will lead to the formation of two
or more Unions." He was wrong, of course, but not just because he underestimated the role of emotion in human affairs,
but because he believed the function of government was to
serve the "interests" of society. The principle of representation
which gave constituents power over government was one way
to see to it that government was responsible to the interests of
its constituents. The other was to divide "a country of great
extent" into "separate jurisdictions." "If this is not done, the
general and local interests will be confounded." But Grimke's
defense of the right of secession was possible for him only on
the assumption that reasonable men would probably refuse to
use a right, so obviously against their interest. He trusted that
the open affirmation of the right of secession would serve to
maintain the Union, not destroy it.

The Social Basis of Freedom

In the midst of his plea for an open avowal of the right of
secession, Grimke observed, "The European doctrine is that in

matters of government it is necessary that statesmen should have both a secret and a declared opinion. The maxim in America should be that the justest use will in the long run be most likely to be made of every right where it is clearly, frankly and unreservedly admitted." Beneath the carefully reasoned constitutional and legalistic arguments Grimke made against the doctrine of nullification and for the right of secession lay a firm commitment to the power of public opinion and an abiding trust in the good sense of the average citizen. Baffled by what to do about slavery, he was still sure that if a solution were ever to be found it would be through "the moral force of public opinion which . . . silently introduces changes which would otherwise have disturbed the whole order of society." So Grimke's discussion of the nature of the federal government brings him, as did his discussion of the role of party politics in a free society, to the nature of public opinion. An exploration of his understanding of that question involves Grimke's view of the social forces that call certain kinds of political institutions into being; it involves a consideration of Grimke's notions about the social conditions that create a sound public opinion and that make freedom possible.

In his chapter on the difficulties in the way of arriving at a "science of government" Grimke remarks that "writers on political philosophy have for the most part employed themselves in studying what is termed the mechanism of government, rather than unfolding the structure of society." He then distinguishes between "negative" and "positive" influences of society upon the institutions of government. The influence is negative when the population "is sunk in ignorance and apathy" and government assumes the character of "a self-existing institution"; it is positive when "the standard of popular intelligence is high and no impediment exists to the exercise of . . . popular authority." For Grimke, the United States was an instance of the latter, a society in which "the people may truly be said to create and uphold the government." To employ one of his further distinctions, a representative republic was the only "natural" form of government; all others were "artificial." The government of the United States was, he thought, the only example of true, natural government in the world. As a student of the forms of government, Grimke places considerable emphasis on social determinism and cultural relativism in his analysis of political institutions. But as a philosophical observer of politics, he insists upon an ideal standard against which all historical forms must be measured. That standard was the principle of constituent power; "the bars" to irresponsible exercise of power must be "truly without, and not within" the institutions of government. Or, in other words, government must be constructed so that it is responsible to the will of the people. In the United States of his time, Grimke thought it was, and he was no mere chauvinist in saying so. If he thought his contemporaries were more given to reflection, if he thought the free institutions of republican politics were capable of still further improvement, it was not because Americans were better than other men; they were simply in a different "situation." Formerly, Grimke wrote, it may have been "sufficient to study the mere mechanism of government, but it is now necessary to look a great deal further and to take in the structure of society as a most important element in the character and working of the political institutions."

In his discussion of the English Constitution Grimke notes that "mixed government" is a consequence of the "mixed character" of the population. There are "permanent classes in society whose interests are opposed to each other," and the English constitution is an institutional recognition of the fact. Then Grimke goes on to say, "In a representative republic, the composition of society is exceedingly uniform." Or, as he had put it earlier: "there is more sameness, more uniformity of character, among the American people than among any other." The great problem facing European nations was how to achieve sufficient equality in social conditions to allow "just and equal rules" for all men in politics. But in America, Grimke observes, "this substantial requisite is already obtained." Here, "the principle of equality has thus found a natural support. It has not been the creature of the laws." So the period in which he wrote was for Grimke "the golden age of the republic" for the simple reason that "Americans commenced where other communities will probably leave off." The third estate might have to struggle with kings and nobles in Europe, but in the United States the people were "almost entirely . . . middle class."

"When I speak of a society which is democratically consti- tuted," Grimke insists, "I do not intend merely a society which has democratic institutions; it may have them today and lose them tomorrow. I intend a society in which not only the politi- cal but the social organization is so advanced as to render free institutions the natural expression of the national will." The social organization which made freedom so easy to maintain in the United States was the simple fact that there were no classes in it. One need only read Grimke's chapter on "The Classes of Society" to see how diffuse the concept of class was when ap- plied to the United States. Grimke may begin by saying "the greater the number of classes the less powerful will anyone be," or that "society is balanced by the various classes of men," but he is not thinking of class in an economic sense. The "orders of men," as he puts it, comprise the "young and the old, the rich and the poor, capitalists and laborers, the rural and town population, professional men, and lastly, the parties of majority and minority." Generational differences are equal in importance to wealth for Grimke, and the division of rich and poor is not a social division but a personal one: "Industry, sa- gacity and enterprise, though they can be neither seen nor touched, compose at the present day the chief elements of wealth." That is to say, the existence of rich and poor derived from personal attributes, "the result of certain laws of our na- ture," and not from the chances in life determined by the structure of society. Likewise, the division between the rural and town population vanishes upon inspection. "The distinguishing feature then of American society," Grimke observes, "was that the *tiers état*, or middle class, is not confined to the towns but is diffused over the country." In Europe, the bourgeoisie was to be found only in the towns; in the United States "it comprehends in addition a vastly more numerous class, to wit, the country population," and Grimke thought that fact one of "infinite moment" in the study of American institutions. The final result was that in the United States "the middle class has swallowed up all other distinctions in the state." Little wonder that free institutions worked in such a society. It already enjoyed the luxury of a "tacit agreement" among all men.

Grimke celebrated the middle class not simply because America was a society where the "great majority of the people have so deep a stake in the protection of property and in the maintenance of those laws which guarantee personal liberty." The enveloping middle class made free institutions possible because it created shared consensus, and those free institutions in their turn reacted upon society and forced men to be free and prosperous. Ultimately, Grimke's analysis of the virtue of freedom is not that property creates freedom but that freedom creates property. So he is not simply confounding the difference between politics and society when he includes the "parties of majority and minority" in his description of classes. His category derives from the fact that in the United States the individuals who compose the majority and the minority are constantly passing from one to the other because the "middle class may be said fairly to represent the interests which are common to the whole society." The right to property extends to the "man worth a million as well as to one who possesses only two thousand dollars"; and since "the ambition of everyone is to move forward and to rise as fast as possible into the class of the rich," the rule of the middle class also represents the aspirations of those who "commenced life with little or no property." The United States was, in the pithy phrase of a later historian, a society of "expectant capitalists." If parties existed in the United States to act as "the representatives of the various interests of the community," it was also true that Americans could allow parties to "magnify their respective differences" because the "only effect is to set in a more striking light the numerous points of agreement which exist among them."

At this point, Grimke sounds like little more than still another witness to the generally received notion that Americans are unconscious beneficiaries (or victims, as some prefer) of an unexamined consensus, an uncritical devotion to liberal and bourgeois values. Grimke *is* devoted to liberal values in politics, that is, to equality before the law, to equal participation in government through representative institutions, and to the protection of the right to property by the state. He is equally devoted to bourgeois values in society, that is, to sobriety, industriousness, and decency, the civic virtues which the individual citizen internalizes within his own personality in order to make possible freedom from external control. But Grimke is neither unconscious nor uncritical of his own position. He is not, to use the phrase of Louis Hartz, an irrational Lockean, if by "irrational" one means someone who is unconscious of the assumptions which underlie his values because he has not bothered to think about them. To be sure, Grimke is a "Lockean" in the vague and diffuse sense in which Professor Hartz uses the word in *The Liberal Tradition in America,* that is, as a summary reference to the social and economic values of classical, middle-class liberalism. But, more important, he is also a "Lockean" in a much more precise sense, a sense which derives from Locke's *Essay on Human Understanding* as well as the *Second Treatise on Civil Government.* Grimke's celebration of the middle class, his affirmation of the social and political values which we associate with Locke's political theory, derives from his acceptance of Locke's epistemology and his acceptance of Lockean assumptions about the nature of knowledge and about human nature. The ultimate value of freedom, Grimke insisted, was that it created the kind of character which made freedom possible.

Freedom and Human Nature

When the first edition of *The Nature and Tendency of Free Institutions* appeared in 1848, a writer in the *North American Review* remarked that the book had no "outward intellectual form," that it lacked a discernible structure. "No analysis," wrote the reviewer, "at the commencement or close of the work, lays open to us the plan of arrangement which existed in the author's mind. . . . It is a series of sensible, deeply meditated essays, well worth reading, but which would have been far more satisfactory if brought before us as parts of a great whole. It is a quarry of thought, not a temple; a wheat-stack, not a loaf of bread."

Even if one did not know through Grimke's letter to Sarah asking for the name of the author that Grimke had reacted to this review, one would be confident Grimke took the criticism into account when he revised *The Nature and Tendency of Free Institutions* for a second edition. His first sentence in the "Preface to the Second Edition" may be read as a rebuttal: "My design in writing the present work has not been to produce a formal treatise in which the parts are made to hang together by certain prescribed rules of art, but to unfold a system of thought which will exercise the mind, and not the critical skill, of the reader." Yet, Grimke did accept the stricture that his reader might need greater direction in arriving at a full comprehension of the "system of thought" he wished to unfold in his book. He followed his critic's advice and added to the second edition a new first chapter and a new conclusion (in addition to the new chapter on the right of secession). Since

Grimke thought the addition of these chapters pointed more directly to the central theme of *The Nature and Tendency of Free Insitutions,* they provide a convenient entry to the basic assumptions of his social and political thought, assumptions which do not emerge explicitly in the development of his argument. They are assumptions about the nature of man and the nature of knowledge which constitute Grimke's intellectual universe and make possible (and, perhaps, more comprehensible to us) all else he has to say about the nature and tendency of free institutions.

Grimke's new "Introductory" chapter begins with the assertion that "the existence of free institutions presupposes the existence of a highly civilized society," and there follows a lengthy speculation on the origin and development of civilization. The crucial moment for Grimke, the moment when men are no longer "impelled by mere instincts," is when an agricultural surplus draws men into exchange one with another. Two results follow. First, "the circle of their desires will be enlarged and the range of observation and experience proportionally extended. The occupations of society then become more complex and more diversified. Men begin to reflect." Second, "in addition to the inanimate objects with which they will have to deal, their own minds will become the subject of observation. Each individual in order to regulate his own actions will be compelled to make observation of the actions of others; and the range of observation widening with every increase of the population, the understandings of everyone will be sharpened whether they will or no." Commerce, the emergence of a market economy, the development of the notion of property, all these are important to Grimke but all are secondary to the basic influence the development of society has upon man's mind; "it acts upon the mind by presenting it with abundant materials for reflection."

If one turns to Grimke's conclusion, "The Ultimate Destiny of Free Institutions," one will discover that his tempered hope for the "wise and equitable government of society" is presented and argued in precisely the same language. "The actions of men," writes Grimke, "depend upon two causes: the faculties of one kind or another with which they are endowed, and the circumstances which are external to them, including in the last not only the physical world but other intellectual beings, together with the institutions, public and private, in the country where they reside and even those of other countries wherever they are capable of exerting an influence upon them. On the joint influence of these two causes depends the whole conduct and behavior of men. . . . It is impossible to conceive that it should be otherwise, since all actions imply something beyond us, affecting our faculties and at the same time affected by them."

Even one casually acquainted with the sensational psychology of John Jocke will recognize the accent of Grimke's language. Grimke takes from Locke the notion that men have certain "faculties," that all knowledge is the product, first, of experience of an external world and, then, of reflection within the conscious mind. The advance of civilization widens the experience of men and forces them to reflect. Free institutions advance the cause of civilization because they are a further development of the dynamic which underlies civilization itself: "free institutions lead to an association of people of all classes." By multiplying the relations among men and by putting men in the way of the experience of governing themselves, freedom develops the understanding and the need for reflection which finally makes freedom tolerable. Similarly, freedom once established is irreversible because through experience it has, in the strict Lockean sense, become understood. America's influence upon the rest of the world derives from the "material application" of the principle of freedom in the American system of government: "Until then, it is the subject of conjecture, but not an item of knowledge, no more than it is one of experience." Grimke is claiming no less than that "freedom" existed only in the realm of conjecture until realized in the action and experience of the United States; then, freedom enters human history as an item of knowledge.

Closely allied to Grimke's insistence on experience and the development of the understanding is his constant depreciation of imagination and emotion. In the "Preface to the Second Edition," where he deplores his time's "vitiated taste for reading," Grimke rejects books which are "exciting" because they do not serve a "genuine desire for knowledge," and "nothing," Grimke concludes, "contributes more to enfeeble the understanding and even to pervert the moral faculties." Grimke has chosen his words carefully here and they emphasize his ambition for his own book. Grimke, in his own tone as well as in the substance of his argument, presents a society of sensible and sober men who, through experience, reflect on ideas and are not led astray by vain imaginings and exciting visions. Throughout *The Nature and Tendency of Free Institutions,* the power which has allowed kings and priests to rule irresponsibly over men is the untutored condition of the masses whose imaginations are inflamed by what their understandings cannot comprehend. "Kingly authority," wrote Grimke at the end of his long book, "is undoubtedly founded on an illusion of the imagination." That illusion may once have had an "infinite advantage" at a time when it was necessary to create unity in society, "to control the imaginations of men by a supreme imagination." But no longer. Once "more homely faculties have been cultivated at the expense of the imagination, the illusion vanishes."

From the start to the end of *The Nature and Tendency of Free Institutions,* Grimke equates despotism and arbitrary rule with the imposition of the imagination, and freedom and republican institutions with the development of the understanding of men through the experience which freedom forces upon them. Grimke was even suspicious of the remnants of the force of the imagination among a free people: "I should not err if I were to say that it is to the over-exercise of the imagination that the greatest defects are to be traced, even in a country of free institutions." The people may still tend to surrender their judgment to the "showy authority" of the state, but the cure for that weakness comes "when they are cast upon their own resources and compelled to grapple with business as a matter serious concern." So, if the office of the executive in a republican form of government is not so "dazzling," that is its very strength: "It will not affect the imaginations of men so strongly, but it will acquire a firmer hold upon their understandings."

At one point, in a discussion of the extension of the suffrage and the participation of all men in the experience of government, Grimke asks the question, "Why it is that the communication of political privileges to a people imparts so much vigor and activity to their whole character?" Political freedom, he answers, "removes a feeling of degradation," but adds, "one can hardly say that the peasantry of Russia or Austria realize this feeling since, having been habituated from time immemorial to a state of subjection, they can hardly form an idea of the value of the privilege" of participation in politics. The only way to acquire the idea of freedom is through the experience of freedom. So, Grimke concludes, "The great advantage arising from the free communication of the privilege [of political participation] consists . . . in its giving men new faculties and not merely new rights."

Grimke is making an extraordinary claim here. When he writes that "the political institutions of the United States may be described as the greatest experiment which has ever been made upon human nature" he is not simply speaking in the hyperbole of the patriot. He speaks out of a rich tradition in western thought which names experience as the source of all knowledge. Free institutions enlarge the "bounds of human experience" and through that enlarged experience effect no less than a change in human nature. Or, as he puts it in the last paragraph of his book, "The enjoyment of liberty in its highest degree has opened a great volume of experience to the American people and this experience, not the possession of any natural qualities superior to those of other people," is what has shaped the character of Americans. Grimke's sober, empirical and skeptical tone throughout his book should not hide from us his enormous faith in the consequences of freedom for all men. The only way to make a man fit for freedom is to give him freedom. He may have a notion of freedom, but he will not realize a true idea of freedom until his understanding grasps it through actual experience. If a Lockean in such an argument, Grimke is decidedly not the Locke of the *Second Treatise* with its emphasis on certain natural rights common to all men; he is the Locke of the *Essay on Human Understanding* with its constant emphasis on experience as the only valid source for true knowledge.

At this point one could multiply examples indefinitely, but the reader may do so for himself. Whether discussing equality which breaks down barriers between men, political parties which stir men into activity, the voluntary principle in religion which makes each man personally responsible, the inefficacy of ideas derived at second hand through books and education rather than directly through experience—whatever his subject, Grimke has constantly in mind one assumption: "There is but one way in which that perception of what is useful and fit can be gained, but one way in which any sort of practical knowledge can be acquired, and that is by placing those for whom such knowledge is desirable in a situation where they will be sure to realize the consequences which will follow from pursuing opposite courses." Or, again, "Free institutions, if they do not find men absolutely fit for self-government, are . . . wonderfully adapted to make them so."

There was, of course, one group of men Grimke did not think freedom would make fit for self-government, black men held in slavery. Grimke generally did not accept intrinsic differences in human nature. He argued for a common nature which developed in different directions because it was exerted on different objects in its environment. But he excluded the Negro from participation in that common human nature on the grounds of race. "In a democratic republic," Grimke wrote, "the field of human life is more thoroughly laid open than it is anywhere else. All the ordinary motives to reflection are increased because the objects about which reflection is employed are multiplied. Individuals are thrown more upon their own resources. Each has more to do, more to quicken his exertion, more to kindle hope and yet sadden with exertion." Perhaps his own language brought the hopeless slave to mind, because Grimke immediately added: "If the slaves of the south did not belong to a race decidedly inferior to that of the white man, it would be the highest wisdom to manumit them."

One may say of Grimke's racism what Grimke said of David Hume's inability to conceive of the separation of church and state and full religious freedom: "Our speculations of any sort hardly ever rise much higher than the age in which we live." The best excuse for Grimke's belief in the racial inferiority of the Negro, in flat contradiction to his general view of human nature, is to point out that he shared a view of race pervasive in his time. The typology which divided mankind up into "races" distinguished by innate and irreversible traits was the dominant intellectual attitude toward race in the period in which Grimke wrote. The purpose of typology is to classify phenomena by certain defined characteristics but, as one student of race has put it, "classification poses problems, it does not solve them." But the concept of race as Grimke put it to work was not to pose a problem, it was to avoid a problem. It was used simply to exclude the Negro from the benefits of freedom.

Grimke's treatment of the Negro represents the single departure in his book from the logic of his own argument. Though he is otherwise skeptical of abstractions which assert a case without proving it, he has his own abstraction, his own unexamined prejudice, behind which he will not go. When confronted with the Negro, Grimke reverses the entire logic of his argument for freedom and deserts his faith that the experience of freedom creates the character necessary for freedom. When he asks, "How shall we emancipate from civil disabilities two or three millions of people without admitting them to the enjoyment of political privileges also?" he answers by a further rhetorical question, "And yet how can this be done without endangering the existence of the very institutions which are appealed to as the warrant for creating so great a revolution?" The answer to that question might well have been the answer Grimke gave elsewhere: the only way to make a man capable of freedom is to make him free. But Grimke refused to extend this argument to the Negro, to claim for the Negro, too, that freedom does not require in advance a certain character, but, rather, that freedom in itself creates the character appropriate for the conditions of freedom.

Grimke's discussion, then, of the political institutions of freedom takes him inevitably to the social context of freedom and, finally, to a justification of freedom which rests ultimately upon an implicit conception of the nature of man. To separate the three major dimensions of Grimke's argument may, however, do Grimke a disservice. It ignores the integrity of his argument, the way in which each of the categories affect each other. It neglects, to use Grimke's phrase, the "dynamics of freedom." So, finally, one may stand back a bit from Grimke's book and ask the question of his title, what is the general "nature" of free society and what is its future, its "tendency"?

Grimke had read *Democracy in America,* and in *The Nature and Tendency of Free Institutions* he has high praise for

Tocqueville who, like Plato, "visited a foreign land with the single view of seeking instruction and who, to the fine genius of Plato, unites the severe analysis and calm observation of Aristotle." But such extravagant admiration did not lead Grimke to concur with all that Tocqueville wrote about American democratic society in the early nineteenth century. He thought Tocqueville misunderstood the nature of equality in the United States, and he did not share Tocqueville's apprehensions about the tyranny of the majority, what Grimke called the force of public opinion.

Tocqueville, in both his book on America and in *The Old Regime*, believed that the meaning of Western history lay in the inevitable spread of equality. "The gradual development of the principle of equality," he wrote, "is therefore a providential fact. It has all the chief characteristics of such a fact; it is universal, it is lasting, it constantly eludes all human interference, and all events as well as all men contribute to its progress." In the first sentences of the "Author's Introduction" to the *Democracy*, Tocqueville wrote, "Among the novel objects that attracted my attention during my stay in the United States, nothing struck me more forcibly than the general equality of condition among the people. I readily discovered the prodigious influence that this primary fact exercises on the whole course of society; it gives a peculiar direction to public opinion and a peculiar tenor to the laws; it imparts new maxims to the governing authorities and peculiar habits to the governed."

For Tocqueville, there was the danger that under the mortar of equality the articulated structure of society would be ground down to identical and equal particles and that democratic society would run the risk of two opposite but related extremes, the anarchy of isolated, self-interested individuals, or mass conformity where each individual, thinking himself self-sufficient, but like all the others, would be psychologically unable to resist the tyrannous weight of the opinion of the majority of his equal fellows. Although Tocqueville thought equality was God's plan for human history he did not think too well of the plan. His own image of the good society was one formed by the notion of a social hierarchy, a chain of being in which each member of the community belonged to a clearly defined place in the hierarchical order of things. "Aristocracy," he wrote, "had made a chain of all the members of the community, from the peasant to the king; democracy breaks that chain and severs every link of it." The consequence of equality for Tocqueville was this shattering separation of man from man and the rupture of traditional social relationships and social obligations.

Grimke shared Tocqueville's belief that the movement from status relationships among corporate groups to contractual relationships among equal citizens was a great moment in history, and he used the same metaphor of the chain of being to describe it. "A great revolution was effected in the structure of society when the inferior classes lost their dependence upon the higher, when the relations of patron and client, or lord and vassal, ceased. A new relation immediately sprang up. Instead of the dependence being all on one side, the two orders became mutually dependent on each other. Society began to assume the character of a great partnership among the members, instead of that series of ascending links in a chain, one end of which was fastened to the throne." But the social consequence, Grimke believed, was precisely the opposite of what Tocqueville feared.

Grimke did not, as Tocqueville seems to have thought all American democrats did, believe in actual equality among men, nor did he anticipate or desire such a consequence. The obvious question, then, was "why do legislators constantly inculcate the maxim that all men are equal?" For Grimke the answer was plain. First, heuristically, to act *as if* men were equal was the only way to achieve whatever degree of equality was possible; second, pragmatically, "it is not in the power of government to make anything like an accurate discrimination between the inequalities of different men"; third, ideally, to treat all men equally as citizens would do away with artificial distinctions among men and allow the inevitable differences among men to emerge naturally and justly. "The utmost which the citizen can demand," concluded Grimke, "is that no law shall be passed to obstruct his rise and to impede his progress through life. He has then an even chance with all his fellows. If he does not become their equal his case is beyond the reach of society and to complain would be to quarrel with his own nature."

To make a simple distinction, equality for Grimke meant not equality of condition but equality of opportunity. "The same laws which declare that all men are equal give unbounded scope to the enterprise and industry of all. Neither family, nor rank, nor education confer any peculiar advantages in running the career which is now opened. In many respects they even throw obstacles in the way. Men without education, with ordinary faculties, and who commenced life with little or nothing are continually emerging from obscurity and displacing those who have acquired fortunes by inheritance. They constitute emphatically the class of rich in the United States. It is the principle of equality there which introduces all the inequality which is established in that country." Grimke's *beau ideal* was the man on the make who asked only that he be given a fair chance to show that he was considerably more equal than his fellows. The "broad and indiscriminate rule of equality" among citizens, he thought, "obliterates all artificial distinction and yet brings out in bolder relief all the natural inequalities of men."

Nor did Grimke fear that those who lost the race would turn to politics to gain what they lost in society; "as a large proportion of the envious are constantly rising into the ranks of the envied, a powerful check is imposed upon the revolutionary tendencies of the former. They cannot reach, nor after reaching will they be able to enjoy that which is the constant aim of all their efforts without lending an earnest and vigorous support to the laws under which they live." Grimke could say so, of course, only on the assumption that all Americans did have a common as well as a constant aim, that they shared the same goals, and, if failures, would blame themselves and not the social system. Grimke did think Americans shared what he called a "tacit consensus," and, because he esteemed the values which defined that consensus, he was not greatly disturbed that the opinion of the majority had an enormous influence upon the single individual. "No one," he wrote, "who is an attentive observer of human nature can fail to be struck with the amazing influence which the opinion of a multitude of men exercises over the mind. We can stand up and confront a single individual even though we are far from being right, but we recoil with a sort of dread from any opposition to the opinion of a great number." But, having described the reasons why this was so, Grimke accepted the consequence: we live in "a world where a system of opinions and conduct is already established and it does not seem unnatural but rather a necessary consequence of the process by which human conduct is shaped that we should defer greatly to the standard of opinion which is erected, and our deportment . . . should be compressed into a conformity with it and that any revolt against it should be followed with a sense of dread and uneasiness."

Grimke recognized that the stability of American society derived from the simple fact that each individual internalized within his own personality the values of American society. Or, to put it another way, freedom from external control was possible because each individual controlled himself. The self-restraint which Grimke argued was the necessary corollary of freedom was present in American society because, through the force of public opinion, the people controlled each other and, so, did not need to rely upon the coercive power of the state. "I think if anyone will follow carefully and minutely the workings of American society, he will find that the people are fully as much occupied in keeping each other in order as they are in checking the authority of their governments." And, he concluded, "it is only by doing the first that they succeed in doing the last."

At this point, Grimke might have rested in the conclusion that the values of the middle class were so pervasive in American society that they would be self-sustaining through "that invisible power which we term public opinion." But he was not content with so relativistic an answer. He wanted that public opinion also to be reasonable. Otherwise, he could hardly have been so untroubled by the impotence of the single individual in the face of majority opinion. "Public opinion only tends to be right in proportion as it resembles itself to the opinion of mankind," he wrote, and went on to say, "I cannot help thinking that this effect will take place in proportion to the number of men who are in the possession of liberty and who, on that very account, are driven to habits of thought and reflection." Grimke's view of the nature of the development of understanding and reflection among men closed the gap in his argument for him. Liberty would drive men to become as thoughtful as men could be, so the opinion of the majority under the conditions of freedom would come as close to the dictates of reason as men could expect to come.

Grimke also thought that men had to be "driven to habits of thought and reflection" and the ultimate worth, as well as the ultimate safeguard, of freedom was that it drove men to think and reflect. Grimke had, in one respect, a rather low view of human nature. He did not think men would stir themselves; men would not better themselves or advance in understanding unless they were forced to do so. "The human mind," he wrote, "with all its capabilities of thought and action is wonderfully disposed to listlessness, so that it requires the most powerful incentives in order to rouse its dormant energies." The effect of freedom was to rouse the dormant energies of the people and force them to attend to their own interests. This was why "the growth of popular parties constantly keeps pace with the diffusion of industry and property. The diffusion of industry and property, by exercising the mind intently upon small things at first, exercises it earnestly and seriously upon important ones in the end." But it was, Grimke recognized, a serious and strenuous world: "Free institutions introduce heart burnings enough into society. But these only constitute a state of discipline by which men are rendered more wise, more prudent and more just than they would otherwise be."

There is little of the sublime in Grimke's picture of democratic society. He envisions a society of prudent and sensible men, industrious and responsible, holding themselves in check and guarding their own interests by participating actively in the governance of their society. If the vision seems at times a little bleak, one should also remember that such men were free. Or, as Grimke would have it, freedom made such men, and they would continue to be free so long as they continued to accept the heavy burden freedom imposed upon them. Grimke's tempered hope was that the future was on their side. Like many of his contemporaries, Grimke was at times troubled by the assumption that all societies went through a cyclical pattern of growth, and that civilization was followed, inevitably, by decline and fall. But he thought the United States would escape that fatality and "falsify the maxim of Montesquieu that a nation after it has attained a certain height is compelled by some invincible law of its being to decline." He thought the United States would avoid the vices of excessive civilization and the catastrophe of dissolution because "free institutions are endowed with a faculty of self-preservation which is possessed by no other form of government." Freedom forced men to be energetic, imposed experience upon them and inevitably developed their understanding. Freedom perpetuated among men the energy which had started civilization on its course in the first place, and the ceaseless activity and the strenuous burden of freedom afforded, Grimke thought, "a reasonable assurance of the perpetuity of free institutions." Progress was not inevitable—not necessarily God's plan for the world—but it was possible. That was Grimke's cautious hope, and he wrote *The Nature and Tendency of Free Institutions* to enlarge the understanding of his fellow Americans so that it might become probable.

There is always the danger in discovering a neglected figure from out of the past of paying him, in compensation, too great praise. There are good reasons, reasons which may appeal especially to scholars of the early nineteenth century, for rescuing Grimke from obscurity, but there is as much disservice in unstinted and indiscriminate praise as in simple neglect. It is easy to understand why Grimke's contemporaries may have turned away from and forgotten *The Nature and Tendency of Free Institutions*. Grimke's defense of slavery and his cool contemplation of the possible dismemberment of the Union relegated him to a past which blood and battle were supported to have buried. The same coolness may still keep the modern reader at a distance. Grimke's greatest weakness derives from his greatest strength, his image of the nature of man. His depreciation of imagination and emotion provides a foreshortened image of man, one which does not take sufficiently into account man's capacity either for passionate irrationality or for selfless commitment to a good which transcends his particular, individual interest.

Yet Grimke's cool and sober voice should not hide from us his fervent hope for the possibilities of freedom. He may have derided utopian schemes of perfection built upon the benevolence of human nature, but beneath his skeptical and empirical style there lies a great act of faith, the faith that the only way to make men free is to give them freedom. He was too much of his time to extend that faith to the Negro, but we have not yet done so well that we may deride him for his failure. We may properly wish to enlarge the conception of human nature upon which we build our politics, but Grimke may still remind us of the basic premise upon which free institutions are built. Freedom is its own justification, and the only way to make men free is to make them free.

4

MILL, MARX,
AND MODERN INDIVIDUALISM

A CENTURY ago, John Stuart Mill wrote, "If the claims of Individuality are ever to be asserted, the time is now, while much is still wanting to complete the enforced assimilation. . . . If resistance waits till life is reduced *nearly* to one uniform type, all deviations from that type will come to be considered impious, immoral, even monstrous and contrary to nature."

Mill's assertion of the "claims of Individuality" was the essay "On Liberty," published in 1859. It is now, then, more than one hundred years old and custom demands that we do homage to one of the classics of our intellectual tradition. But custom falters before a book which so sturdily denounces custom. The conventional obeisance of respect will not do. Mill, as always, demands a reason and one is not hard to find. When Mill decided to expand a short essay into the small book we now have, he wrote his wife that "nothing seems to be more needed—it is a growing need, too, for opinion tends to encroach more and more on liberty." The need still grows and we still have use for Mill.

213

One use is some perspective on ourselves. We live in a loud and insistent present and now on all sides we hear that the American is an organization man lost in the lonely crowd of mass society. About the longest perspective brought to bear on this faceless man in a gray flannel suit is the accusation that John Dewey started it all by preaching something called adjustment in education. But to read Mill is to remember that our problem is at least a hundred years old. Mill thought it was older. He first had the notion of writing a book on liberty while climbing the long steps to the Capitol in Rome. From that grand perspective the present looks like the thin edge of time. We remember that problems are made in the past and solved in the future. The present loses much of its shrillness and we can, as Mill would have us, think coolly and rationally about the problem of the individual in the modern world.

Tocqueville remarked that "an abstract term is like a box with a false bottom; you may put in it what ideas you please, and take them out again without being observed." Others than Tocqueville have looked with distrust on the magic quality in language, but he is useful here since, according to the Oxford English Dictionary (although it has the date wrong), he is the source of our word, "individualism," using it to describe American society in its Jacksonian phase. It is hard to believe that the word, now so pervasive and various in its significance, is that recent. But even in a little more than a century, times have, to put it softly, changed. We may use the same word, but we may mean different things.

Also in 1859, Marx published the "Critique of Political Economy," his preface to which is the classic statement on the economic interpretation of history. Marx's argument there that it is not the individual who is primary, but society, that "it is not the consciousness of men that determines their existence but, on the contrary, it is their social existence that determines their consciousness," swept away all the assumptions which made Mill's liberal belief in the individual possible. But it was also Marx who had written "we shall have an association in which the free development of each is the condition for the free development of all." That could easily be Mill, but it is "The Communist Manifesto." One does not, I think, readily associate Marxism with an ideal of individualism. Yet one of the most stinging phrases in that polemical classic, the "Manifesto," is the condemnation of the property-owning middle class because "in bourgeois society capital is independent and has individuality, while the living person is dependent and has no individuality."

One's first reaction is right. Mill and Marx do not finally mean the same thing when they talk about individuality. One might object that one cannot use the same word to mean different things, but that would be to deny what we know. Marc Bloch, that brave French historian, observed that, "to the great despair of historians, men fail to change their vocabulary every time they change their customs." Particularly in America because our characteristic depreciation of ideas has made us prone not to worry much about words. Tocqueville is an interesting instance. Americans in the age of Jackson were acting out a social philosophy without much self-consciousness about what they were doing. A foreigner came to provide the word for the action. If intellectuals now sometimes feel like outsiders in America, it may be that they now play the rôle of foreigner to the immense activity of American life.

There is enough truth to be seductive in the notion that it is well for a society not to be too careful in achieving the nice coherence between all its parts so dear to the intellectual. Change is accomplished more easily when men can adapt tradition to changed circumstance by gradually adapting their ideals through changing the meaning of words. But seductiveness need not lead to prostitution. We may discover light for our present concern about the individual by concerning ourselves with Mill and Marx, by discovering that the word, "individualism," can contain quite different, even opposed, systems of value. We may discover that ideas help, even today, even ideas a hundred years old.

Mill saw two threats to the individual, one political, the other social. The political threat, formidable enough, was, Mill thought, a matter of institutional arrangement and he was more concerned with the social. Mill had read his Tocqueville well. "Like other tyrannies," he wrote, "the tyranny of the majority was at first, and is still vulgarly held in dread, chiefly as operating through the acts of public authorities." But when "society is itself the tyrant—society collectively over the separate individuals who compose it—its means of tyrannizing are not restricted to the acts which it may do by the hands of its political functionaries." The real danger was "the tyranny of the prevailing opinion and feeling." Without civil penalties society still could "fetter the development, and, if possible, prevent the formation, of any individuality not in harmony with its way, and compel all characters to fashion themselves upon the model of its own."

All this sounds familiar enough. We become, as our modern sociologist would have it, "other-directed." The prose has changed, much the worse for us, but the problem is the same: "how to make the fitting adjustment between individual independence and social control." Despite the popular image of him, Mill was not trying to deny social control; he was trying to find its proper limit. And he found it, he tells us, in "one very simple principle." Society, whether by force of law or coercion of public opinion, may not interfere with the self-determination of any individual except on the ground of "self-protection." "The only purpose for which power can be rightfully exercised over any member of a civilized community, against his will, is to prevent harm to others." To compel a man to do other than he would is just only when "the conduct from which it is desired to deter him must be calculated to produce evil to some one else. The only part of the conduct of anyone, for which he is amenable to society, is that which concerns others. In the part which merely concerns himself, his independence is, of right, absolute."

As Mill says, this is a very simple rule. So simple that it is almost no help at all. Mill's principle merely shifts the debate to different ground. What part of my action concerns others? What part merely myself? Mill seems not to have realized what a drastic abridgement of individual liberty the protection of society might involve. Not only because, in our complex and interdependent society, it is hard to think of an action of any importance that does not concern others, but also because it is still harder to think that society would surrender its right to decide what does constitute a threat to it. Mill puts us back in the hands of the majority once again and for a social philosopher who so feared the caprice of public opinion, Mill asks a great deal of the same public when he asks it to draw a narrow circle around its opinion of what concerns it. Freedom is not much good if it does not apply to matters that count and it is doubtful if the majority will be less tyrannous in deciding what counts than in enforcing its will afterward on those who disagree. Without undue casuistry, one could push Mill's simple principle to the unhappy conclusion that about the only liberty left is to think one's thoughts to one's self. But that would be to mock the meaning of words.

It is necessary to insist that despite Mill's place in our intellectual hagiography as the "saint of rationalism," "On Liberty" is essentially hortatory, not argumentative. It convinces by an appeal to our emotions, not to our intelligence. It is a hymn to liberty, not a textbook in its justification. Caroline Fox, Mill's contemporary, called "On Liberty" "that terrible book, so clear and calm and cold." Many have continued to confuse Mill's cool style with the quality of his thought. But if we can forget his reputation, we can see that Mill's most famous essay rests essentially on one grand assumption that he refuses to question. The unchallenged belief that Mill finally built his case upon was, as he puts it, that man's "errors are corrigible. He is capable of rectifying his mistakes, by discussion and experience." That is, in his moral and intellectual capacity, man is rational. He has reasons, not just opinions.

As far as man's opinions were concerned, Mill was as much a relativist as any of our modern cultural anthropologists. He knew that it hardly bothered a man that "the same causes which make him a Churchman in London, would have made him a Buddhist or a Confucian in Pekin." And as keenly as any Marxist, Mill knew that man generally decides upon self-interest and that "wherever there is an ascendant class, a large portion of the morality of the country emanates from its class interests."

But Mill escaped cultural or economic determinism by distinguishing carefully between opinion and conduct on the one hand and reason on the other. Regarding the follies discernible in the history of opinion and custom, Mill wondered, "Why is it, then, that there is on the whole a preponderance among mankind of rational opinions and rational conduct? If there really is this preponderance—which there must be unless human affairs are, and always have been, in an almost desperate state—it is owing to a quality of the human mind, the source of everything respectable in man either as an intellectual or as a moral being, namely that his errors are corrigible. He is capable of rectifying his mistakes, by discussion and experience." It is his faith in reason that buttresses Mill's plea for the freedom and the primacy of the individual.

But as Mill plucks rationality from the nettle of foolish opinion, how, one wonders, can he look about him and claim, even hesitantly as he does, a preponderance of rational conduct and rational opinion in a society whose morbid fear of discussion is the very target of his essay? Because he must. Mill's primary commitment was to the self-sufficiency of the individual person. In "A System of Logic," when the conflict between cause and effect and freedom of the will threatened to submerge the individual, Mill "had no hesitation," as his biographer says, "in using his great powers to bend the logic." Such an issue may make us think kindly of the humanist, but not so well of the philosopher. Mill believed with his heart, not his head, that there *must* be a thread of rationality running through the botched tapestry of human affairs. If not, human affairs are in an "almost desperate state."

We, in the twentieth century, are perhaps more ready to admit that human affairs are in a desperate state. Precisely because we have lost the capacity to believe in the efficacy of human reason. Our skepticism runs deep, however much we may fear where it bears us. The argument could be developed but we now know all its terms. Man's capacity for self-deception, privately, according to Freud, and socially, according to Marx, looks to us so great that reason seems a slender reed against which to lean our faith in the individual. Society seems to us so real that the individual looks to be but a shadow of its will. Bereft of Mill's supporting belief, we are in danger of surrendering our individual wills to the group with which we work, the class to which we belong, or the society in which we live. And just as early nineteenth-century American society acted out an ideal of the individual without bothering to define it, we may again today be acting out a different ideal without much awareness that it runs violently counter to much of our professed belief.

However much a rationalist Marx was himself, his assertion that "being determines consciousness, not consciousness being," struck a radical blow at the sufficiency of reason to provide a basis for a social philosophy. For the Marxist an escape lay in the future, but until the ultimate success of the proletariat, man's "reasons" were simply a mask for his material interests.

But Marx did more than just weaken the basis of faith in Mill's brand of liberal individualism. He captured its very ideal and, in the process, inverted its very terms. Marx claimed to stand for true individualism. Just as he thought that Hegel's idealism stood on its head, rather than on the solid footing of reality, Marx condemned bourgeois society for having its most cherished ideal upside-down. When Marx, in the "Communist Manifesto," derides the freedom and independence of bourgeois individuality as nothing more than false values which cloak the economic interests of the middle class, the purpose might seem to be purely polemical. Yet by deriding "bourgeois" individualism, Marx implies, at least, that there is some other kind of individualism which is more than a rationalization of one's economic position in society, that there is a valid individualism just as there is a valid organization of society. And this, of course, is where Marx arrives: "In place of the old bourgeois society, with its classes and class antagonisms, we shall have an association in which the free development of each is the condition for the free development of all."

It will surprise only those who have not read Marx that he arrives where Mill began. But that is precisely the difference. For Marx, the ideal community in which the free development of each individual is compatible with the development of all individuals was to be arrived at, to be won only at the end of the unfolding of history. For Mill, the ideal was to be recovered; the free society was to be the premise of history, not its conclusion.

One of the difficulties in reading Marx is to decide whether he really believed in the conclusion of history, a conclusion in the sense of the realization of the ideal of the classless society in which man for the first time leaps into freedom. For polemical purposes, for the coffee-house conspirator, it was psychologically necessary, perhaps, to have a determinate goal, an ideal society in which all conflict and change were resolved and the wolves laid down with the lambs. But the question whether Marx believed that historical change had an end has a logical urgency about it, especially when one tries to understand what kind of individuality will finally be achieved when the false individuality of the bourgeoisie is put aside.

The theoretical difference between Marx and Mill is put sharply in one of Marx's theses on Feuerbach: "the human essence is no abstraction inherent in each single individual. In its reality it is the *ensemble* of the social relations." With those few words, all Mill's assumptions are gone. There is no unhistorical quality, reason or any other, which somehow defines the individual and, more importantly, assures his individuality whatever his social or historical position. The individual becomes simply an embodiment of the material conditions in which, at any historical moment, the individual has being. All subjective life, all ideas, become "the product, in the last analysis," as Engels wrote, "of the economic stage which society had reached at that particular epoch."

The individual has, in this view, no individuality; he is simply a function of the practical relations on which his class position is based. To put it more starkly, the individual has no reality. Reality becomes the attribute of the developing material conditions of society.

At this point, the follower of Marx will surely cry out that this presentation develops the very "mechanical" materialism which Marx set out to destroy. The exposition here is not "dialectical," it does not recognize the development of necessity into its opposite, freedom. Marx, in another of the theses on Feuerbach, wrote that "the materialist doctrine that men are the products of circumstances and upbringing and that, therefore, changed men are the products of other circumstances and changed upbringing, forgets that circumstances are changed precisely by men." Man's will, in this view, is effective at those points where changing circumstances and human will coincide. Man is not completely free, free to accomplish whatever he will. But he is free to instrument change. Freedom, the Marxist says, is the recognition of necessity.

Now, enough has been written about this famous formulation to make a simple observation on it difficult. Engels, with Marx's editorial approval, wrote that "Hegel was the first to state correctly the relation between freedom and necessity. To him, freedom is the appreciation of necessity. 'Necessity is *blind* only *in so far as it is not understood.*' . . . Freedom of the will therefore means nothing but the capacity to make decisions with real knowledge of the subject." Engels is perfectly right in saying that "uncertainty, founded on ignorance, which seems to make an arbitrary choice . . . possible, shows by this precisely that [man's judgement] is not free, that it is controlled by the very object it should itself control." True, the more real knowledge I have of the problem I must solve, the narrower my range of choice. But that is not to make my choice *free*. It only makes me less *blind* to the choice I must make (if knowledge finally discloses that there is only one possible course of action). If the freedom of the individual is to be an ideal embodiment of the objective, necessary conditions in which he lives and moves, then one can, if one wants, say that freedom and necessity are identical. But for most of us, it is nothing more than verbal legerdemain to say that freedom is its opposite, however trippingly the word, "dialectical," comes from the tongue.

For Hegel, freedom is the growing recognition of necessity because freedom and necessity are not resolved in history, but at the beginning and the end of history in that ultimate abstract ideal in which all contraries are resolved into one. The Marxists, however, saw in such a notion only metaphysical rubbish. Their concern was with actual men in their changing social and historical relations. The end was to come when society, by seizing the means of production, finally puts an end to all conflicts between men, puts an end to classes and their limited ideologies, puts an end to the state, and finally puts an end to change itself.

It is a stirring ideal, certainly, and it is more to our discredit than to Marxism itself that the very grandness of its conception has become chiefly a means of ridicule. In this apocalyptic vision, man becomes god-like; the Marxist would say that he becomes truly human, that all class history is the history of man's animal evolution. Man knows all, therefore he wills all. Knowledge and power, freedom and necessity are one and the same. The ultimate heaven to be won on earth solves the problem. Man must submit to necessity to gain freedom; man must lose his individuality in order to win it. The program may mean the denial now of all it promises to achieve, but it would be an unwise critic who scorned the power of such an appeal to stir men to heroic effort.

But an irritating practical question obtrudes itself. At one point in the "Manifesto," Marx speaks of the diminution of the individual in the modern world and here his remark has nothing to do with the distortions created by class ideology: "Owing to the extensive use of machinery and to division of labor, the work of the proletarians has lost all individual character, and, consequently, all charm for the workman. He becomes an appendage of the machine." These words could easily have been written by a humanitarian reformer, like William Morris, or a utopian socialist, like Charles Fourier, either of whom Marx would brand as sentimental for turning away from the real and necessary condition of the future, the emergence of an industrial and technological society, with its inevitable concomitant, large-scale organization and collective, rather than individual, activity. But if the division of labor and the extensive use of machinery are necessary postulates for a socialist society, how will the worker be rescued from the joyless routine of production which diminishes the individual to a function of the collective whole? Even after social control is to make the leap into freedom possible, the intense organization of economic life would remain a necessity.

Whatever Marx's errors (and it has become a ritualistic necessity in our time to insist always on the errors whenever one finds a grain of truth in Marxist thought), Marx was surely right about one thing, the necessary growth of organization, planning, and mutual interdependence in society as a result of a system of production built upon technology and advanced industrialism. All modern societies, not only those that aspire to socialism, must face the fact that they are at the mercy of conditions which make the old ideal of individualism, based on the assumption of the autonomy of the single person, no longer credible, let alone possible.

What kind of "individualism" is, then, possible? Marxism, whether social change has a stop or not, would seem to face a dilemma. The individual must submit to the discipline of the party until socialism is achieved, or to the discipline of the collectivity in order to maintain socialism once achieved. But in Marxist thought, as in much of human thought, the dilemma was avoided by the wonderfully simple device of changing the meaning of one of its terms. There is no conflict between the individual and the collectivity, because the collective will is the will of the individual, rightly understood. One is to realize his individuality by participating in the will of the group. The idea is as old as Plato, of course, and individualism becomes an ideal of belonging, not an ideal of separateness.

At this point it is clear that individualism has two versions. Mill and Marx, if we take their names as shorthand representations of large movements of thought, stand at opposite poles. The individualism of one is the complete negation of the individualism of the other. In America today, we tend, I think, to use the word in Mill's sense; we talk as if we believed in the primacy of the individual person. But our desperate concern about what has happened to that individual gives evidence that we feel confused. We feel that confusion without understanding it.

Despite our talk, we have now for a long time acted quite differently. Our concern today about the organization man stems from the fact that, certainly without ever having read Marx, Americans have begun under the impact of the necessary organization of their economic life to develop in their actions a definition of the individual as a member of the collective. At its most innocuous level, this means simply that an individual should be able to get along with others, to adjust to others. At its most serious, it means a submersion of the individual in the group. The individual is defined by his function; one's rôle in the organization becomes one's real self. The rest is mere appendage. Without an apologist of the new order to make us more self-conscious, we may be all unwittingly developing a conception of democracy which postulates a general will as tyrannous as Plato's or Marx's.

Here we find, I think, two uses for the ideas of Mill and Marx. First, we can choose, establish an intelligent degree of coherence between our ideals and our actions. One may, upon reflection, decide that Marx is right, that true individuality lies in transcending one's narrow self and committing one's self to a greater will. The will of God embodied in a church; the laws of history embodied in a party; the good of society embodied in a corporation: these are not strange and unusual creeds. But one still must judge. Our second use is with Mill. Before choosing to commit one's self, there must be reasons for choosing. There must be more than mere belonging; there must be a standard for belonging.

Far more than Mill, we may be aware of the limits that hedge the power of reason and we do well not to expect too much. But that is no cause to abandon society to rule by some other force. Man's reason may not be much but the relative certainty to be reached by it is all the certainty that is given to man. To say this is to run counter to much of the opinion of our time and one could soften the statement by a certain amount of verbal cushioning. But the desire not to offend is too much the vice of our age. One need not deny any man the comfort of belief arrived at by special revelation or intuition, by appeal to tradition or to any other authority greater than his own intelligence. But if he wishes others to share that belief, he must give reasons that move the mind. More importantly, if on the basis of his own private moral certainty, any man wishes for public power, political or social, he must do more than stigmatize his opponent as immoral. He must submit to the cardinal morality of a democratic society, discussion, the dialogue which accepts the primacy of every individual person, even the most detested opponent. As Mill said over one hundred years ago, there is much left to do.

5

THE IDEAL OF INDIVIDUALISM AND THE REALITY OF ORGANIZATION

"Such was individualism in its two aspects—
all things unto all men."

(Thomas Mann)

THE PURPOSE of this essay is to trace the history of the ideal of individualism in American culture and then to use that history in order to understand better the deep concern for the place of the individual in contemporary American society. Our society, like all modern industrial societies, is characterized by economic and social interdependence, specialization of activity, and large-scale organization—social phenomena that pose troublesome problems for traditional American attitudes toward the relation of the individual to society. One way of coming to grips with our predicament is to see how we came to it in the first place.

"The profit of studying history," George Santayana once said, "lies in something else than in a dead knowledge of what happens to have happened." Yet no good historian—and the adjective will quickly exclude those who may disagree—would suggest that history will give us ready and pat answers to problems in the present. What history can do is enlarge our experi-

227

ence of the events that have entered into the shaping of the present in which we live and move and, thus, make us more aware, itself a virtue, and perhaps through awareness better able to act. Since my final purpose is to bring an excursion into the past to bear upon the present, perhaps it will serve that purpose to begin in the present.

There is an embarrassment of riches when one looks for a contemporary text from which to begin. One thinks of the fortieth anniversary issue of *Time* magazine, The Individual in America, with its cover story on Lincoln, "the greatest, the classic, the archetypical individual in the American imagination," who knew about the organization man because "in a sense he was one himself, and a good one." But I have chosen as my text an article from *Fortune* magazine for two reasons: it is shorter and therefore more adaptable to my needs; but more important, it comes from a magazine that addresses itself specifically to the leaders of American business.

A few years ago—in 1951 to be precise—in the political stalemate following the end of the Second World War, the editors of *Fortune* looked about and discovered half the world on their right hand and half on their left. There seemed to be no ground to stand on between "fascist totalitarianism," the world of the right, and "paternal state socialism," the world of the left. So *Fortune* decided to establish one. In a world made cold by the winds of change, America, in its fat and warm contentment, seemed to offer too visible a target. Although what the editors of *Fortune* were after was what they themselves called a "middle of the road" solution, they packaged it handsomely under the brand name of "the permanent revolution."

The irony cuts deeper than that. The "third force" that the world needed to combat fascism and socialism was that old American tradition, "individualism." The editors faced the cliché without flinching:

Americans are fond of saying that the state exists for the individual, not the individual for the state. Despite its truistic character, this aphorism has enormous meaning. A proletarian approach, which subordinates the individual to the group or class, represents for the American, not an advance but a reaction . . . . If a really dynamic third force is to be created . . . the principle of individualism must constitute its foundation.

But the dynamic principle of a conservative revolution based on the ideal of individualism had some awkward facts to face. The editors went on to say:

In our time, individualism has clashed with the whole industrial development, mass production and the division of labor. The key to industrialization is not independence but interdependence; no individual is self-sufficient; each is involved with others in complicated relationships. Dominating all this is the modern corporation, an organization of vast powers, which exacts of its managers purely impersonal decisions. It is little wonder that men have turned to the state to protect themselves in such a world.

The world of the state was, of course, the world of fascism or socialism. Yet, if America was to maintain its conservative, permanent revolution, it had to remain true to what the editors of *Fortune* took to be the basic proposition of American society—private, individual responsibility. To turn to the state would only further compromise the integrity of the industrial American, dependent on his fellows but lonely in a world of impersonal decisions. *"The solution is to be found,"* discovered the editors, so delighted that they put their discovery in italics, *"The solution is to be found not through a growth in government, but through a growth in the stature of the individual."*
The dialectic begins to pick up speed here, and one has to watch closely.

The concept that appears to be emerging, as the answer of the modern individual to this challenge, is the concept of the *team*. It is an old concept but it is being put to new uses. As a member of a team an individual can find full opportunity for self-expression and still retain a dynamic relationship to other individuals . . . the concept of the team has the power to challenge the individual to seek his self-expression, not along purely egoistic channels. . . . A community—big or little—is created, and through it the individual finds a higher expression of himself.

If one stops as one reads that the individual is to realize himself as part of a team, if one stops to wonder what happened to that reactionary, proletarian danger of immersing the individual in a group, one will see the same thing happened to it that happened to that independent individual. The group has become community; interdependence has become team play; complicated relationships have become dynamic relationships. "Community," "team," "dynamic": these are all plus words. We respond to them positively and happily, perhaps even mindlessly. Unless we watch the verbal magic, we will not notice that the individualism put in the hat at the beginning is not the individualism that pops out at the end.

The traditional American individual, once wrapped warmly in the pleasant connotations of self-reliance and independence, reappears as that well-known fellow, the other-directed individual, trying to find out who he truly is by relating himself to others in his society.

Now, the semanticist will find a certain perverse delight in all of this, but the historian will find a text. What the editors of *Fortune* did was to run over a century of American history through a single article. The projector works so fast that we tend to see only the blurred confusion. However, rather than blame the operator we might better be thankful for seeing what we may well have been missing in the slow-motion version of history.

At the beginning when Americans spoke of individualism, they meant the kind of independence the editors of *Fortune* point to in their beginning. Individualism meant the primacy of the individual person, the denial of social restraint, freedom from involvement with others. After an awkward transition in which they tried to make this ideal apply to conditions that made it increasingly anachronistic, Americans have begun to shift the connotations of the word in precisely the fashion that the editors of *Fortune* do when they draw to their conclusion. Individualism comes to mean participation in society. One achieves a higher expression of one's self through the organization of society. The early version, that is, *freedom from* society, was essentially negative; the modern version, that is, *freedom to cooperate* in society, is essentially positive.

What Americans have been doing for more than a century is gradually changing their system of values under the protection of big, umbrella words like "individualism." The word stays the same; it provides comfort against the rude weather of change. But the meaning moves, and we come out from under the umbrella in a different climate altogether.

The concept, individualism, appeared first in France as "*individualisme*," after the French Revolution. Prior to the Revolution the French word for individual, *individu*, was used to describe someone who did not belong to any of the corporate bodies that constituted society, someone who had no social identity. After the Revolution when all corporate bodies had been abolished, the word *individualisme*, used by conservatives, liberals, and socialists alike, first appeared to describe the evil and antisocial impulses of self-interest. This is also Edmund Burke's charge against the French Revolution—that the political philosophy of the Revolution with its celebration of abstract rights would lead to the point where, in his words, "the commonwealth itself would, in a few generations, crumble away, be disconnected into the dust and powder of individuality, and at length dispersed to all the winds of heaven."

In Europe, then, individualism meant the atomization of society, a threat to the common good, the suffocating dust of equality. Notice, however, that Burke uses the word "individuality," not "individualism," and for a good and simple reason. The word was not yet available to him; it had not yet come into the English language. According to the *Oxford English Dictionary*, "individualism" made its appearance in English in 1835 with the translation of Tocqueville's justly famous *Democracy in America*. The *Oxford English Dictionary* happens to be wrong in its particulars but still generally right. It has the date of the translation of Tocqueville wrong; it should be 1840. Also, there are a few other uses of the word in English prior to the translation of Tocqueville, but the *Oxford English Dictionary* is right in the sense that "individualism" came into the English language in response to the need for a word to describe the social philosophy of America in the 1830's, the period of Jacksonian democracy. So, since the attribution is correct in the terms that count, let us begin with Tocqueville, because he clearly sets forth the original meaning of the word.

Tocqueville and the Novelty of Individualism

In describing the attitude that developed because of the conditions of social equality in America, Tocqueville found himself at a loss for a word to name the social philosophy of Americans. So he introduced a new one. "*Individualism,*" he wrote, emphasizing the word, "is a novel expression, to which a novel idea has given birth." Tocqueville's English translator, Henry Reeve, felt the same sense of something new. When he translated the word from the French, he simply dropped the

French "e" from its end, rendered it as "individualism," and put a note at the bottom of his page: "I adopt the expression of the original," he explained, "however strange it may sound to the English ear . . . because I know of no English word exactly equivalent to the expression."

What Tocqueville wanted to describe by using his new word was a social philosophy he had discovered in America concerning the relation of the individual to society. His need for a new word is the best measure we have of his sense that the future, which he thought was embodied in America, meant a radical departure from the past of Europe. But Tocqueville was not happy with the texture of the world that he saw unfolding before his eyes. What in Europe seemed odious—the notion that the individual was superior to society—was in America "a mature and calm feeling." Tocqueville was at pains to discriminate the social philosophy of individualism from sheer egoism, sheer selfishness, but he thought that Americans, in developing a social philosophy that detached the individual from his fellow men, might come to as mean a failure as if they had acted from mere thoughtless selfishness. "Selfishness," he wrote, "originates in blind instinct; individualism proceeds from erroneous judgement more than from depraved feelings; it originates as much in deficiencies of mind as in perversity of heart." The judgment is the typical European critique: Americans mean well, but they lack mind. With all the good heart in the world, Americans, thought Tocqueville, were organizing society around a notion of the individual person, which would in the long run destroy all social virtue and end in social disaster.

Yet, Tocqueville recognized that in Jacksonian America individualism was an ideal of behavior, not simply an antisocial impulse. In attributing so much power to an idea, Tocqueville was no Platonist. As much as any modern sociologist he knew that social conditions have their characteristic intellectual counterparts. In his analysis, individualism was the idea, social equality was the condition. The tendency of the American to look to himself alone was, thought Tocqueville, a function of his environment. However, as a member of the *petite noblesse* of French society, Tocqueville could not face the logical consequences of social equality and individualism without considerable apprehension. His image of the good society was formed by the notion of a social hierarchy, a chain of being in which each member of the community belonged to a clearly defined place in the hierarchical order of things. "Aristocracy," he said, "had made a chain of all the members of the community, from the peasant to the king; democracy breaks that chain and severs every link of it." It was this shattering separation of man from man, the rupture of all social relationships and social obligations, that defined individualism for Tocqueville:

> As social conditions become more equal, the number of persons increases who, although they are neither rich nor powerful enough to exercise any great influence over their fellows, have nevertheless acquired or retained sufficient education and fortune to satisfy their own wants. They owe nothing to any man, they expect nothing from any man, they acquire the habit of always considering themselves as standing alone, and they are apt to imagine that their whole destiny is in their own hands. Thus not only does democracy make every man forget his ancestors, but it hides his descendants and separates his contemporaries from him; it throws him back forever upon himself alone and threatens in the end to confine him entirely within the solitude of his own heart.

The Democratic Hero: The Autonomous Individual

There is much one might say of Tocqueville's bleak adumbration of the myth of the self-made man, but for present purposes I would like to make one simple point about it. Tocqueville deplored the consequences of individualism, but from his context it is apparent that Americans did not. What Europeans feared, Americans celebrated. What was for Tocqueville a danger, was for the American Democrat an intoxicating ideal. Whereas, to make society possible at all, Tocqueville sought countervailing tendencies against individualism, so American a spokesman as Ralph Waldo Emerson wrote in his journals in 1840, the same year in which Tocqueville published: "In all my lectures, I have taught one doctrine, namely, the infinitude of the private man."

A considerable body of assumptions lies behind so bold an assertion, but in insisting on the individual as the ultimate reality in society Emerson was a characteristic spokesman for his time. In the early nineteenth century, Americans did not like the state any more than the editors of *Fortune* do today. "The less government we have the better," that was the rallying cry of Jeffersonians and Jacksonians alike. "The antidote," said Emerson, in almost the precise words that *Fortune* was to use more than a century later, "is the influence of private character, the growth of the individual." Emerson went on, in a long series of remarkable negatives, to strip this full-grown individual of every conceivable extrinsic support:

> The appearance of character makes the State unnecessary. The wise man is the State. He needs no army, fort, or navy—he loves men too well; no bribe, or feast, or palace, to draw friends to him; no vantage ground, no favorable circumstances. He needs no library, for he has not done thinking; no church, for he is a prophet; no statute-book, for he has the law-giver; no money, for he is value; no road, for he is at home where he is; no experience, for the life of the creator shoots through him. . . . He has no personal friends.

The figure of this grandly isolated man, nakedly alone, without any helpful circumstance, without the accumulated knowledge and the traditions of the past, homeless, gladly bereft of friends, is a chilling ideal—unless, that is, one can share the assumption that makes it possible. Emerson and most Americans of his time could embrace this figure because of the calm belief that there was an order that existed apart from society, a natural order, which ultimately validated the rejection of the artificial order of society and the state. As Emerson put it elsewhere, "you take the way from man, not to man." This centrifugal thrust was kept from spinning madly away by a deep trust in a natural order, which guaranteed social unity. So society emerges miraculously as the sum of all the individual rejections of society.

I have said that in this kind of assertion Emerson was a characteristically American thinker; he was. One can see the same attitude of thought, the same conception of the relation of the individual to society, in Jacksonian political thought, in economic thought, in revivalistic and evangelical Protestantism, in literature, and in the popular ideals of American society in Emerson's time—the America that we sometimes tend to forget was the object of Tocqueville's analysis. The mood rises to a climax by the end of the nineteenth century in the historical interpretation of the meaning of American history in the hands of Frederick Jackson Turner and his followers in the frontier interpretation of our history, the notion that the meaning of American life lies in the movement out of society, away from others, to a new beginning.

The Unforeseen Consequence of Individualism

What happened to that heroic individual, standing alone, independent of others, the editors of *Fortune* put quite well: "The key to industrialization is not independence, but interdependence." From where we stand, looking backward, it surely seems ironic that an ideal of independence and simple harmony should have been formulated by a society on the verge of complexity and conflict, the society of industrial America. Actually, the unintended consequence of the ideal of uninhibited individual action, of this negative theory of the state, of the denial of the reality of society, was to accelerate the powerful energies of an acquisitive capitalism and to lead finally to where we now stand. Richard Hofstadter has observed that "the same forces in American life that had made Jacksonian equalitarianism possible and had given to the equalitarian theme in the agrarian romance its most compelling appeal had also unleashed in the nation an entrepreneurial zeal probably without precedent in history."

The processes of machine industry and technology which characterize the modern world have made organization, the rationalization of activity, specialization, and social interdependence utterly necessary. The first response of Americans to the world that they had made was to try to keep the social benefits made possible through the economies of large-scale organization and, at the same time, to invoke and maintain an ideal of individualism which organization and its logical consequences were rendering obsolete. Whatever the consequences (we can see them easily, because we have experienced them), Jacksonian America drew its emotional energy from the belief and assumption that there existed a simple, natural order, which would emerge spontaneously and unbidden if each individual went his own separate way.

It was, of course, the very fluidity and openness of Jacksonian society that provided a material basis for the heady optimism of this ultimately anarchic ideal of individualism. For an historian looking back on early America, the social circumstances bulk large; they may properly be primary in his assessment of the age. But for those living in the age, there was also an ideal, a moral basis for their optimism, a "cosmic optimism" built on a belief in a cosmic natural order, which undergirded and validated the ideal of the free and autonomous individual.

The original ideal of individualism in Jacksonian America was a secular jeremiad, an exhortation to begin over again, sloughing off the complexities of society by returning to a nat-ural state of grace. Somewhat ironically, it was the material expansiveness of the society that made it possible to entertain such an ideal, to believe in the possibility of constantly begin-ning anew, of turning away from society to create one's own future. More ironically, it was the same material expansiveness, itself accelerated by the lack of social restraint implicit in the ideal, that finally destroyed the ideal itself. There were two "natures" in American society: the normative Nature of the Jeffersonians, the Jacksonians, and the Transcendentalists; and a physical nature of coal, iron, and oil—the raw materials of the vast industrial and technological society in which we now live. The unforeseen consequences of the Jacksonian program was, as I have already said, to liberate the energies of industrial capitalism and, thus, to accelerate the creation of our modern complex world.

The American Democrat described by Tocqueville—the man who saw about him no one much richer or more powerful than himself, the man who had acquired the habit of consider-ing himself as standing alone and who imagined that his whole destiny was in his own hands—found it increasingly difficult to square his beliefs with the world he found about him. Not that the effort was not made. The years after the Civil War saw the apogee of the cult of the self-made man in America, the spawn-ing of an immensely popular literature on success, and the ap-pearance of the Horatio Alger stories. These phenomena repre-sent in their different ways attempts to assert the old belief that success, or, on the more uncharitable side, failure, lay in one's own character and not in society. Robert Bremner's study of the discovery of poverty in America is instructive in the problem facing the prevailing view of the relation of the individual to society.

The Discovery of Society

Social-service work, generated by the pressing needs of displaced immigrants, the squalid conditions of cities whose growth outstripped the capacity for control, and the general helplessness of those at the bottom of the new industrial economy, began as one might expect it to begin. It began with an appeal to individuals to change their way of life, to better themselves, to solve their problems by an act of will. It may seem a gratuitous insult to us today, but the Association for Improving the Condition of the Poor went about its work in the New York slums by distributing free copies of Benjamin Franklin's "Way to Wealth." A people who felt that they owed nothing to society found it hard to blame society; nurtured on the belief that the individual was all, they found it difficult to see anything more than purely individual wills operating atomistically to create society. But as social-service work became increasingly organized and information on poverty and the ills that went with it was amassed and exchanged among social-service workers, the brute fact obtruded itself that poverty was a social phenomenon and not simply a function of individual character. Experience finally teaches, but the teaching, in this case, was slow and painful.

The response of social-service workers—those most dramatically exposed to the shaping forces of society—suggests a way of comprehending much of the confused thought of the late nineteenth century. It is the simple observation that people perceive reality largely from the angle of vision provided by the concepts that they derive from tradition. They will persist in seeing the world from their inherited perspective even when, from our later perspective, it seems to us to make little sense of their world. Take, for example, the idea of the self-made man and, closely associated with it, the cluster of notions that we have come to call the "gospel of wealth."

The Self-Made Man

The very phrase "the self-made man," with its connotation of a radical self-sufficiency, was itself a heritage from the Jacksonian period. A nice irony surrounds its birth. The phrase was fathered in 1832 in a speech by Henry Clay in behalf of a protective tariff for the infant industries of Kentucky hemp manufacturers, Clay's constituents, whom he described as "enterprising self-made men." Clay seems not to have been bothered by the incongruity of self-made men seeking the paternalistic support of the state, and the discrepancy has made it easy ever since to write parodies of the idea of the self-made man. But the discrepancy should alert us to the fact that the successful man represented more than just success to his contemporaries; he presented a whole constellation of values, especially the beauty of the American way of life and the capacity of the unaided individual to make his own way in the world.

When, in 1897, Vanderbilt University unveiled a statue in honor of its benefactor, Cornelius Vanderbilt, Chauncey M. Depew gave the address which drew the popular moral:

> The American Commonwealth is built upon the individual. It recognizes neither classes nor masses. . . . We have thus become a nation of self-made men. We live under just and equal laws and all avenues for a career are open. . . . Freedom of opportunity and preservation of the results of forecast, industry, thrift, and honesty have made the United States the most prosperous and wealthy country in the world. Commodore Vanderbilt is a conspicuous example of the products and possibilities of our state and elastic conditions. . . . He neither gave

nor asked quarter. The same country, the same laws, the same open avenues, the same opportunities which he had before him are equally before every other man. . . . He was not the creation of luck nor chance nor circumstances.

There was, of course, the one circumstance—the great, good fortune of living under the equal laws of the American Commonwealth—so that such ritualistic celebrations of the self-made man were at the same time secular hymns of nationalistic self-congratulation. One need not be too astute to suspect that these rhetorical set pieces were serving some purpose other than a fair description of reality, when a New York newspaper found the fact that J. P. Morgan was born with millions to his name no hindrance to citing the traditional maxim. Despite the fact, the *Tribune* observed, that Morgan had "no traditions of the steerage, in him were the qualities of the self-made man, and by his own efforts he traversed relatively as many rounds of the ladder as did many other financiers who began with nothing."

When evidence and conclusion part company so blatantly, one senses a strain in the culture, some imperious need that desperately needs an answer. The terms of the answer are clear enough: If you are not a success, look to yourself, not to the system, for the reason for your failure. The easy convertibility of the cult of self-help into praise for the American way of life implies that questions were being raised about that way. Chauncey Depew's remark that Commodore Vanderbilt "neither gave nor asked quarter" suggests that success involved a fierce struggle and that the road to it was not quite so broad and open as the ideal would have it. But, given the terms of the answer, those who protested were in the uncomfortable position of being un-American. Those not eminently successful, those who sought power through the organization of workingmen or security through pension systems, were told, for example, in 1883 by Mr. Norvin Green, President of the Western

Union Telegraph Company, which had just defeated a costly strike by its operators, that his company was against unions "simply to protect the free will of each individual" and that pensions were "not in accordance with the genius of our Government or our country."

There were those in the society who did not have to wait for the later researches of historians to discover that the cult of the self-made man was not an accurate transcription of social reality. It was in 1901 that the Right Reverend William Lawrence of Massachusetts published what soon became a famous piece, "The Relation of Wealth to Morals," in which he maintained that "in the long run, it is only to the man of morality that wealth comes." The Bishop realized that "we, like the Psalmist, occasionally see the wicked prosper, but only occasionally" because, as he triumphantly concluded, "Godliness is in league with riches." As a preacher, Bishop Lawrence told a little parable to dramatize his abstract moralizing:

> As I was beginning to write this paper an Irishman with his horse and wagon drew up at my back door. Note that I say *his* horse and wagon. Twenty years ago that Irishman, then hardly twenty years old, landed in Boston, illiterate, uncouth, scarcely able to make himself understood in English. There was no symptom of brains, alertness, or ambition. He got a job to tend a few cows. Soon the American atmosphere began to take hold. He discovered that here every man has his chance.

There is no need to follow Bishop Lawrence's Irishman until he becomes "a capitalist, and his yearly earnings represent the income on $30,000"; the point is made succinctly. The Irishman "made his own way" in the inspiring American atmosphere. "Twenty years ago" would take us back to 1881, and it so happens that we have the story of another Irishman, clearly not the Bishop's, but one who, like him, came as an immigrant to the United States and by hard work saved money and bought himself a horse and wagon to go into the carting business in order to set himself up as a capitalist. In 1883, a Senate committee inquiring into the relations between labor and capital called this Irishman, Thomas B. McGuire of New York, before them to relate his career.

Whether because of the "American atmosphere" or not, McGuire made himself understood quite forcibly. "I embarked something like $300 in the business, thinking I might become something of a capitalist eventually, but I found competition so great that it was impossible for me to do so." Although he lacked such sophisticated terminology as "favored entry into the market" or "the economies of large-scale organization," McGuire knew what had happened to him. He described for the committee how the railroads had their own trucking companies with representatives aboard the trains, so that there was no business left at the depot for independent operators like himself. Furthermore, given the size of their operations, these subsidiaries were able to maintain their own blacksmith shops and buy feed for their animals in large quantities at cheaper prices. With higher operating costs and no entry into the market, McGuire was soon, as he put it, driven to the wall. Out of work in 1883, he was openly contemptuous of the possibility that "politicians," the Senators he was addressing, would do anything to redress the conditions under which he thought the working man had no chance at all.

The Senate committee was clearly upset, especially when, in response to the question whether he would go to work for room and board for himself and his family and twenty dollars a month, McGuire answered, "I would be willing to do better than that. If they will guarantee me food, clothing and shelter for myself and family for twenty years, I will give them my services for nothing." A few days later Jay Gould followed Mr. McGuire to the stand before the same committee and was asked the somewhat leading question, "Of the men who conduct business enterprise and wield the power of capital in this country today, what proportion do you think are what are called 'self-made men'?" He answered, "I think they are all 'self-made men'; I do not say *self*-made exactly, for the country has grown and they have grown up with it. In this country we have no heirlooms or handing down estates. Every man has to stand here on his own individual merit." One of the senators, however, the chairman of the committee, Senator Blair of New Hampshire, could not forget McGuire. He said to Jay Gould, "We have had a man six feet high, who has driven a truck team, and who has more intellectual capacity than half, or perhaps any, of the members of Congress, offering here before this committee to agree under contract to work diligently and faithfully for the next twenty years for anybody who would give him employment and agree to maintain himself and his family."

Gould did not comment on what he thought of the intelligence of congressmen, but he did say, "Well, I know there are a great many cases of actual suffering in a large city like [New York]. . . . I have noticed, though, that generally if men are temperate and industrious they are pretty sure of success. In cases such as the one you describe I could almost always go back behind the scenes and find a cause for such a person's 'misfortunes.' "

The fascinating thing about Jay Gould's response is that he is doing more than just dismissing a bit of contrary evidence. His logic implies that this country has no unequal laws, that every man stands on his own two feet; therefore, if a man is a failure, there *must* be a personal cause for what are called his "misfortunes" but are really his just deserts. Just as with Bishop Lawrence, the adverb "generally" will take care of rude exceptions, but the confidence that these can only be exceptions is an unquestioned article of faith. If the self-propelled American Democrat owes nothing to anything outside his own character, then, if he is a success, he must deserve it, and if he is a failure, he deserves that too.

The Gospel of Wealth

It is hard not to be cynical about Jay Gould's reaction, especially given the character of the witness. But hypocrisy is not too useful an analytical generalization for the historian, especially when, as in Gould's case, the sentiment is so widely shared by others at the same time. It makes more sense simply to conclude that many Americans in the late nineteenth century, a moment of massive and rapid social change, were attempting to impose a cultural ideal, inherited from the past and deeply cherished, onto a present to which the ideal had little, if any, relevance. The same generalization holds true for the gospel of wealth, although the gospel of wealth had an immense psychological advantage over the idea of the self-made man. It, too, incorporated the notion that the source of success was in the individual, but it yoked with that notion the idea that the man of wealth labored not for himself but for others, that he was a trustee who spent his life in the service of society. As Andrew Carnegie put it, "Individualism will continue, but the millionaire will be a trustee for the poor; intrusted for a season with a great part of the increased wealth of the community, but administering it for the community far better than it would or could have done for itself."

Throughout the late nineteenth century, Andrew Carnegie was held up again and again as an exemplum of success in America. His story was a paradigm of the American story—democracy triumphant, to invert the title of one of his books. The poor immigrant boy arrives on the shores of the new nation, which abounds in endless opportunity. The son of a workingman, he has little opportunity for formal education and is forced by circumstance to seek work at a tender age. His first job is a lowly one, but by diligence, cleverness, and good luck he rises to the top in short order. The story had been told before the brassy age of American industrial expansion that followed the Civil War, but it came into its own with the appearance on the American scene of men like Carnegie.

In 1889, near the peak of his success, Carnegie published in the *North American Review* a statement of his social philosophy—what he called "this intense individualism"—in an essay named simply "Wealth." Ralph Henry Gabriel has pointed out the significance of the year. It came in the midst of revolt by farmers against northeastern capitalism, after the terrible railroad strikes of the 1870's, and just three years after the Haymarket Riot in Chicago. As Gabriel says, one might expect Carnegie's essay to be an *apologia*, a somewhat embarrassed defense of the concentration of wealth of which he was so outstanding an example. But such was not the case. Carnegie began his essay with a sober account of the high price that society pays for its material advancement, the division between "castes," the concentration of the labor force into large factories, and the suspicions and mutual distrust between labor and capital, but only to conclude that even "accepting conditions as they exist, the situation can be surveyed and pronounced good." In Carnegie's view the concentration of wealth was inevitable, so the only question to be asked was how concentrated wealth could best be used for the good of society. His answer was the gospel of wealth—in Gabriel's words, "an elaboration of the doctrine of the free individual of the American democratic faith and . . . a result of the discovery that this tenet had important utilities in the new industrial capitalism."

Looking back on Carnegie's career, we tend to see his wealth as a result of the great price that society was willing to pay for the organization of one of its basic industries. Historians differ on whether the price was too high or not, but they all agree that the reward was made possible by the emergence in America of a national economy and the consolidation of individual enterprises into massive collective organizations. Yet, in Carnegie's philosophy, there is none of this. His essay resolves wealth into purely personal terms, the capacity of the

single individual: "The experienced in affairs always rate the
MAN . . . as not only the first consideration, but such as to
render the question of his capital scarcely worth considering;
. . . we might as well urge the destruction of the highest existing type of man because he failed to reach our ideal as to
favor the destruction of Individualism, Private Property, the
Law of the Accumulation of Wealth, and the Law of Competition."

Carnegie thought there were three ways a man could dis-
pose of his wealth. He could leave it to his family, he could
bequeath it at death for public purposes, or he could administer
it during his lifetime for the public good. Carnegie rejected the
first two. For the first, he thought it "not well for the children
that they should be so burdened"—at first glance a charming
sentiment, yet congruent with Carnegie's basic notion that
wealth should come to the individual because of his worth and
not by an environmental accident such as birth. For the second,
in addition to the fear that legacies do not generally realize
their donor's wishes, Carnegie shrewdly realized that "it may
fairly be said that no man is to be extolled for doing what he
cannot help doing. . . . Men who leave vast sums in this way
may fairly be thought men who would not have left it at all,
had they been able to take it with them." Carnegie was radical
enough for his time to suggest that the state, through death
taxes, should confiscate up to one-half of the wealthy man's
estate. He thought the disposition to do this "a cheering indica-
tion of the growth of a salutary change in public opinion."

So there remained only one way for the man of wealth to
discharge the responsibility of wealth—to administer it himself
during his lifetime:

> This, then, is held to be the duty of the man of Wealth:
> First, to set an example of modest, unostentatious living, shun-
> ning display or extravagance; to provide moderately for the le-
> gitimate wants of those dependent upon him; and after doing so

to consider all surplus revenues which come to him simply as trust funds, which he is called upon to administer, and strictly bound as a matter of duty to administer in the manner which, in his judgment, is best calculated to produce the most beneficial results for the community—the man of wealth thus becoming the mere agent and trustee for his poorer brethren, bringing to their service his superior wisdom, experience, and ability to administer, doing for them better than they would or could do for themselves.

As Mr. Dooley was to say, every time "Andhrew Carnaygie" gives a speech, "he gives himself away." The individualism of the early nineteenth century was built upon a belief in the equality of all men—not only social, economic, and political equality, but a rough equality in their personal capacities. Carnegie retained the freedom, the intense individualism, for the man of wealth but at the price of a thoroughgoing paternalism for his poorer brethren. Since the man of wealth is bound only by his own private judgment of what is good for society, the only check against his economic power is the assumption that he shares, even in his superior wisdom, the same values as his inferior and poorer brethren. At a moment when, as Carnegie himself testified, there was little but suspicion and mistrust on either side, it is difficult to understand the acceptance of his message.

Part of the answer may lie in Carnegie's brilliant success in weaving together nearly every major strand of the American tradition into a blanket approval of the concentration of wealth in the hands of individuals who recognized no control outside themselves. Simply to enumerate the elements of his argument is to grasp some of its force: A secularized version of the Protestant Ethic of hard work and stewardship; the idea of progress; the sanctity of private property and the competition of laissez-faire classical economics; and a vindication of the free and responsible individual.

All these minor themes play in and around Carnegie's major

one, the affirmation of present conditions. Surprisingly, at least for an essay making so much of service to others, the conclusion comes to the fact that "those worthy of assistance, except in rare cases, seldom require assistance." You cannot help a man; he must help himself. You might, as Carnegie did, put libraries in his way, so his capacity for self-help could exercise itself, but "it were better for mankind that the millions of the rich were thrown into the sea than so spent as to encourage the slothful, the drunken, the unworthy." The best that can be said for Carnegie is that he was candid enough to apply this to the sons of the rich as well as his poorer brethren.

The persistent, one would like to say passionate, appeal to the intrinsic personal qualities that determine success in the literature of the self-made man and the gospel of wealth in the latter nineteenth century was probably neither cynical nor hypocritical. American society had for a long time prided itself on being equalitarian, and one of the distinguishing virtues of the American Democrat was supposed to be that his success was due to his own unaided merit. Any other source of success was somehow alien and un-American. Status in a society can be described in a number of ways, which, in turn, break down into objective (birth, wealth, authority, power) and subjective (character, intellect, personal charm) characteristics. Those who had the obvious objective attributes (wealth and power) were not content simply to enjoy their perquisites. They had to believe that they deserved those perquisites, that they had the personal qualities that merited them. As Max Weber said in a different context, "the fortunate [man] is seldom satisfied with the fact of being fortunate. Beyond this, he needs to know that he has a *right* to his good fortune. He wants to be convinced that he 'deserves' it, and above all, that he deserves it in comparison with others. He wishes to be allowed the belief that the less fortunate also merely experience their due. Good fortune thus wants to be 'legitimate' fortune."

In this view, ideas are rationalizations, and there seems no sense in denying that the process of self-justification was, consciously or not, going on. There are few at any level of society who construct images of themselves that are not rather flattering self-portraits. But the rub comes when we realize how widely admired these self-projections were. The successful, the men of wealth, were, in Harry Stack Sullivan's nice phrase, the "significant others" in the late nineteenth century. The society collaborated in the work of imputing personal qualities to those who possessed the objective power, justifying them, and in so doing, justifying the society to itself. Those who had power and prestige were felt to merit power and prestige, because to say otherwise was to say that the old ideal of individualism was dead. But, as I said at the beginning of this excursion into the idea of the self-made man and the gospel of wealth, the increasing social and economic organization of American life was putting severe strains on the ideal of the free and autonomous individual. Worse, there were those who spoke with authority, like John D. Rockefeller, who said, "Individualism has gone, never to return."

The context of John D. Rockefeller's blunt remark was that cooperative activity was a necessary consequence of large-scale technological production. The editors of *Fortune* recognize this in their article, when they observe that the key to industrialization is not independence, but interdependence. One can say, in a general sense, that somewhere toward the end of the nineteenth century, Americans began to discover the reality of society. As they did, it became increasingly difficult to insist that the individual was all in face of this growing awareness, but there was another way to preserve the emotional sanctions of the ideal of individualism. That was to change its meaning. A new meaning was implicit in the very technology built upon the machine, which was subverting belief in the original ideal of individualism.

The Idea of the Machine

One can get at the matter by stopping for a moment to consider the machine itself, abstractly, as the material embodiment of certain ideas. This may seem a curious way of speaking. Normally, when we speak of ideas, we think of the written or spoken word, but second thought makes us all aware that institutions, even the common objects surrounding our daily lives, embody certain attitudes; they objectify ways in which we think about our world. The cities we live in, the factories we work in, the buildings we dwell in—all these "speak" to us, if only we will listen.

To think of the machine in this fashion is quickly to recognize that the machine clearly embodies certain ideas. A well-designed machine is an instance of total organization, that is, a series of interrelated means contrived to achieve a single end. The machine consists always of particular parts that have no meaning and no function separate from the organized entity to which they contribute. A machine consists of a coherent bringing together of all parts toward the highest possible efficiency of the functioning whole, of interrelationships marshalled wholly toward a given result. In the ideal machine, there can be no extraneous part, no extraneous movement; all is set, part for part, motion for motion, toward the functioning of the whole. The machine is, then, at once a perfect instance of total rationalization of a field of action and of total organization. This is perhaps even more quickly evident in that larger machine, the assembly line.

A society that chooses to enjoy the benefits of the power that the machine makes possible—that is, a society committed to mechanization, a society that accepts the logic of functional interdependence and increasing rationalization of its material life—is also committed inexorably to increasing organization of its economic and social life, to more and more precise articulation of its interrelations. In response to the machine, or, more accurately, to attitudes implicit in the machine, not only new patterns of social life but even new values begin to emerge. To reverse Emerson's dictum, in the social world created by industrialism we take our way to man, not from man.

All this is rather abstract, so let me restate it by an historical anecdote, a homely example of the way in which what I have described analytically worked out in historical practice. The purpose of this story is simply to show in action the cast of mind embodied in the machine itself—that is, the tendency toward rationalizing the work process, the drive toward increasing organization, and, finally and most importantly, the emergence of an ethic of the organization, describing the individual in terms of functional fitness, or in more popular language, defining the individual in terms of his ability to contribute to the group.

Frederick Winslow Taylor and Rational Organization

The historical anecdote concerns the work of Frederick Winslow Taylor, the man who is generally credited with being the father of "scientific management" in our country. The particular example from Taylor's work is the "shovelling experiment" he conducted in the yards of the Bethlehem Steel Company in Pennsylvania in the 1890's.

Taylor had been called in by the Bethlehem Steel Company as a management consultant and allowed, at first, to introduce efficiency only into the most menial tasks in the work process. The steel yard was a big one, almost two miles long by about a quarter of a mile wide, and the company employed 400 to 600 day laborers who owned their own shovels and worked in large gangs, moving material ranging from light ash and coke to heavy ore about the yard wherever needed.

Taylor first ran a series of tests to decide the optimum shovel load for a first-class worker. As he put it, "we would see a first-class shoveller go from shovelling rice coal with a load of 3½ pounds to the shovel to handling iron ore with 38 pounds to the shovel. Now is 3½ pounds the proper shovel load or is 38 pounds the proper shovel load?" There is not space to describe the series of interesting tests that Taylor devised to arrive at the proper load for a shovel, but by experiment he came to the conclusion that 21½ pounds was the ideal weight for a first-class shoveller.

As Taylor told the story, a number of things followed. First, a variety of kinds of shovels had to be designed to handle different kinds of materials. That also meant building shovel rooms in the various parts of the yard, so that a gang would have the proper tools at hand. To eliminate the waste motion of wandering about so large a yard, it meant, as Taylor said, "organizing and planning work at least a day in advance," so that when men checked in, they would be at that day's work. This meant, Taylor reported, building a labor office for a planning staff—a bureaucracy, as we would say. Large maps of the yard were then necessary to show at a glance the location of different kinds of work and the location of men. Furthermore, the installation of a telephone network was essential for more effective interior communication. Once the yard was mapped so that one could see at a glance the relationships in time and sequence between different jobs, it led, naturally enough, to the reorganization of the yard itself, so that materials could be delivered or dumped in a more logical sequence.

One can see readily enough what happened. Taylor's attempt to make the crudest physical act of labor efficient led inexorably to a further organization of every aspect of the production process. Logically at least, total efficiency could be attained only when the entire plant was totally organized, when all parts in the process were related in the most efficient way, one to the other. Although this homely example is fairly simple —and I have chosen it partly because its very simplicity enables quick description—there is a good deal implicit here. Let me point to just three things: First, the sheer material success of Taylor's experiment; second, the cast of mind, the historical style, dramatized by Taylor; and, third, a problem in social values implicit in the machine and in an organized society.

The Achievements of Rational Organization

First, not only those who have to meet a payroll will be interested in the concrete results of Taylor's work. The Bethelehem Steel Company previously had 400 to 600 men at work in the yard gang. After three years under Taylor's system, 140 men were doing the same volume of work. At the same time that the labor force was cut so drastically, the actual cost per ton of material moved also dropped by 50 per cent. Taylor reported that during the last six months of the three and one half years that he was with Bethlehem, the saving to the company was at the rate of $78,000 per year *after* paying the additional costs of the planning staff, new shovels, and new overhead. At the same time wages went up 60 per cent.

These figures do more than satisfy our curiosity. We can see here in microcosm the basic character of our productive power—a standardized process leading to a reduction in unskilled labor, an expanded output with, at the same time, a decrease in unit cost, rising wages, and an increase at the managerial level of planning. These are characteristics not only of Taylor's small experiment but also of the general direction of our economy from his time to ours.

There is a moral here too. No society is willingly going to surrender the tremendous material benefits that flow from the rationalization and organization at the heart of the industrial system. We tend to take the enormous benefits of organization too much for granted. We hear so much today about the threat of organization to personality, to social values, even, ironically, to the efficiency of our organizations themselves that we may be tempted to think that some social panacea lies in the rejection of organization; this is clearly not true. Even if we want to—and I do not believe we want to—we cannot reject the machine upon which our society is built, and the machine inexorably demands rationalization of effort and planning and their concomitant, large-scale organization.

The Ethic of Productivity

The second point involves the style of thought symbolized by the machine and set to work by Taylor. The subjective attitude—the curious combination of the drive toward productivity along with an intensely self-conscious rationalization of the means toward that end—is perhaps as important as the material success itself. Once organization is introduced at any point, the trend toward further organization is irreversible, but one will quickly recognize that organization says nothing about the goal to be pursued; it only points to the best way to achieve whatever goal one chooses to pursue. In Taylor's work there is always the unquestioned premise that efficiency and increased productivity are their own justification, ends in themselves. What Taylor did was to stand outside the work process, consider all its parts, and put it together again in its most logical order; this is what we mean by saying that he rationalized the work process. But Taylor never questioned the unstated premise that work is its own measure of value. Quite the contrary, testifying before a Congressional committee inquiring into his system, he explicitly accepted that criterion: "In my judgment," Taylor said, "the best possible measure of the height in the scale of civilization to which any people has arisen is its productivity." Only in modern Western civilization could that remark have been made. In the East—in India and China at least, until they too decided to "modernize"—in ancient Greece, and in Christian Europe until the end of the Middle Ages, it was the most obvious and axiomatic piece of orthodoxy that action was a means to the end of life, which was contemplation. In Taylor's world and in the world of modern industrialism this view is completely reversed; thought is a means to further action. Action, Work, Productivity— choose what word you will—these have become ends in themselves.

This reversal of values, the celebration of work and activity themselves, did not, of course, come about simply as a consequence of the machine. Quite the opposite. The psychological shift preceded industrialism, and perhaps it had to. The attitude of mind that Taylor represents has been in the making a long time in Western civilization. A machine-oriented civilization represents the convergence of numerous habits, ideas, and modes of living, as well as technical instruments. If we were to trace the origin of these habits back in history, we would probably follow the trail all the way back to the monasteries of the Middle Ages. At least, Werner Sombart, the German historian of capitalism, says with a certain heavy-handed irony that the Benedictine monks were our first capitalists. What he means is that it is in the monasteries of the Western world after the collapse of the Roman empire that we see the imposition of order and control on everyday life, although for supernatural ends, of course. The revolution in men's attitudes toward work in the world comes when the Reformation destroys the monasteries and turns their ascetic discipline toward work in the world with a consequent blessing of work, order, and industry.

The Functional Individual

Instead of turning back to the past I would like to turn ahead to our own present, to our own future, to a problem implicit in the growth of organization spawned by the machine. There is a third aspect to Taylor's work, which involves a problem in social values implicit in any highly organized society. It is the emergence of a social ethic in response to the movement toward organization.

Frederick Winslow Taylor got at the matter in a single sentence. In his book setting forth the principles of his system, Taylor said bluntly, "In the past the man has been first; in the future the system must be first." Taylor had the great virtue of seeing clearly the consequences of what he was doing, but he was also aware, especially because of hostility toward the Taylor system, that the consequences he saw and desired ran counter to many of the cherished ideals of his culture. A society that had always put the individual person first was going to find it hard to adapt to a system that insisted that the individual had importance only as a functioning part of some larger social organization. Not the least fascinating aspect of Taylor's work is the way in which he tried to adapt the old ideal of the primary importance of the individual to a system that itself relegated the individual to a secondary order of importance. You can see this transvaluation taking place in Taylor's own words:

> Let me say that we are now but on the threshold of the coming era of true cooperation. The time is fast going by for the great personal or individual achievement of any one man standing alone and without the help of those around him. And the time is coming when all the great things will be done by the cooperation of many men in which each man performs that function for which he is best suited, each man preserves his individuality and is supreme in his particular function, and each man at the same time loses none of his originality and proper personal

initiative, and yet is controlled by and must work harmoniously with many other men.

Now, we may shrink from such phrases as "man . . . is controlled by" and man "*must* work harmoniously with" others, but notice that Taylor is trying to redefine the meaning of the individual in order to escape the harshness of his conclusion. In his statement the person is defined not simply by being, but by doing.

In response to the new conditions of an industrial society built upon the machine, Taylor is trying to formulate a social theory that sanctions these new conditions by defining the relation of the individual to society just as he has defined the relation of part to whole in his system of industrial efficiency. The person achieves his individuality by discovering the function for which he is best suited and in which he can best contribute to the whole, which is greater than he is, and to which, as one part, he must contribute. To generalize very broadly, freedom in the ethic that Taylor is struggling to formulate changes from negative freedom, that is, freedom from restraint by the group, to positive freedom, that is, freedom to do that which contributes to the group.

The goal of organization means the death of the ideal of the free, primary, autonomous person standing alone, aloof from involvement with his fellows, heroically self-sufficient. The conflict is obvious enough. But suddenly there is a way out. Each individual realizes himself by performing that function for which he is best suited, as Taylor put it; or, the individual finds a "higher expression of himself" through his dynamic relationship with others, as *Fortune* put it.

So, if we smile at the editors of *Fortune*, we must smile at ourselves as well. There are many ways to accommodate change. A favorite one is man's happy ability to keep on talking one way while acting another, as in the case of the self-made men and the stewards of great wealth in the late nineteenth century. Another, as intellectuals themselves best know, is to redefine the terms of the argument, so that it turns out that you and your opponent have really been talking about the same thing all along.

Two Versions of Individualism

In American history in general, as well as in *Fortune*'s treatment in particular, we have then two meanings of "individualism." One, the original meaning, said that the individual was an individual to the degree that he was separate from society and free from the institutions and restraints of society. The other, defined in a world quite different from the equalitarian and open society of the early nineteenth century, says that an individual is an individual to the degree that he participates in society. The individual becomes himself by furthering the good of the collective group, large or small, of which he must become a functioning part. But to use a word like "collective" reminds us of the proletariat, and, as *Fortune* warns us, to submerge the individual in the group is supposed to be a philosophy of reaction in America, a betrayal of the American proposition of individual responsibility.

We have done our work so well in a fit of contented absentmindedness that many Americans will surely protest that this second meaning is not a valid meaning of individualism. It may not be valid for those who like a degree of logical consistency, but it is a meaning. The editors of *Fortune* insist it is; Frederick Winslow Taylor said so long ago; Herbert Croly in *The Promise of American Life*, a political textbook for the liberal reforms of both Roosevelts in this century, defines true, "constructive" individualism so; and this second meaning permeates all the pages of John Dewey's political and social thought. Our recent immensely popular president, Mr. Eisenhower, always insisted that "more than ever before, in our country, this is the age of the individual. . . . There is no limit . . . to the temporal goals we set ourselves—as free individuals joined in a team with our fellows."

At this point, the historian might simply conclude and go no further. But I began by saying that I intended to bring this long historical excursion to bear upon a present problem. The problem is familiar enough. From all sides we hear that the American is an organization man lost in the lonely crowd of mass society, that the American has ceased to be a self-reliant individual, and that this is all somehow a betrayal of the American way of life. In the popular version, about the longest perspective brought to bear on this faceless man in a gray flannel suit is the accusation that progressive education started the problem by preaching something called "called "adjustment." But the problem is much older than that, and a long historical process has gone into its making. If you accept my account of the historical process, then there are three logical ways one might attack the relationship of the ideal of individualism to the reality of organization in modern America.

The first would be to restrict the word "individualism" to the early nineteenth century, to insist that the word has significance only in a discussion of the historical context that gave rise to it. The simplicity of this solution has a certain appeal, but one would be sanguine indeed to think that he could legislate out of existence a word with such massive emotional associations. It ignores the very terms of the problem—that is, that it *is* a problem, that American culture has a deep affective stake in the historical connotations of the concept of individualism and will not lightly surrender it on the grounds of being responsible to some intellectual demand for historical accuracy and logical consistency. Yet, it is a solution that some intellectual historians might accept.

The second answer would be to decide upon reflection that the real meaning of the word *should be* the collective sense, that the individual realizes himself by committing himself to some worthy enterprise larger than himself, that the older ideal of autonomy was simply an egoistic mistake, a mistake made possible by the peculiar and special circumstances of a passing moment in our national history. Despite its identification with the positive hero of the authoritarian mind, this version of individualism is a concept not totally alien to American culture, as we have already seen. If it were totally alien to our culture, there would be no problem. In the context of the necessary organization of our economic and social life, Americans have begun to develop a native definition of the individual as a member of the group. At its most innocuous level, this means simply that the individual should be able to get along with others, to adjust to the demands of living and working with others. At its most serious, it means a submersion of the individual in the group. The individual is defined by his function; one's role in the organization becomes one's real self. The rest is mere appendage. The will of God embodied in a church; the law of history embodied in a party; the good of society embodied in a corporation; or even the good of society, the national interest itself—these are not strange and unusual creeds in our time. Yet, they are creeds that are difficult for Americans to accept, even when they act in terms of them, because of the very past out of which American society has come. Again, this second solution may be acceptable to some, but not, I think, to Americans generally.

There is a third answer to the problem, which, in turn, has so many problems in it that it may not be an answer in any responsible sense of the word. It is a political answer, not in the narrow sense of the government but rather in the wider sense of the structuring of all the institutions which affect our daily lives. But to suggest it requires first a comment on the history that I have just recounted.

The paradoxical thing about the ideal of individualism in Jacksonian America, which celebrated the individual to the point of denying the reality of society, is that it was, in its very rejection of social forces, itself a social ideal. That is, only a particular kind of society could have generated an ideal that denied society. It took an outsider, a foreign observer like Tocqueville, to see that the heroically self-reliant American was possible only because of a widely shared consensus on matters that counted. The general will, which Rousseau had to hypothesize in order to make society possible at all, was in America the general experience under conditions of approximate social equality. In similar fashion, the violent swing to an opposite ideal still calling itself individualism but with radically different connotations, an ideal that makes the individual a part of society, an ideal that at its furthest reaches attributes reality to society and makes the individual simply a shadow of its will —this too is the product of our history.

All this is simply to say that the historian can describe two different systems of values both going under the name "individualism" that verge toward opposites—one toward the isolated person, the other toward society—and be descriptively correct in saying that at different moments in our history Americans have moved toward one and then the other. But the critical historian must then say that to put the question in terms of one *or* the other, of the individual *versus* society, is a false question. To put the matter in its baldest terms, to be a human being at all is a social achievement; the human animal is simply animal without society. At the same time, society, conceived as something apart from the human beings who compose it, is simply an abstraction—a convenient one so long as we remember it, a monstrous one if we forget it. Such resounding platitudes, however, leave us nowhere but in that comfortable American position, the middle of the road, unless one asks what follows. On the one hand we can ask what kind of individuals we want, and on the other what kind of organizations we want.

The first of this linked pair of questions admits no answer. To describe attributes that say that one is an individual only if one possesses particular qualities is to violate the very integrity of the individual person. Here we are at the emotional heart of the problem that troubles contemporary America—the notion that you can properly make no demands on the individual that are not his demands too. To do otherwise is to bully the actual, empirical individual, with the added insult that you are doing it to get him to be what he really wants to be, what his ideal self demands if only his ignorant actual self would recognize it. To construct a social definition of the nature of the individual and impose it on actual individuals would result, ironically, in a uniformity that tolerated no individual differences.

At this point criticism is driven back to history once again. It is true that the notion of consent—the idea that the individual must first accept emotionally and intellectually what power demands before power is legitimate—is itself an historical ideal; that is, it is relative. It has no universal, transcendental sanction behind it. It is the achievement of a particular history, a particular culture. There are cultures, not only in the past but also in the present, that would find such an ideal exotic or incomprehensible. However, it is an ideal that has informed American culture throughout its history. It is what we mean when we say that America is democratic. A democratic society is one in which those in positions of power, public or private, are responsible for their decisions to those whom their decisions affect. That definition forces us, then, to ask how the organizations of our modern, complex society might be made responsible to the individual and serve the ends of a democratic society.

An actual example is the best way to proceed. In the 1930's, when the United Auto Workers were locked in a fierce strug-

gle with the management and owners of the automobile industry, the union was powerful because the worker identified
himself with the union. As one might expect, the literature of
the union movement in its militant phase provides an excellent
source of illustration for what we have called the positive version of individualism. The worker, by a disciplined and dedicated commitment to the union, to the group of which he was
a part, realized his own interest—not simply his immediate self-
interest, but more importantly his own identification, his sense
of who he was and where he was in a society fashioned somewhat closer to his desires. But having achieved recognition and
having won his battle with management, the worker discovered that the union was itself no organic unitary thing; he discovered opponents in his own leadership. He did not have to
read Michels on the "iron law of oligarchy" to discover that
the leaders of any organization develop interests that conflict
with the interests of the constituent members. The ideal of the
union allowed for no such discrepancy, no such internal conflict, just as the ideal of positive individualism assumes a con-
gruence between the ends of the group and the self-realization
of the individual member. But conflict arose.

At this point, the leadership of the UAW performed an act
of considerable political intelligence. They built into their or-
ganizational structure a Public Review Board, an impartial
agency with the power of final adjudication to which the
membership could appeal some decisions made by the leadership. By this action, the UAW has tried to bring its organiza-
tional structure into line with the theory of democracy that
holds that leaders must be responsible to the individuals whom
their decisions affect. Unless that theory is to remain empty
rhetoric, there must be some means by which those affected
can protest and, furthermore, they must feel free to exercise
those means. The UAW Review Board is one attempt to create
the means; such institutional safeguards allow the individual to
participate in group action without surrendering himself en-

tirely to a point of reference lying entirely outside his own self. Obviously, a staggering number of problems still remain, but some such feature must be present in the structure of the organization before other problems can be faced at all, and some such feature is the only means of guaranteeing to the individual some importance in the bureaucratic style of life that we call the organization.

What this comes down to is the need for a certain kind of organization. Our choice is not between organization and something else. It is a choice between organizations that serve our needs and ideals and organizations that do not. One of the humanly disturbing features of the modern world is that the individual, drawn tighter and tighter into a network of functional relations with a greater and greater number of other individuals, feels an increasing depersonalization, the sense of emotional distance that accompanies actual physical dependence. To borrow a word from biology, our relations are increasingly symbiotic. The classic example of such a relation is the embryo in the womb, dependent directly on the mother for nourishment. Today, we depend on an untold number of others to do their work, so our life may go on. These kinds of social relationships are not only necessary; they must exist (as they do) at some level of unawareness much as the functioning and organization of the nervous system in our body. But, to pursue the analogy, the social skills of specialization and organization must serve some larger end than simply intake and output. If Americans insist that society exists to serve the individual, not the individual to serve society, then we must show more imagination with the organization of our organizations in order to bring them at least within hailing distance of our professed ideals. As one looks about, one can fairly say that there is almost no evidence of such imagination at work in our society. We see, instead, cynicism masking itself in praise of the individual. Thus, *Time* magazine in its issue on The Individual in America says: "Like all freedoms, this freedom of choice is also a burden, and that is one reason why there is so much 'conformity.' . . . To expect every individual to take in all of life through a thinking man's filter—to have his own independent, personal convictions about politics, ethics, culture—is to ask the impossible. It is, in fact, to ask for a mass elite."

It is. In all its outrageous innocence, this is what America has asked for from the beginning—sufficient individual character to control the realities of society. It may be impossible, but it will surely be impossible if we decide so beforehand.

6

THE POLITICS OF DESIGN

"What a very little fact sometimes betrays
the national character!"

Andrew Jackson Downing (1849)

EMERSON ONCE remarked that the scholar needs a far horizon
line. I had the great good fortune to write this essay in an ideal
Emersonian setting, in the quiet of a room at the Center for
Advanced Study in the Behavioral Sciences in California where
one glass wall gave upon a distant scene, through the gnarled
branches of blue oaks, over the red-tiled rooftops of the Stanford campus, to the blue and green and rust colored salt-flats of
the lower reaches of San Francisco Bay, to the bare burned-
brown masses of the range of mountains beyond. One oak
could not quite blot out the blocky, aggressive thrust of Stanford's Hoover Tower, but even its egotism retired into the
reaches of space beyond it.

One felt there what Emerson meant. He meant more than
the sheer delight such a prospect has for the eye. He meant the
need the scholar has to hold the world at a certain remove in
order to do his proper work, to get some perspective, as we
say. Even more for Emerson, the soft circle of the far horizon
symbolized his confident trust that the contradictions of the

confusing present would resolve themselves and blend into the perfect oneness of a harmonious whole. We still have need for some perspective on our daily lives, even if we may no longer share Emerson's trust that if only we will take the long view the crooked will somehow make itself straight. Even while beguiled by the prospect from the eastward slope of the low hill on which the Center sits, one cannot forget that the Camino Real with its shrill vulgarity runs through the middle distance, that the fill and the filth of cities on the shore threaten the very existence of San Francisco Bay, and that the research plants of a war economy which have made Stanford's land a great capital asset have also pulled the population with them which threatens all the land around.

My room with a view, then, is proof of the easy condition of the critic of our culture and our environment. All one has to do is look: there are such glaring irreconcilables all about us that one need only describe them to seem percipient and use words like "paradox" and "tension" to seem profound. There is a danger in the ease, though, the danger of being trapped in the very present one hopes to assess and so defeated by letting the immediate moment determine the limits of criticism. At a time when the conditions of change threaten radically to cut us off from any usable past, we need the past all the more to gain some perspective on ourselves.

The job of the historian is to enlarge our experience of the present, to escape its tyranny by amplifying our sense of the contours of the moment in which we live and move, making us more aware, itself a virtue, and through awareness perhaps better able to act. Playing the role of historian, I wish simply to raise a question, to ask through an examination of two selected moments in the past what political and social values are implicit in ways in which we have shaped our physical environment. To answer that question in the past tense will lead, I hope, to an imperative in the present tense. Those who create our environment today must be conscious that their choices are not just aesthetic choices. They are political choices. They imply views about the nature of man, the relation of the individual to society, the nature of the good society. Normally, when we talk about the expression of social and political values we think of the word, either spoken or written. But things too speak to us. They embody ways in which we think about the world. They stand as objective symbols for subjective states of mind. They express preferences. True, we cannot step out of our skins and be fully and objectively aware of all which is implicit in our actions and our preferences but, if we are to use the power which now promises chaos to achieve some human end, we need to be as self-conscious as possible about what we think it means to be human. If we see in the work of designers in the American past a material statement of the pervasive cultural ideals of their time, perhaps we will be readier to accept the need to recognize our own and realize them in our work or, perhaps, reject them for something better.

In 1815, Hezekiah Niles, the editor of *Niles' Weekly Register*, the single most important newspaper in early nineteenth-century America, remarked that the distinguishing feature of the American character was "the almost universal ambition to get forward." One of the chief moods of Jacksonian America was this enterpreneurial psychology, this high level of economic aspiration. But the almost universal ambition to get forward required auspicious social circumstances. Relatively speaking, the American economy up to 1815, the date of Niles' remark, was a static economy. America had not yet entered what today we have come to call the "take-off" period of economic growth. The relatively underdeveloped potentiality of the American economy in, say, 1815 did not provide the occasion to realize the ambition which Niles commented on; in other words, the economy sharply limited the ability of most men to realize their ambition, however powerful it may have been. But once the United States developed internal means of communication, growth and opportunity appeared where physical and economic obstacles had before stood in the way. After 1825 (the date of the completion of the Erie Canal), the boom in transportation and the rapid expansion of the economy gave substance and a tremendous impetus to American ambition. Americans, in an optative mood, embarked on what Emerson called a "Saturnalia of faith," a faith that their future was inevitably glorious. Yet, at the same time, the conditions of rapid social change and physical movement generated an undertone of anxiety in Jacksonian America, a fear that the simple virtues of an ideal republic were endangered by the gospel of the main chance, the ambition to get forward.

Andrew Jackson Downing, horticulturist, landscape gardener, and architect of rural homes, lived his short and full career in these years of change. His life and work bear a curious relationship to his age. Superficially, it seems almost too pat that he was born in 1815 (the year in which General Andrew Jackson began his national public career by his astonishing victory at New Orleans), and died in 1852 in the explosion of the steamboat *Henry Clay*, an embodiment of the technological change, named after the statesman who welcomed it, which brought disaster to the rural world of Downing's America as well as to himself. But that is simply the kind of dramatic fitness with which history sometimes delights the historian.

On first consideration, Downing seems out of place in his time. Unlike most Americans, especially then, but even now, he lived all his life in one place, in the Hudson River Valley, near the outskirts of Newburgh, overlooking the river. In an age we remember as the age of the common man, he was fastidious, gently aloof, with aspirations to being something of an aristocrat; his ideal was always the English country gentry, even more the English country lady who was as much at home on the farm lands of her estate as at her elegant dinner table. In his work, Downing had an eye on two enemies: the drab, slatternly condition of the American village and the pretentious and vulgar eclecticism of the new wealth rising in the city. In the place of both, he argued for "fitness" in houses and landscaping.

Andrew Jackson Downing is generally remembered today as an anticipation of our own time, a temptation the historian always faces of assimilating the past into the categories of his own present. To a point, such an evaluation of Downing has a certain merit. He writes often in a voice which is familiar to us, with an emphasis, to use our terms, on functional design. Because Louis Sullivan and Frank Lloyd Wright have intervened we are at home with Downing when he writes in *The Architecture of Country Houses* that "however full of ornament or luxury a house may be, if its apartments do not afford that convenience, comfort, and adaptation to human wants, which the habits of those who live in it demand, it must always fail to satisfy." Downing not only urged that a house should boldly declare the living habits of those within it, he argued also that the materials which went into it should show the same honesty:

> Material should *appear* to be what it is. . . . When we employ stone as a building material, let it be clearly expressed; when we employ wood, there should be no less frankness in avowing the material. There is more merit in so using wood as to give to it the utmost expression of which the substance is capable, than in endeavoring to make it look like some other material.

He had a special scorn for the pretentious towers and battlements of false Gothic made from slender one-inch pine board. Like Wright again, he thought that so far as possible buildings should be constructed from materials native to the region.

All such prescriptions for design Downing gathered under the heading, "fitness." Beauty came first "intellectually considered," as he put it, but practically considered, it could be achieved only by putting it last and beginning with "convenience" and "comfort," the utilitarian aspects of the art of design. "In the country places which [novices] create," he wrote, "the casual visitor may be struck with many beautiful effects; but when a trifling observation has shown him that this beauty is not the result of a harmony between the real and the ideal,— or, in other words, between the surface of things intended to be seen and the things themselves, as they minister to our daily wants—then all the pleasure vanishes, and the opposite feeling takes its place."

Downing went even further than contemporary functional design has presumed to go. Beyond his demand that a building should declare its use and take bold advantage of the materials which went into its construction, he aspired to an architecture which would figure forth the very character of its inhabitant:

> The most casual reader will understand from our suggestion, that if a man's house can be made to express the best traits of his character, it is undeniable that a large source of beauty and interest is always lost by those who copy each other's homes without reflection. . . . We would have the cottage, the farm-house, and the larger country-house, all marked by a somewhat distinctive character of their own, so far as relates to making them complete and individual of their kind; and believing as we do, that the beauty and force of every true man's life or occupation depend largely on his pursuing it frankly, honestly and openly, with all the individuality of his character, we would have his house and home help to give significance to, and dignify that daily life and occupation, by harmonizing with them.

Such a prescription would have the architect become moral psychologist as well as designer and it is understandable that not much follows such exhortations in Downing's work. Functionalism for Downing did not stop with building, use, site, and materials. He demanded that it express the character of the individual and, finally, even the national character of the American people: "to make the outward form of all about us express our best ideal of life, to mould it so that it shall evince, not merely the borrowed and accepted form of the books and schools of art, but the deeper essence of the life, and character, and manners of the people, and even the families that inhabit it—that should be the ambition and the goal of the domestic architect of any country."

Yet, to dwell solely on the emphasis of functionalism in Downing's work, however much that may raise his work in our current estimation, is finally to violate that work and Downing's main intention. The historically inclined critic will do well to adapt Gordon Allport's advice to practicing psychologists, namely, to "develop skill as an oculist, training himself to look *at* his spectacles and not merely *through* them, and training himself to look both *at* and *through* the spectacles of the client with whom he deals." Neither of Mr. Allport's ideal states are capable of realization. As I have already said, one cannot stand fully outside one's self and look objectively at the values through which he perceives experience; neither can one, however empathic, enter fully into the total experience of the past, not only because some of that totality is irretrievably lost but because one knows where the past led to, namely, one's own present. We know what those in the past could never know: what came after. But this need not imprison us in the present. There is still the record, however partial, and we can do rough justice to the past in its own terms and not just in ours.

However much Andrew Jackson Downing insisted on use and fitness, he could never go so far as to say that the useful was the beautiful. He was still involved in an aesthetic which drew a line between the two. He thought the truth was "undeniable, that the Beautiful is, intrinsically, something quite different from the Useful. It appeals to a wholly different part of our nature; it requires another portion of our being to receive and enjoy it." Some platonic hierarchy of ideal form is in Downing's mind when he argues that "a head of grain, one of the most useful of vegetable forms, is not so beautiful as a rose; an ass, one of the most useful of animals, is not so beautiful as a gazelle; a cotton-mill, one of the most useful of modern structures, is not so beautiful as the temple of Vesta." Speaking from this side of his mind, Downing can forget his own criterion of "fitness" and speak of beauty in a design as the "embellishment" of "rude and rough forms." At such moments he lapses into the genteel tradition in American thought which consigns power and utility to the rude masculine world and elevates beauty and culture to the feminine. "Whenever any thing especially tasteful is to be done," Downing wrote,

> we have to entreat the assistance of the fairer half of humanity. All that is most graceful and charming in this way, owes its existence to female hands. Over the heavy exterior of man's handiwork, they weave a fairylike web of enchantment, which, like our Indian summer haze upon autumn hills, spiritualizes and makes poetical, whatever of rude form or rough outlines may lie beneath.

We can look *at* as well as *through* those softly-tinted spectacles and may rightly lay them aside. They will not do for our eyes, but they provide a clue to the element in Downing's work in architecture and landscape gardening which finally involves his aesthetic in certain social and political preferences. Downing thinks that the rude and rough material world can be etherealized and made poetical because, despite his anticipations of a utilitarian and functional view, he worked mainly within the conventions of a tradition, received from England, built upon a theory of association derived from the sensationalist psychology of John Locke. The reason Downing could think the rose more beautiful than the head of grain was that "there is the *infinity of associations* which float like rich incense about the rose, and that, after all, bind it most strongly to us; for they represent the accumulated wealth of joys and sorrows, which has become so inseparably connected with it in the human heart."

Downing here speaks out of a considerable tradition in the history of taste in Western thought. His belief that we are moved by certain objects because of the subjective associations which certain stimuli arouse in our mind derives directly from eighteenth century British aesthetics, especially as it related to the "improvement" of the grounds of a country estate, a literature Downing knew well. The prinicpal theoretician of the problem of association was Archibald Alison in his *Essays on the Nature and Principles of Taste* (Edinburgh, 1790) which went through four editions by 1815. Sir Uvedale Price, whose work on the picturesque Downing called "elegant and masterly," expressed concisely the materialist psychology and the associational aesthetic which Downing assumed:

> All external objects affect us in two different ways: by the impression they make on the senses, and by the reflections they suggest to the mind. These two modes, though very distinct in their operations, often unite in producing one effect; the reflections of the mind, either strengthening, weakening, or giving a new direction to the impression received by the eye.

By the 1840's in the United States, such views on the matter of taste were uncritical assumptions.

In another context, one might well pay considerable attention to Downing's importance as a critical agent in the transmission of the influence the old world played on the new but, as enticing as that subject is, what is immediately important in Downing's work is to discern what pattern of associations was in his mind and was implicit in the work he did as designer; in other words, to lay bare what ideal image of the nature of American society he wished to achieve through his work. In rural architecture, Downing was perhaps the major figure in

the reaction against the vogue of classicism; he was an out-
spoken champion of the Gothic and its derivatives. In landscape planning, he rejected the abstract pattern of the formal
garden and spoke for the picturesque, the *jardin anglais* as it
came to be called because of its dominance in English gardening.

Downing recognized that "to the scholar and the man of
refined and cultivated mind, the *associations* connected with
Grecian architecture are of the most delightful character," but
he rejected the classical mode, first on the sensible ground that
a temple did not easily adapt itself to a home, but more importantly because of the very associations connected with it. "In
Grecian art," he says, quoting Humboldt's *Cosmos*, "all is made
to concentrate within the sphere of *human* life and feeling.
. . . With them, the landscape is always the mere background of a picture, in the foreground of which human figures
are moving. Passion, breaking forth in action, invited their attention almost exclusively; the agitation of politics, and a life
passed chiefly in public, withdrew men's minds from . . . the
tranquil pursuit of nature." The Gothic, too, had its "romantic
associations" and Downing prized them, but it was the tran-
quilizing effect of rural Gothic which comprised its chief value:
"under its enchanting influence, the too great bustle and excite-
ment of our commercial cities will be happily counterbalanced
by the more elegant and quiet enjoyments of country life."

It may seem an immense imaginative leap from the bracket-
style, cottage *ornée* of rural Gothic to the aggressive commer-
cialism of American cities, but the chain of associations which
makes it possible is clear in Downing's writing. The formal
order of classicism is, for Downing, an expression of man's will
to power and dominance over nature; it is appropriate to passionate action and the agitation of public life. "Though there is
no positive beauty in a straight or level line," he wrote, "it is
often interesting as expressive of *power*." He would tolerate

the classical mode in public buildings and in the formal gardens in their grounds because it fittingly symbolized society's imposition of order, but in domestic architecture he sought some counterforce to the "feverish" quality of American life, most obvious in the city. "We must look," said Downing, "for a counterpoise to the great tendency towards constant change, and the restless spirit of emigration, which form part of our national character." A citizen of the new world, Downing admired "its very spirit of liberty and progress, its freedom from old prejudices, and the boundless life and energy that make the pulses of its true citizens—either native or adopted—beat with health and exultation," yet he feared the excess of that freedom and energy.

Downing had read Tocqueville's magistral analysis of American society, *Democracy in America,* and shared Tocqueville's uneasiness about the restless energy and drive in Americans which posed a threat to the stability and order of society. "One does not need to be much of a philosopher," wrote Downing, "to remark that one of the most striking of our national traits is the SPIRIT OF UNREST. It is the grand energetic element which leads us to clear vast forests, and settle new States, with a rapidity unparalleled in the world's history; the spirit, possessed with which, our yet comparatively scanty people do not find elbow-room enough in a territory already in their possession, and vast enough to hold the greatest of ancient empires." This was, as he put it, "the grand and exciting side of the picture." But there was another, less agreeable side. "The *spirit of unrest,* followed into the bosom of society, makes of man a feverish being, in whose Tantalus' cup repose is the unattainable drop. Unable to take root any where, he leads, socially and physically, the uncertain life of a tree transplanted from place to place, and shifted to different soil every season." Although Downing admired the energy of the American people, he valued "no less the love of order, the obedience to law, the security and repose of society, the love of home," and was deeply convinced that "whatever tends, without checking due energy of character, but to develop along with it certain virtues that will keep it within due bounds, may be looked upon as a boon to the nation." All his work, in architecture, in gardening, and in horticulture, was offered as such a boon. He wished to attach his restless fellow men to a home and a garden, to give them roots in "one spot of earth," an "Eden of interest and delights."

Even a passing familiarity with Downing's time will show that he was in no way unique in his attitudes. His demand for individual character which, without losing its admirable energy, would contain itself within the bounds of the good of society has a precise parallel in Emerson's writings; his view of nature (he speaks of spring as the "wonderful resurrection of life and beauty out of the death-sleep of winter . . . a fore-shadowing of that transformation and awakening of us all in the spiritual spring of another and higher life") is Thoreau's, although without Thoreau's capacity to translate that vision into remarkable prose. Closer to Downing's own idiom, one thinks of the pastoral vision of Thomas Cole or the painters of Downing's own world, the Hudson River School. The American Art Union, in promoting its lottery sales of paintings, made the same argument for our landscape painters that Downing did for rural architecture:

> To the inhabitants of cities, as nearly all of the subscribers to the Art-Union are, a painted landscape is almost essential to preserve a healthy tone to the spirits, lest they forget in the wilderness of bricks which surrounds them the pure delights of nature and a country life. Those who cannot afford a seat in the country to refresh their wearied spirits, may at least have a country seat in their parlors; a bit of landscape with a green tree, a distant hill, or low-roofed cottage;—some of these simple objects, which all men find so refreshing to their spirits after being long pent up in dismal streets and in the haunts of business.

Downing's work is in significant part a response to the un-settling conditions of rapid social change in American society in its expansive phase. Recent work in politics and economics and sociology on "the emerging nations," as the title of one book names the materially under-developed countries of the world, has led us to see rapid economic growth not simply as beneficent progress but as a "profoundly destabilizing force." The United States escaped many of the most profound conse-quences of the social instability which attends rapid change but the stresses and anxieties are clearly there to see in the early nineteenth century. What is important about Downing's work is not that he shares a widespread concern about the unsettling consequences of America's powerful energy, but that he trans-lates that concern into an aesthetic choice. Like many in his time, Downing had an anti-urban bias, but most significantly he translates that bias into an aesthetic. The straight lines and the formal order of the reigning classical style are, in his mind, associated with the will to power and the enterprising mastery over nature which he sees most nakedly in the city. In response, he turned to the Gothic and the picturesque and argued for them as counterbalancing weights against the aggressiveness of an acquisitive society with its desire to "get ahead."

The irony in Downing's career is that, popular as he was, his most popular book was *The Fruits and Fruit Trees of America* . . . which from 1845 to 1856 went through four-teen editions. He also edited John Lindley, *The Theory of Horticulture . . . Upon Physiological Principles* (1852); Lindley was a Professor of Botany in England and Secretary of the Horticultural Society of London and Downing's editorial work was mainly to adapt his prescriptions to American condi-tions. This side of Downing's career, as pomologist and horti-culturist, represents a stage in the beginning of what today we would call "scientific" agriculture. As he wrote in his intro-duction to Lindley, "Besides the higher gratification which Horticulture affords, when its principles are understood, the

increased profit, derived from the superior quality and augmented quantity of the products, and the greater certainty of
success in culture, should not be forgotten."

Downing was justly appalled at the wastefulness and short-
sighted exploitation of the land in American agriculture but
there was little need for him to insist on "increased profits,"
"augmented quantity," and "success." The American farmer,
no less than his brother in the commercial city, had his eye on
the main chance. The farmer in the United States has never
been attached to the soil in the manner of his European coun-
terpart. He has been, from the beginning, an exploitative capitalist working in a different medium. The success of Downing's
Fruits and Fruit Trees suggests that writings which increased
the American farmer's cash crop stood a better chance than
essays which put forth the "higher gratification" of agriculture. In pleading for the embellishment of rural homes, Downing had imagined the happy result:

> The stout farmer, who once looked upon his acres only as a
> laboratory for transmuting labor into gold, now takes a widely
> different view of his possessions. His eyes are opened to the
> *beautiful* in nature, and he looks with reverence upon every
> giant remnant of the forest, that by good luck escaped his mur-
> derous axe in former days. No leafy monarch is now laid low
> without a stern necessity demands it; but many a vigorous tree is
> planted in the hope that the children of *his* children may gather
> beneath the spreading branches, and talk with pious gratitude of
> him who planted them.

That image of bucolic harmony was to remain a dream.

On his first page in *Rural Essays*, Downing wrote, "Angry
volumes of politics have we written none; but peaceful books,
humbly aiming to weave something more into the fair garland
of the beautiful and useful." He was right that none of his
books is angry, but they are political, not political in the sense
of talking about politics but in the sense of embodying a politi-

cal ideal, an ideal of a pastoral middle ground between the chaos of the raw frontier and the brutal power of the new city. Whatever judgment the student of architecture passes on the merits of Downing's work, the cultural historian will value it as a statement in the idiom of art of a concern which was central to the thought and the emotions of his time, and still important to ours. Downing's work is prophetic of the position of contemporary conservationism, although the final protective line has retreated before the suburbs to the wilderness. As Sigurd Olson has said, the wilderness means "more than just the preservation of rocks and trees and scenery. It is a battle for the minds that have become increasingly engrossed with the machine."

Because of the machine, we live in a world radically different from the world Andrew Jackson Downing wished to bring into being. His vision of the American future was abortive; it remains the road not taken by America. The road taken was the freeway to success, busyness, and an industrial technology built upon the machine—the straight line of power. If Downing's unease was a response to the uncertainties generated in the "take-off" period of American economic growth, it is hard to find terms adequate to the altitudes of full power later in the century. The simplicity of the Jacksonian period seems truly a pastoral idyll in our national history from almost any subsequent vantage point. Edward Atkinson, writing toward the end of the nineteenth century, put the matter succinctly: "Nothing is constant but change."

From a population of roughly 30 million in 1860, the United States grew to somewhat more than 75 million by 1900. Of that increase, roughly 10 million were immigrants; at the same time that 10 million people, uprooted from their native cultures, moved into a way of life new and strange to them, an even greater number of Americans were changing their style of life, moving from rural to urban environments. Not only was there a sharp shift from farm to city, there was unceasing movement within the farm population itself. In one Nebraska township, twenty years after the initial settlement, more than fifty percent of the original cultivators had sold out and moved on. The number of factory workers multiplied by a factor greater than ten during the second half of the nineteenth century, "a rate far too rapid for social adjustment," as two students of American enterprise have pointed out. A whole new class came into being during these years. In the census of 1870, there appeared for the first time what we now name the "new middle class," clerks, employees of the new bureaucracies, and salaried professionals. They numbered slightly more than 750,-000 in 1870 and increased phenomenally to more than five and one-half million by 1910. All the neat charts which try to capture in graphic terms the drastic speed of change of the late nineteenth century, lines describing the increase of power, output of physical goods, the elaboration of the transportation and communications network, the rise of national and world population, all show a nearly right angle upward turn somewhere around 1870 to 1880.

Henry James, returning to the United States in 1905, could only see *"the will to grow . . .* everywhere written large, and to grow at no matter what or to whose expense." The sense of stumbling in the dark which pervades the pages of *The Education of Henry Adams* captures better than any volume of statistics the immediate human consequences of new sources of power at work. As one ordinary, bewildered woman put it, "The trouble is that the simplicity of life is gone."

There are a number of ways of looking at the consequences of rapid economic and social change for taste and design in the period around the turn of the twentieth century, but the ways one will find in almost any standard account are almost uniformly unfortunate. The author of a major work on the relation of art to American life is content with this order of generalization: "America seized upon every known style of building with a predatory zeal which marks her genius for business exploitation"; or, "Ornament was applied to structure with as reckless a disregard for truth as could be found in any mining company's prospectus and originality consisted in being lawless." One is at a loss to know what loose analogy is in the writer's mind, or whether some positive and causative relationship is being asserted between the predatory instincts of American business, the lawlessness of a mining company's prospectus, and the rampant eclecticism of the taste of the time. The same writer, discussing the obvious eclecticism of Downing's time, the 1840's, speaks of that generation of Americans as only too glad to separate forms from their historical context and to play freely with them, so eclecticism apparently need not be a simple and direct manifestation of business vulgarity. One might still make a case and argue indirectly that business enterprise is one acute instance of the lack of historical consciousness, an absence of a sense of the past, an intensification of an attitude long present in American society; that is, a reader might, by his own effort, establish a connection between these two "critical" statements about eclecticism in the 1840's and at the turn of the century, but one feels that a false rhetoric has interposed between the author's intelligence and his job of work. Those who wish to argue a relationship between the forms of art in a culture and the larger patterns of the culture itself will have to take that task seriously; if not, the precise, cautiously factual monograph will prove far more satisfying than the large, eye-catching generality which implies a relationship no one intends to entertain.

One profitable way of looking at art in the period of the late nineteenth century is to examine it in its institutional form, that is, quite apart from any formal aesthetic concern and see it simply as one of the many social institutions affected by the conditions of change in society. What was happening suddenly and all at once everywhere in the late nineteenth century was the emergence of an interdependent and advanced technological society, the development of a national economy of a modern national state, all this carried through by the industrial and communications revolution. One of the major consequences was the thrust toward increasing specialization of skills at all levels of the society, from productive skills to professional skills. The American Medical Association had been formed before the Civil War, but the American Bar Association did not come into being until 1878. The Engineers formed their society in 1871 and quickly split off into mechanical and electrical engineering associations in the 1880's. Immediately after the Civil War there existed an organization called the American Social Science Association which carried forward the old tradition of taking all knowledge as its province, but it rapidly splintered into the American Historical Association, the American Economic Association the following year, and by the end of the century politics and sociology had also formed their own professional groups.

In other words, just as the organization and rationalization of the economy went forward, so did organization and specialization in all fields of knowledge go forward in these years. In the 1870's, seventy-nine professional societies were formed; in the 1880's, 121 professional societies were chartered; in the 1890's, there were 45. What was happening in the institution of art can be suggested quickly by a cluster of dates. The decline of the old apprenticeship system and, a closely related phenomenon, the notion that every man should be his own architect (the gentlemanly school of architecture) can be indicated by the fact that 1856 saw the last, at least the last of the best, of the architectural *vademecums*, Minard Lafever's *The Architectural Instructor*. In the very next year, 1857, the American Institute of Architects is formed. By 1866, we have the first professional school of architecture at M.I.T., followed quickly by

Cornell under the leadership of men like Charles Babcock, then at Illinois, and at Syracuse. So, in these years, together with the beginnings of industrial training to serve the demands for productive skills in the economy when an older system of supply has ceased, one observes in art and architecture the founding of institutions to support professions which had lost their old means of continuity.

Mr. A. J. Bloor, who was secretary and archivist for the AIA, pointed out as early as 1869 the need for professional organization to sustain work in the arts. He said,

> However else American architects may differ, none of us surely can blind our eyes to the fact that we cannot, isolated, yield each other the support that we may if we stand all over our common country on a common platform of professional principles. We are the organized representatives of an active and every year more potential profession; and practical men, for practical purposes, must accept the facts around them. If the architectural calling in this country, contrary to its antecedents in the other hemisphere, finds itself destitute of the art-atmosphere . . . deprived . . . of the protective guild appliances of the middle ages, and in its totality without the governmental appliances of recent times; while, at the same time, it is surrounded on all sides by well-concerted and powerful organizations in the interest of other professions and of commerce, manufactures, and finance—with which, nevertheless, in the universal struggle for self-preservation, it has, in a certain degree, to compete—how can it adequately perform its duty either to the age and nation, or to itself and its successors, without some similar self-sustaining combination. We need our special platform from which to train the public . . . while, at the same time, we protect ourselves from the jealousy, the misunderstanding and ignorance of each other, of our clients, and of mechanics.

Bloor's vision of what the AIA could and should do was quickly realized. Ultimately it was called upon by the Federal Government to adjudicate conflicts in contracts between practicing architects and the government. Then, in 1886, it ruled in its own convention that it would act as mediator only for the members of its own professional organization. In the minutes of the meeting the reason for this ruling was the press of business on the officers of the organization, but one needs little imagination to see the effects of such a rule. The AIA was becoming the official spokesman for the profession of architecture, the government implicitly recognized it as architecture's voice, and not to belong to it was to suffer a real disadvantage. In other words, by the late 1870's and 1880's, the architects were organizing the enterprise of architecture in ways precisely comparable to entrepreneurs in other fields of the economy. One can catch some of the contemporary human flavor of this trend in the words of Daniel H. Burnham in 1887:

> More important than anything yet attempted to be done by any society is the compiling and publishing of a code of ethics for architects which of course shall show what is good, *but especially what is professionally damnable in our dealings with each other*. Let this be rendered in strong, clear type, and put upon the desk of everyone, and it will at once have a most salutary effect upon the fee-cutting, back-biting, backstairs-climbing crowd, and remove temptation from the lives of those yet uncorrupted.

It was during these years that Mr. Rockefeller was trying to establish the same kind of gentlemen's agreement in the oil industry, trying to impose order upon the chaotic conditions of competition. There is a striking similarity and the AIA was legally even more successful because by 1894 both Federal and State Courts, in the absence of any contract to the contrary, accepted the AIA's schedule of fees as legally binding. By that time, Mr. Burnham was becoming a trifle uneasy and implored the society not to lay themselves open to the charge of being a trade-union instead of a deliberative society of professional men.

Put simply, one sees in the economy and in the general culture in these years a quest for order, that is, the attempt to master the rapid change which the society was undergoing. Art, as an organized institution, participates in this general trend. To consider art and society from this perspective would be to treat the sociology of art, but there were important consequences for taste as well as for institutional organization. To name just one: the eclecticism of the period, rather than being the predatory instinct of raw industrial capitalism, was probably more the result of the kind of teaching that was institutionalized. The kind of teaching was itself a product of technological innovation, that is, cheap means of reproduction which made a sedentary tour of world art all too easy. If one reads the descriptions of courses printed in the Proceedings of the AIA in their annual conventions, one might find oneself more in sympathy with Louis Sullivan, even at his primitivistic and Whitmanesque worst, bewailing reason and the mind, when he cries out against "utterly purposeless education" and awaits the young genius, inspired by the divine "afflatus" to lead architecture out of the wilderness of eclecticism.

Though certain aesthetic consequences do follow from even an institutional perspective on the various arts of the time, there is another and rather more directly interesting way of looking at the relation of design to culture in the period. The quest for order, apparent in the organization of the institutions of art, can be seen also in the emergence in these years of an attempt to formulate an aesthetic appropriate to the conditions of what E. H. Carr has called the "new society."

The disorder men were trying to master was most present, certainly, in the urban chaos of the late nineteenth century, the urban chaos generated in part by industrialism and technology. One can get at the matter of an attempt to formulate an aesthetic in response to such change through a few sentences from a speech by Frederick Law Olmsted, the landscape architect. The occasion of the speech was a discussion in 1903 of L'Enfant's plan for the Capital City in Washington in the attempt to make that plan still operative in the twentieth century. Olmsted said, "In any complex [social] work of art which must be the product of many minds working through a considerable time, like a national capital, or a university, or a public park, the only hope of a successful issue lies in the adherence of the various designers to a consistent plan or ideal, definite or indefinite, conscious or unconscious." He then pointed out how "unconscious" ideals once operated. "In the unsophisticated work of the middle ages, and again in large measure during the height of the renaissance, such consistency was secured through the almost universal adherence of the people to a rather narrow range of mutually harmonious ideals." In other words, people achieved a style, Olmsted thought, by doing what comes naturally. "It was not necessary," he went on to say, "for the citizens of that charming old city of Chester on the Dee to hold a meeting and vote upon a style of architecture for the city, or to adopt a definite cornice height or to take any self-conscious measures toward making their city a beautiful artistic composition." The people of Chester acted intuitively in conformity with the genius of Chester. Now, said Olmsted, in contrast with the slow incremental growth of style in those days, people can stay at home and invent new fashions or consciously select and buy them "ready made, some from Paris, some from Japan, and some from the *Ladies' Home Journal.*"

Olmsted is arguing that the conditions of the modern world have made an unconscious idiom impossible and because of this, he says, "we get the confusion and contradiction, the loudmouthed clash of divergent and opposing artistic expressions, which mark not only our cities and the more concentrated units of single streets and squares, but even our college quadrangles and groups of government buildings." So, in conclusion, in talking about L'Enfant's plan for Washington, Olmsted said that it "stands as the great example in the lesson we are learning that freedom, from the unconscious restraint of definite tradition and limited environment which once controlled all artistic efforts, imposes upon us the needs of a sophisticated self-restraint with regard to each part of a large design, within the limits of some one consistent character consciously adopted as appropriate to the purpose of the design as a whole."

We recognize the accents of this, of course. Olmsted is arguing the need for functional planning, for the self-conscious mastery of the environment in which all parts will relate to the whole. What I would like to suggest is that if the machine created disorder, it also provided an ideal by which order might again be realized in the society.

Consider the machine itself, for a moment, abstractly, as the embodiment of certain ideas. If one thinks of the machine in this fashion he quickly recognizes that it is the clear embodiment of certain ideas. A well-designed machine is an instance of total organization, that is, a series of interrelated means contrived to achieve a single end. A machine consists always of particular parts that have no meaning or function separate from the organized entity to which they contribute and whose interrelationships are marshaled wholly toward a given result. In the ideal machine, there can be no extraneous part, no extraneous movement; all is set, part for part, motion for motion toward the functioning of the whole. The machine is, then, at once a perfect instance of total rationalization of a field of action and of total organization. A society which chooses to enjoy the benefits of the power that the machine makes possible, a society committed to mechanization, is also committed, inexorably, to increasing organization of its economic and its social life, to more and more precise articulation; in two words: to *planning* and *organization*. The result was that a self-conscious ideal of functional relationships began to penetrate American thought, both its ethics and its aesthetics, toward the end of the nineteenth century.

For one example, Frederick Winslow Taylor, an industrial engineer, remembered as the "father" of scientific management in the United States, testifying before a House Committee, said,

> Let me say that we are now but on the threshold of the coming era of true cooperation. The time is fast going by for the great personal or individual achievement of any one man standing alone and without the help of those around him. And the time is coming when all the great things will be done by the cooperation of many men in which each man performs that function for which he is best suited, each man preserves his individuality and is supreme in his particular function, and each man at the same time loses none of his originality and proper personal initiative, and yet is controlled by, and must work harmoniously with, many other men.

In his work as an industrial engineer, Taylor's goal was to relate the part to the whole in the productive process to achieve maximum efficiency, which is what we mean by saying he rationalized the work process. In response to new conditions which his own work helped to create, Taylor in his remarks here is trying to formulate a social ethic which sanctions these conditions by relating the individual to society just as he had related the part to the whole in his system of industrial efficiency. The person becomes a person by discovering the function for which he is best suited; one achieves his individuality by participating in some whole which is greater than one's separate self, by becoming a functioning part of some larger collective organization.

The notion, implicit in the organization of an industrial society and explicit in Taylor's testimony, was widespread in American culture around the turn of the century. It is the central notion of Herbert Croly's "constructive" nationalist political thought, the assertion that one must pursue that calling which best furthers the national interest; it pervades the educational and ethical thought of John Dewey; it is marked in the beginnings of professional sociology at the time, especially in the writings of Albion Small and Charles H. Cooley. By the end of the nineteenth century Downing's vision of a pastoral middle ground which, supported by belief in an ideal natural order, would keep the power of society at a certain distance had largely vanished. There began to emerge a social ethic of functional adaptation to society.

If we return to Olmsted's words, we can see there the same cultural pattern of values put in the idiom of aesthetics. In a society where rapid change has destroyed the unconscious authority of tradition, Olmsted concludes that we must give up an old notion of freedom and turn to a self-conscious and planned effort to impose order upon the social landscape, that every element in a design must be related to a total plan, which is what we mean by functional planning.

We have read much about the effects of technology and the machine upon the arts, whether the structure of a building or the internal, subjective vision of the artist himself, but far more critical is the way in which an aesthetic of functionalism is implicated in technological change itself, is part of the very cast of mind symbolized by the machine. In 1901, looking out on the towering black mass of Chicago's buildings by night, Frank Lloyd Wright said, "If this power must be uprooted that civilization may live, then civilization is already doomed." Wright's architecture was, as he liked to say, "prophetic" because it put in architectural terms a problem American culture has yet to solve in other terms, the terms of politics and social organization. Rather than an unplanned for, simple and inevitable harmony, Wright realized that the

> single secret of simplicity [was] that we may truly regard nothing at all as simple in itself. I believe that no one thing in itself is ever so, but must achieve simplicity—as an artist should use the

term—as a perfectly realized part of some organic whole. Only as a feature or any part becomes harmonious element in the harmonious whole does it arrive at the state of simplicity.

There Wright is speaking of design. He spoke in the same accent when he called his architecture an "architecture for democracy" because his ideal of a democratic society was "the highest possible expression of the individual, as a unit not inconsistent with a harmonious whole."

Andrew Jackson Downing and Frank Lloyd Wright were both critics of their times, both had visions of society which went beyond the present conditions of society. Yet, at the same time, both were very much part of their times: Downing, in his commitment to a natural order which was available to man as a standard to place over and against the artificial order of society; Wright, in his hope that man's power was capable of imposing order upon the disorder it seemed to promise. Like most intellectuals, or artists, if one prefers, they were inside and outside their culture at one and the same moment. If we project a line of development from Downing through Wright to our own present, their work poses a critical problem for us.

Downing's ideal of a cultivated middle ground between the raw frontier and the frenetic city fell victim to the will to power he saw symbolized in the straight lines of man's determination to control nature rather than live in harmony with it. Wright, accepting the uses of power, the vision of created order as well as the techniques of technology, hoped to use that power to realize once again a harmonious human scale which power, unchecked, threatened to destroy forever. The styles of both embody political aspirations as well as aesthetic choices.

Today, our society, sustained by an accelerating and quickly changing technology, is so clearly a complex of inter-related parts that we must now accept the need for foresight, coordination, and planning. The same need, recognized but certainly not acted upon, is there in the physical texture of modern society, the very environment in which we live and move. Specialization, itself a necessary condition of a rationalistic and technological society, has led to a real dilemma. The assumption which permits specialization, which tolerates the division of labor, is that somewhere someone is putting the improved parts together again. A Ford assembly line would hardly be an advantage if a Ford car did not roll off the end of the line. One of the assumptions which once made division of labor and specialization of activity tolerable was the notion that an order exists quite apart from the inquiring mind, that the order is in nature and radically separate from human intelligence. If one amasses enough facts, or enough "truths," order will eventually emerge because each fact has its place in some pre-existing order. This assumption has its parallel in the belief that if each man pursues his own particular good the general community will inevitably prosper, or in the belief that if each man exercises his reason separately that all thinking men will somehow arrive at an identical answer. Such assumptions were implicit in much of eighteenth and nineteenth century thought. In each case, the belief that the ends will take care of themselves left the individual free to act vigorously in his particular sphere unhampered by nagging doubts about the final effect of his action. The result was a spectacular release of energy.

In recent years this atomistic view of knowledge and society has given way in nearly every area of thought. The dominant words in the intellectual vocabulary of the twentieth century are "pattern," "context," "relation," and "form." The individual fact, the individual person, the individual transaction takes on its meaning only in relation to other facts, individuals, and transactions. This can be observed in gestalt psychology, the physics of relativity, the stress on context in literary criticism, and the culture concept of modern social theory. These tendencies in various areas of contemporary thought represent the idea that reality is a whole, not a sum of separate parts. So the movement away from extreme specialization is itself part of a larger pattern which seems to be expressing itself in nearly every area of the modern world.

If there is to be a human order at all, man must create it. It will not emerge spontaneously and unbidden from the separate activities of separate men. The critical question then becomes: what human values, what view of man, what view of the political order, are implicit in the shape of our modern environment and in the minds of those men who play a central role in its creation. Is it possible to elicit from those men who play a central role in the making of man-made America a self-conscious awareness of what defines a healthy human order and to ask how their work is an attempt to reach it? Or, has the centrifugal process of specialization and self-concern gone so far that there is no common ground, that all the king's men can never put the pieces back together again? Does the chaos of our physical environment simply mirror a deeper chaos in our moral and political order?

7

HERBERT CROLY: THE PROMISE
OF CONSTRUCTIVE
INDIVIDUALISM

TOWARD THE END of *The Promise of American Life,* in a discussion of the meaning of excellence, Herbert Croly wrote that, however fine his work, an individual must "make some sort of a personal impression." He must achieve "a more or less numerous popular following." The criterion raises difficult problems for the meaning of excellence in an egalitarian culture but, for the moment, Croly's measure is a useful measure of his own success. His following was less rather than more numerous. Published in 1909, with two more printings by 1911, *The Promise of American Life* sold only about 7,500 copies. Croly did not reach a large audience, but he reached a great audience. He reached a generation and more of intellectuals whose careers help to define the meaning of modern American life: Felix Frankfurter, Walter Lippmann, Edmund Wilson, Learned Hand, Robert Morss Lovett, Henry L. Stimson, and many others. More directly, *The Promise of American Life* brought Mr. and Mrs. Willard Straight to Croly, and the result was the founding of *The New Republic* in 1914 with Croly as its chief editor until 1928, two years before his death.

So Croly satisfied his own standard: *The Promise of American Life* created a following. It did because it spoke to the needs of its time. As Felix Frankfurter was to recall, "the rallying cry was progressivism and in Herbert Croly it found its philosopher." In this view, Croly stands in the classic posture of the intellectual, making explicit what is implicit in the events of his time. That achievement is enough to demand our attention. Croly makes a further demand upon us, though. It is fair to say that American society has not yet faced up to the questions Croly put to it in 1909. Despite the plethora of President's Commissions and books on our national goals and national purpose, *The Promise of American Life* remains the best analysis we have in the twentieth century of the basic questions facing a powerful industrial society that claims to be democratic.

The Promise of American Life may transcend the moment in which Croly wrote, but that moment is important. As Felix Frankfurter put it, "Behind the diverse and discordant movements for reform to which [Theodore] Roosevelt gave voice lay the assumption that the traditional hopes of American democracy had been defeated by social and economic forces not contemplated by the founders of our nation. But there was lacking a thoroughgoing critical analysis of the ways in which Americanism had become merely a formal creed." Croly's book supplied the analysis. What Theodore Roosevelt acted out and symbolized on the stage of politics, Herbert Croly thought out and articulated in his book. Yet, if Croly is partly to be understood as the philosopher of progressivism, one must admit that at first glance he seems an unlikely candidate for the post. When Croly's book appeared, Theodore Roosevelt, an ex-president at fifty, was on a safari in Africa. Judge Learned Hand sent Roosevelt a copy of *The Promise of American Life*, while Roosevelt, in response to a letter from Henry Cabot Lodge, had already ordered a copy of his own. Eric Goldman has entertainingly described the occasion: "Everything was bully. . . . Delighted with his nine lions, five elephants, thirteen rhinoceroses, and seven hippopotamuses, Roosevelt swung off on a grand tour, lecturing Egyptian nationalists on the beneficence of British imperialism, dining with the King and Queen of Italy and finding their etiquette something like that of 'a Jewish wedding on the East Side,' spending five rapturous hours astride a charger while the troops of the German Empire goose-stepped in review. Somewhere in the course of it all, he whisked through dozens of books, including Herbert Croly's *The Promise of American Life*." When Roosevelt returned to the United States, he invited Croly to lunch.

One can imagine the contrast. Edmund Wilson has left us a record of what a meeting with Croly could be like: "One's first encounters with Herbert Croly were likely to be rather baffling. It was never easy for him to deal with people, and if the visitor himself were at all diffident, he would be likely to find the conversation subsiding into a discontinuous series of remarks, more and more haltingly delivered by himself, to which Croly would mutter responses more and more fragmentary and more and more imperfectly audible. At last the visitor would lose heart and stop, and a terrible silence would ensue. The atmosphere would become taut with panic." Since *diffident* is not the word one readily assigns to Theodore Roosevelt, silence probably did not ensue, but rarely has American political life brought together two such opposites as the ebullient Teddy Roosevelt and the scholarly, withdrawn Herbert Croly. Nor should too much be made of the meeting. Croly has received credit for converting Roosevelt to the New Nationalism of the campaign of 1912, but Charles Forcey has shown conclusively that the relation between Croly and Roosevelt was a matter of similarity and not a matter of sequence of cause and effect. If Roosevelt was a function of his time, so was Croly; both the active politician and the intellectual in politics came by different paths through a common political landscape to their meeting.

Croly conforms closely to Richard Hofstadter's description of the "Mugwump" type, the educated, middle-class, Republican reformer whose impulse toward political action is as much moral and aesthetic as it is economic. But the generalization hides as much as it reveals; it hides the particulars of Croly's career. Before *The Promise of American Life* made Croly one of the important journalists of American politics, his preparation was remarkably inauspicious. His education at Harvard was undistinguished and interrupted, and Croly did not actually take a degree there until 1910 when the degree was largely a matter of recognition for his book. Before 1909, his writing was in the field of architecture and he worked as an editor of the *Architectural Record*, but that was a magazine founded by his father and the post seems not a matter of Croly's personal distinction. He was nearly forty before Croly found his role in life.

The most important formative influences on Croly were his parents, David Goodman Croly, an Irish immigrant, newspaperman, and reformer, to whom *The Promise of American Life* was dedicated, and Jane Cunningham Croly, an independent and aggressive woman who, writing under the pseudonym, Jenny June, was our first lady columnist as well as the editor of important women's magazines such as *Godey's Lady's Book*. David Goodman Croly was one of the leading American disciples of the ideas of Auguste Comte and young Herbert was actually baptized into the religion of humanity. Comteism was one of the many *systèmes* which bobbed to the surface in the wake of the social destruction of the French Revolution and the Napoleonic wars. Intellectuals sought by verbal incantation to contain the incipient social chaos and to provide some new principle to fill the vacuum left by the shattered authority of the Christian Church. Comte's thought was, broadly, an attempt to fuse the scientific positivism and belief in progress of the eighteenth-century enlightenment with the emotions and conservatism of a religious tradition. Comte saw himself as the prophet of a new epoch in the history of civilization founded socially on the peaceful power of industry, supported emotionally by a mystical vision of fraternity—a new Christianity stripped of supernaturalism—and administered by an intellectual elite. Although Herbert Croly explicitly rejected his father's faith in Comte's positivistic religion of humanity, one can still discern corresponding emphases in his book: his commitment to what he names at one point "the religion of human brotherhood," his acceptance of the energy and power of industrialism, and, most critically, his approval of leadership by an elite defined by personal excellence.

Croly's mother was probably most important, intellectually that is, for implanting in her son a marked insistence on the value of a job well done quite apart from any invidious pecuniary measure of worth. The epithets are, of course, Veblen's and the notion of satisfaction in craftsmanship apart from its cash reward was not peculiar to the Crolys. Charles Forcey has pointed out the influence on Croly of Robert Grant's novel, *Unleavened Bread* (1900), the story of the frustration of a potentially great architect by the stifling materialism of American culture. Forcey is correct in insisting that Croly's concern for politics grew largely out of his sense that America held excellence in little esteem and that Robert Grant's novel and Croly's reaction to it provide a convenient measure of the fact. But Croly did not have to turn to a novel to become aware in 1900 of the degrading effects of materialism in American culture. In 1883, Mrs. Croly, testifying before a Senate Committee on the relations between Labor and Capital, read into the record one of her own columns on the conditions of working girls in New York City. "It is an infinite pity," she said, "that all the appeals that are made to [workers], nearly all the evidence of sympathy that reaches them, come in the shape of demands for wages. . . . This has a distinctly detrimental influence . . . there is no enthusiasm for work, or the attainment of excellence, and the only object set before any employé is to do as little, and that as poorly as possible for the money he or she receives. This is immoral, and the results are as bad for employer as employed. It is not a question for the conscience of the worker whether the work is sufficiently paid; it is whether it is well done." Herbert Croly was to make that criterion the essential measure of the worth of a democratic culture. If American society did not nurture a disinterested concern for excellence in one's special calling, then American society would have failed to fulfill the promise of a democratic culture.

Croly was at Harvard in those golden years when William James, Josiah Royce, and George Santayana were all members of the department of philosophy. Santayana is named directly on the last page of *The Promise of American Life* as a witness to Croly's belief that "The principle of democracy *is* virtue." Although unnamed, the influence of James and Royce also pervades the pages of *The Promise of American Life*. Royce's book, *The Philosophy of Loyalty*, had been published just the year before Croly's and his notion that men must be loyal to something greater than themselves is implicit in Croly's insistence on loyalty to the nation. Comparing the nation to a vast school of collective experience, Croly insisted, in Roycean accents, that "everybody within the schoolhouse—masters, teachers, pupils and janitors, old pupils and young pupils, good pupils and bad, must feel one to another an indestructible loyalty." Underneath Royce's generalized claim for the need for loyalty, however, Croly speaks in the pragmatic and experimental voice of Royce's philosophical antagonist, William James. For James, the pragmatic test of the truth of an idea was the degree to which it performed a mediating function between old ideals and new experience. That idea was truest (for

James, truth was not absolute and admitted the comparative degree) which best performed this mediating role, which absorbed the maximum of new experience with a minimum jolt to the fund of old values. The pragmatic test is Croly's test again and again. Of the American creed, he wrote, "It must be constantly modified in order to define new experiences and renewed in order to meet unforeseen emergencies. But it should grow, just in so far as the enterprise itself makes new conquests and unfolds new aspects of truth. Democracy is an enterprise of this kind." Those words are in the spirit of William James. Yet the sentence preceding them is: "There can be nothing final about the creed unless there be something final about the action and purposes of which it is the expression." By yoking the two remarks, Croly accomplished the not inconsiderable feat of using both James and Royce to argue for a pragmatic and experimental quest in the spirit of loyalty for the ultimate good of the national interest.

Beside Croly's parents and his teachers at Harvard, who were, after all, the leading social philosophers of his time, there were other influences on the shaping of his thought, most notably John Jay Chapman to whom Croly pays explicit tribute in his book. But his yoking of James and Royce should alert us to the fact that Croly used books and ideas, used them to define his perceptions of the world he found about him and his purpose was wholly defined by his reaction to that world. His father may have schooled him in the religion of humanity, his mother may have held up to him the high standard of selfless excellence, Santayana and Royce and James may have provided him with concepts and an intellectual vocabulary, but American history presented him with a problem. To understand what that problem was takes us, as it did Croly, to *The Promise of American Life*.

The Promise of American Life is a tendentious book. Croly
has an end in view, and the sweeping summary of American history with which he begins his book points constantly to his
ultimate purpose, the economic, political, and moral reform of
American society. The argument is cumulative and Croly's historical chapters at the start are there to provide a solid foundation for Croly's new design for the structure of American society. Arthur Schlesinger, Jr., has made the same analogy: Croly
was interested in architecture and the merit of his style lies not
so much in the particular as in the architectonics of his general
plan.

The substance of the promise of American life consists, for
Croly, of three elements, "an improving popular economic condition, guaranteed by democratic political institutions, and resulting in moral and social amelioration." No one of the three
can be sacrificed. Democracy, however defined, must result in
generally shared economic benefits; the general welfare may
only be reached through the procedures of democratic institutions; both economic democracy and political democracy must
result in the improvement of the impalpable moral dimension
of American society, what one generally means by the quality
of American life. Croly's triadic definition is worth emphasizing at the start because his commitment to all three dimensions
of the promise of American life involves him ultimately in a
problem which resists a fully satisfying solution: how to reconcile individual personal excellence with popular democratic
institutions. But that is to anticipate the end of the argument.

Croly's first task is to persuade his reader that the reform he
is about to call for is not radical but is, instead, deeply conservative. That is, in rejecting much of the traditional way of
American life he lays claim to the sanction of being traditional
in a deeper and more important sense. He does so brilliantly by
insisting that *the* tradition in American life is the rejection of
tradition. The peculiarity of America has been not the brevity
of its history, he asserts, "but in the fact that from the begin-

ning it has been informed by an idea." Turning away from Europe and the traditions of the past, the American has from the start of his national experience been oriented toward the future, to the potential goal to be realized and not to the past achievement to be preserved. America is, as we say, the land of promise. "Thus," Croly argues, "the American's loyalty to the national tradition rather affirms than denies the imaginative projection of a better future." The American who does not have a "prophetic" outlook on the future, who does not cherish some ideal purpose yet to be realized, is un-American. "In cherishing the Promise of a better national future the American is fulfilling rather than imperiling the substance of the national tradition." The image of that better future "must in certain essential respects emancipate [Americans] from their past." The American may have to sacrifice traditional ways of realizing the vision of a better future, but it is that utopian vision which defines the American tradition, not the particular means used to achieve it.

What Croly wishes to repudiate is the optimistic fatalism which has led Americans to believe that a philosophy of drift will lead inevitably, under providential auspices, to a glorious conclusion. If the conditions of the present were the same as the past, perhaps so. But conditions have changed, and Americans must realize, says Croly, that the promise of a better future "will have to be planned and constructed rather than fulfilled of its own momentum." The sanguine notion that if each individual pursues his own self-interest he will, perforce, serve the general interest no longer persuades simply because the traditional American notion of individual freedom has led to "a morally and socially undesirable distribution of wealth." Croly's argument is pragmatic in the technical sense of judging an idea by its consequences, and interesting because he argues from no simple-minded notion of economic determinism. He is not simply saying that new conditions demand new values. He is saying that the new conditions are themselves the consequence of old values and one must begin by changing the values of American society before it is possible to affect the conditions. The transformation must go forward on both levels, of course, but Croly's emphasis is on the major importance of an *edifying*, to use his favorite word, constructive national purpose.

However unlike Theodore Roosevelt Herbert Croly was personally, he was close to him in one essential respect, his strenuous moralism. Croly derives from the same emphasis in American life as that triumphant boy-scout in the White House when he insists that if the promise of American life "is anything more than a vision of power and success, that addition must derive its value from a purpose; because in the moral world the future exists only as a workshop in which a purpose is to be realized." The words *moral* and *discipline* and *purpose* crowd Croly's pages because he speaks out of a considerable tradition in American political rhetoric. Like some latter-day Jeremiah, he has come to call Americans out of the corruption they have fallen into, to exhort them to return to their unfallen ways before they drift off into the pursuit of mere power and success. The tone has persisted in American life from John Winthrop to such various sons of the Puritans as John Foster Dulles and John Fitzgerald Kennedy. It provides the emotional background for Croly's reading of American history, because for him the American people can become a nation only in so far as they self-consciously commit themselves to a collective purpose.

Croly esteems Hamilton and dislikes Jefferson for this very reason. Hamilton, with all his faults, and Croly sees them clearly, had at least some conception of a national interest which was greater than the sum of individual interests. Jefferson's weakness, for Croly, is that he simply did not know what he was doing: he "sought an essentially equalitarian and even socialistic result by means of an essentially individualistic machinery." Hamilton failed because he violated one of the three constituent elements in the meaning of the promise of American life, respect for democratic institutions. But he had one great virtue: "He knew that the only method whereby the good could prevail either in individual or social life was by persistently willing that it should prevail and by the adoption of intelligent means to that end." Croly's problem ultimately becomes whether he can reconcile Hamiltonian means with Jeffersonian ends.

The polarity defined by Hamilton and Jefferson plagues all of American history in Croly's reading. He is at his scathing best with the middle period of American democracy, with the Jacksonians and the Whigs. The Jacksonians instinctively embodied a nationalistic impulse toward social democracy but mindlessly "expected to reach it by wholly negative means— that is, by leaving the individual alone." They succeeded politically because they embodied the aspirations and ethos of their time; they failed politically because they could not see that the impulse toward a national spirit "brought with it organization, and organization depended for its efficiency upon a classification of individual citizens according to ability, knowledge, and competence." The Whigs, on the other hand, suffered the double disaster of prostituting their political program to achieve popular success and then failed to win: "they abandoned their standards, and yet they failed to achieve success."

The hero of American history and the hero of *The Promise of American Life*, Croly's *beau ideal* for the possibilities of a fully developed democratic personality, is Abraham Lincoln. Lincoln is a type of "the kind of human excellence which a political and social democracy may and should fashion," fairly comparable with "the classic types of consummate personal distinction." In Croly's admiring hands, Lincoln becomes a symbol of the potential in American democratic culture, and Lincoln's role in the book is crucial. Croly wishes to destroy the image of Lincoln as "simply a bigger and better version of the plain American citizen." Not at all, insists Croly. It is true that one of Lincoln's great virtues is his humane and humble identification with his fellow Americans; such democratic identification with the people made Lincoln's political success. But in Croly's hands, Lincoln also becomes an indictment of the very people who gave Lincoln his triumph. The average American of Lincoln's day "was fundamentally a man who subordinated his intelligence to certain dominant practical interests and purposes. . . . He was wholly incapable either of disinterested or of concentrated intellectual exertion." Lincoln, on the contrary, "was precisely an example of high and disinterested intellectual culture." For Croly, the fact that Lincoln studied Euclid out on the American frontier makes him "in his way an intellectual gymnast." Lincoln "enjoyed the exertion for its own sake." Lincoln never became alienated from the average American, but he grew beyond him, became "more than an American," because he trained his intelligence "to enlighten his will."

Lincoln is not only the personal hero of *The Promise of American Life*, he is for Croly crucial to American history because his leadership of the North to victory against the moral evil of slavery led not just to the emancipation of the Negro but to the emancipation of "the American national ideal from an obscurantist individualism and provincialism." After Lincoln, Croly moves quickly to the present because the essential issue has been joined: whether the individual energy and democratic sentiment of the American people can be harnessed, through intellectual discipline and disinterested excellence, to the national good. Yet, for one hostile to the immoral consequences of the increasing concentration of great wealth in the hands of a few, Croly takes a tolerant view of the men of great wealth in the latter nineteenth century. He anticipates modern historical scholarship in stressing the contributions of industrial statesmen as well as the evils of the Robber Barons. The railroad, the emergence of a national market, the economies of scale pushed America away from a society of roughly equal individuals of great energy and untutored capacity toward a society of economic organization and the specialization of skills. The danger was the emergence of classes, of "social classification," as Croly put it, but the advantages were obvious, given Croly's predilections.

The dangers were the result of the license given unscrupulous energy by the old tradition of individual action free from social restraint, but "the concentrated leadership, the partial control, the thorough organization thereby effected, was not necessarily a bad thing. It was in some respects a decidedly good thing, because leadership of any kind has certain intrinsic advantages." Croly recognized that economic concentration of power had the practical advantage of eliminating the waste of competitive capitalism and the possible advantage of providing the instrument of economic organization for the service of the American people. In the absence of any public sentiment for social control, he saw no reason to point an accusing finger at those who profited greatly. The Robber Barons were simply "cultivated plants" which had grown up riotously in the "American political and economic garden" under the "traditional methods of cultivation." Like Marx, Croly saw the excesses of industrial capitalism as a necessary stage in the evolution toward a higher kind of social organization; he saw virtue in necessity, even if to conclude that unchecked economic power had finally to be made subservient to the general welfare.

The great virtue of industrial and economic organization for Croly was that it demanded expertness and not "mere energy, untutored enthusiasm, and good-will." The experts required by new circumstances had to depend upon "careful training and single-minded devotion to a special task, and at the same time proper provision had to be made for coordinating the results of this highly specialized work. More complete organization necessarily accompanied specialization. The expert became a part of a great industrial machine. His individuality tended to disappear in his work. His interests became those of a group." The sequence was, for Croly, not only in the nature of things; it was admirable—so long, that is, as the American people could be aroused to see to it that the interests of the group were expanded to the interests of the whole people.

The future Croly envisaged as the satisfaction of the promise of American life did not include the dismantlement of large scale economic organization. He had nothing but contempt for the reactionary vision of William Jennings Bryan; unlike the later position of Woodrow Wilson and Louis Brandeis, he thought that to restore economic competition, as in the Sherman Anti-Trust Law, was not to institute a reform but "simply a species of higher conservatism." This is not to say he did not see dangers. He wrote his book because he did. He recognized that the earlier homogeneity of the American people had given way to the distinction of classes. He recognized the political dangers of uncontrolled economic power in the hands of irresponsible men. He recognized the degrading influence of a standard which measured worth only by wealth. Yet he accepted the new conditions of specialization and organization in economics and politics and labor because they "imposed discipline upon the individual." They forced the individual to become a specialized instrument and to find his place through cooperative activity with others. For Croly, this was the path to true individuality as well as to the collective good. "Individual distinction, resulting from the efficient performance of special work, is not only the foundation of all genuine individuality, but is usually of the utmost social value."

Before turning to Croly's solution of "the social problem," the danger of economic privilege to the general social good and the viability of democracy, it is worth emphasizing the transvaluation of values he has engineered in his treatment of American history. At the beginning when Americans spoke of freedom, they used the word in the classical liberal sense. One was free to the degree he was free from restraints by others. The definition is essentially negative in the sense that the conditions of freedom are conditions of freedom *from* control. This was the ideal of the Jeffersonians and the Jacksonians whose political battle-cry was "That government is best which governs least." The notion of freedom extended to society as well as to the state. The single individual was primary and society was secondary. One was an individual to the degree that he was free from involvement with others, except those casual associations he voluntarily chose to affiliate with. The apologist for this position was Emerson, and its symbol, as Croly saw, was Jackson.

For Croly, freedom and individualism take on an opposite meaning. Freedom becomes positive in its connotation; that is, one is free to do that which is good. One becomes free, one becomes an individual, by discovering that function which best furthers the good of the collective group, however defined. For Croly, the group to whom ultimate loyalty is due is the nation, and perhaps the severest criticism of Croly is that his imagination reached no further than the nation-state as the highest and best form of human association. In this reading of the meaning of freedom, one is an individual to the degree that he participates in society. The individual literally becomes himself, achieves his identity, through the process of national collective action. Throughout *The Promise of American Life*, the former definition is named as "destructive" individualism, the latter, "constructive" individualism. In the background of his thought, Croly has some notion of society as an organism. Further, he not only accepted, he celebrated the complex, interdependent world of a technological society because it realized his ideal of the relation of the individual to society.

In Croly's usage, then, the center of reference shifts from the self to society, from the spontaneous, unfettered, undisciplined individual to the disciplined, controlled, trained individual. The shift verges toward a danger and Croly is not immune to its risks. This danger is that the nation, the national interest, will become so diffuse in its meaning that actual individuals will be sacrificed in the name of some indefinable higher good. Croly's language often conveys just such a threat. It is one thing to say the nation must go to school to learn its lessons; it is another to say that "the exigencies of such schooling frequently demand severe coercive measures, but what schooling does not?" In comparing the nation to the inevitable ship of state, Croly can write: "Even the best of [Americans] have not learned the name of its ultimate destination, the full difficulties of the navigation, or the stern discipline which may eventually be imposed upon the ship's crew." Or, again, in the battle and the risk to achieve the promise of American life, "the heroes of the struggle must maintain their achievements and at times even promote their objects by compulsion." The note Croly sounds at the outset, "like all sacred causes, [the American ideal] must be propagated by the Word and by that right arm of the Word, which is the Sword," reverberates all through the pages of *The Promise of American Life*, even if only in a minor key.

Yet Croly could not, finally, go back on his definition of the promise of American life. An elite, armed with coercive power, could effect a more equal distribution of the economic goods of society; it might even force men to be better than they are. But it would have violated the middle term of Croly's three-part definition: "guaranteed by democratic political institutions." Croly's ultimate problem is how to get people to accept his vision of functional freedom, of self-realization through self-disciplined acceptance of a good larger than one's own immediate, selfish good. What can one do to jolt Americans out of the optimistic fatalism which Croly saw all about him? How could one achieve the national interest without the sacrifice of democracy and without destroying the promise of American life in the very desperate attempt to realize it?

Croly did not accept a populistic, majoritarian notion of democracy. "The popular and the national interests must necessarily in some measure diverge." Majority rule had no binding moral authority for Croly. He wished to substitute the concept, national sovereignty, for popular sovereignty. "The people are not Sovereign as individuals," he wrote. "They are not Sovereign in reason and morals even when united into a majority. They become Sovereign only in so far as they succeed in reaching and expressing a collective purpose." At this point, Croly has set foot on the royal road to anti-democratic thought and the fact that his program is best described as a form of national socialism, with its contemporary connotations, has led some to see fascist leanings in Croly. But, although he set a foot in that direction, Croly refuses to go further. He remains, at bottom, obstinately an American democrat.

What Croly finally comes to is simply an act of faith. He exhorts each person to pursue excellence in whatever work or place he finds himself and to transform his fellows, educate them, by virtue of his example. This may seem perilously close to the position Croly rejects, the notion that if each man pursues his individual interest he will somehow further the general interest. But Croly is not being simply pious when, at the conclusion of *The Promise of American Life*, he asks the general American citizen to become something of a hero or a saint. He dissents from the mediocrity of American life, but he dissents as one of "the children of the Faith," one who believes that human nature is such that man, if freed from the ignoble standard of the selfish accumulation of wealth, is capable of choosing to pursue excellence and the good of all men. The appeal would be pious if Croly were not willing to engage in the many radical reforms he proposes throughout his book: the

redistribution of wealth through confiscatory taxation, the so-
cialization of areas of natural monopoly in the economy, the
limitation of individual income to a decent maximum and, most
radically, given the traditional American emphasis on work and
success, the guarantee to each citizen of "a certain minimum of
economic power and responsibility."

These were radical demands on the traditional ways of
American society but for Croly they were simply pragmatic
means by which society acted now (it might act differently
after the fact) to realize the possibility of a better society, better morally as well as economically, a society in which each
man did his best to further the good of his fellow man. The
challenge Croly put to his America has not yet been answered
in our America. The piety is familiar but the political action
which might translate rhetoric into reality remains yet to be
taken.

PART IV

THE VALUES OF AMERICAN CULTURE: THE INTELLECTUAL AND THE UNIVERSITY

1

THE INTELLECTUAL:
CLERIC OR CRITIC?

IS THE MAIN FUNCTION of the University teaching—that is, the transmission of knowledge and the values of the culture to future generations? Or, is the main function of the University research, the discovery of new knowledge? The tension generated between those two questions we recognize as basic to the definition of any institution of higher learning. It is a tension that has a long history which derives from different ways of looking at the University, different ways of looking at the meaning of education, different ways of looking at the nature of mind itself.

One view had it—and to venture a sweeping generalization, one may say it was the dominant view from the time of Plato to nearly the end of the eighteenth century—that the educated man was that man best conversant with the classics of Western civilization. His triumph was to be a cultivated gentleman, an embodiment in the present of the vitality of a tradition to which he adapted himself. He did not presume to create his own norms. He did not search for new principles of action.

315

Rather, he sought to discover the rules for right action by a careful scrutiny of the past. He conformed to its prescriptions. He was, in other words, a traditionalist.

Somewhere toward the end of the eighteenth century, and markedly by the nineteenth, the conception of the nature of the intellectual underwent a dramatic shift. The intellectual or artist became someone who was original, who escaped the rules of the schools, who transcended the limits of convention, whether intellectual or social, and embodied novelty and variety in his work, perhaps even in his personality. The notion, set forth at the beginning by Plato and which had ruled for so long, that works of thought or imagination were imitations of some reality outside the self, gave way to the notion that the self, the individual genius, unencumbered by the past or convention or the demands of society, was the source of truth or beauty. The classical ideal of learning as the assimilation of and preservation of the past gave way to the modern notion of learning as the discovery of the new.

That is a sweeping sketch of a long and complicated tradition, one in which I have left out all the shading and preserved only the starkest outlines. But let me point to a way, a homely way, in which we in the University are still involved in the terms of this confusion about the meaning of knowledge and the meaning of education. We are, wittingly or unwittingly, products of past history. The only virtue in the study of the past is to make us more aware, more self-conscious, of the complexities and dimensions of our problems in the present. Only those willfully innocent of history are surprised to discover that their day-to-day problems are old problems, indeed, and that the terms were set down long ago.

Today, one of the demands of those who teach in the University is that they do scholarship which, as the pat phrase has it, is an original contribution to knowledge. Among my own acquaintance in the profession, there are hardly one or two who have made an original contribution to knowledge, if we take the word "original" in any serious sense. I would go further and say for 99 and 44/100 percent of the faculty I know, that if they had a truly original idea, it would present such a threat to all their established and comfortable notions they would be so embarrassed by its presence they would hardly know where to put it, where in the desk to hide it away.

What I say will surely come as no surprise to anyone in education, and yet—and yet—we persist in the notion that the University must seek a faculty that is on the frontiers of knowledge, striking out in new directions, leading us by the light of their original minds. The man who modestly sets himself the still enormously ambitious task of assimilating what others have said, the lessons of the past, of becoming, in other words, a responsible embodiment of the tradition of the past, the man who does not presume to be an "original," who is content to write books setting forth what he has learned and how he thinks it bears upon the present, such a man is hard put to find a name for the calling he modestly pursues that does not seem mildly depreciatory, mildly condescending. The word "dilettante" today is simply pejorative. We forget that it derives from the meaning, "to take delight in." Like the word "amateur": one who is in love with something. Can we look about ourselves and say candidly that our society would be the poorer if more of us took a delight in things of the mind and objects of the imagination? Today we need desperately what once was meant by the amateur and the dilettante, but we are so afraid of words like conventional and traditional that we refuse to admit the worth of such a personality.

Yet we feel still the pull, the emotional claim, of the opposite position, which insists that in a world of drastic, whirling change the past is no sure guide and that we must face, right front and courageously, the demands of new experience and new situations which demand new ideas and new modes of action. That double allegiance—on the one side to the notion of the University as the conservator of tradition, most especially in its teaching function, and on the other side to the notion of the University as the innovator and explorer of the new, most especially in its research function—that double allegiance takes us to the heart of the matter, to a tension implicit in the very nature of the University, a tension in the very nature of the life of the intellectual.

To define the tension that I think is inherent in the nature of the University, even in the life of the mind, I have to begin with that dread word, conformity. We are terribly fearful of conformity. We are sure it is all about us. We know all about the mass society, but we never see our face in that faceless mass of others who are conformists. It is always others who conform, not us, and it is a terrible thing to be one of the others. Yet, at least half the reason the University came into being in society was to make some like others, that is, to shape the present generation into an acceptance of the needs and the mores of society, to make it, in other words, conform to the expectations of society. As historians today like to put it, the University is a function of its society. That puts it the way intellectuals like to put it, abstractly. Specification is better.

The oldest, the earliest, of European Universities was devoted to medicine; its purpose was to train doctors. In England, at Cambridge, in the year 1316, a college was founded for the express and special purpose of providing clerks for the King's service. At our own Cambridge, in Massachusetts, Harvard was founded in 1636 to provide a learned ministry to preach the word of God when the day came that the original clerical band had died out. When Harvard was debauched by the seductions of infidelity and deserted the Congregational faith for Unitarianism, colleges like Amherst sprang up in the western part of the state to preserve young men in the ways of their fathers and to protect them from the Babylonian corruption of Boston and Harvard Yard. Finally, our whole magnificent system of public, state-supported Universities had its origins in the Morrill Act, the land-grant legislation by the Federal Government in 1862, for the express purpose in the words of that legislation "to teach such branches of learning as are related to agriculture and the mechanic arts . . . in order to promote the liberal and practical education of the industrial classes."

From Europe, through England, to our own country, institutions of learning have come into being to serve the needs of their society. Here the relation is direct and pragmatic. Universities have trained doctors and clerks and clerics because society wanted and needed doctors and clerks and clerics. Today we need businessmen and engineers and physicists and the Universities will go on as they always have and train men in the skills necessary to meet the demands of their society. At this level, the adaptation of the University to the demands of the society, its conformity, if you will, to the imperatives of society, is direct and largely, I think, untroublesome.

But there is another and deeper way in which the University, and all education, acts as agent in the process we call perhaps by other names but which we may call conformity. That is, education from top to bottom, from the earliest years to the latest years, is an agent, and an increasingly important agent in our world, of initiating the oncoming generation into the mores and values of the culture—our way of life, as we like to say. Quite apart from the skills it may teach or the expertise it may train, education ceaselessly initiates the young into society by instructing the student in the system of thought and imagery that underlies the values and aims of the culture. It provides considerable emotional sanction for prescribed forms of social behavior; it brings the student into close and intimate relation with intangible loyalties—the ethos, the principles, the approved norms of society. Education, in this perspective, is simply one of the ways, as Bernard Bailyn has stressed, in which a society, a culture, transmits itself across generations. The faculty, in this view, belongs—to use a favorite word of Coleridge's—to the clerisy, that is, the clerks of tradition whose job it is to transmit the past to the future, to maintain the traditions and the values of the culture that supports them. The faculty and the University are, in this view, the personal and institutional representatives of society to maintain and give expression to the values of the culture. Because of that role, they enjoy a high degree of social esteem as well as material support as the official spokesmen of the culture.

But once you set a man to thinking, curious things are bound to happen. At this point an ironic consequence follows. In the very act that society assigns the intellectual, that is, in preserving and transmitting the values of the culture, in expressing and giving voice to the values that inform the culture, intellectuals are driven inevitably toward heresy. One needs to be careful here. By heresy I do not mean simply the out-of-hand rejection of, the mindless rebellion against, the values of the culture, but something much more complex. In the very act of formulating and articulating the values of the culture, the intellectual is driven to see tensions and even contradictions within the system of values that society knows and cherishes as tradition. The intellectual makes society uncomfortable because he makes it face choices between goods, different values, neither of which it wishes to surrender. But the intellectual, once you set him the task of giving voice to the meaning of tradition, will point out that one cannot always have it both ways. To use a simple example: as a society, we esteem both liberty and equality, but the historian will quickly remind us that only in special social and economic circumstances may we enjoy both, that at different moments one may have to give way to the other. In other words, in recovering the tradition, the intellectual makes us, at least those who will listen, realize that tradition, our way of life, is no simple unitary thing to be carried comfortably about like a tape in our pocket to measure our approximation to or our deviation from tradition in our actions in the present. Instead, tradition suddenly turns into an elastic measuring rod, relative to the conditions of the present. Its definition is not simply a matter of turning to sacred texts and reading what is writ there. It is, rather, a matter of serious commitment to the present as well as to the past. So, even as cleric, even as conservator of and embodiment of the tradition of the past, the intellectual is, in accepting that role, plunged deeply and inevitably into the battles of his own time.

Let me offer a simple example of what I mean when I say that the intellectual in recovering and giving voice to the values and the tradition of a culture does, in that very act, become a critic of tradition. The example has to do with a single event in the year 1893, the World's Columbian Exposition, the Chicago World's Fair, the famous White City built on the shores of Lake Michigan to celebrate the four hundredth anniversary of when Columbus sailed the ocean blue and blundered onto America. The organizers for the Fair did have a formal opening in 1892 to preserve the round symmetry of the year but the Fair did not actually open until 1893. A great deal went on at that Fair which is of considerable interest to the student of American culture, but I want to use just two matters connected with it.

First, this was the place where in 1893 the great American historian, Frederick Jackson Turner, delivered his famous paper, "The Significance of the Frontier in American History," a thesis so influential in the interpretation of American history that it is fair to say that it dominated the writing of American history for forty years, until it came under attack in the Great Depression.

Second, the Fair, marking four hundred years of American experience, was supposed to signal the coming of age of American society, to dramatize its place among the civilized nations of the world, so it stimulated Nathaniel S. Shaler to put together a large three-volume work, done by many hands, called *The United States of America*. Shaler was a professor of geology at Harvard University and Dean of the Lawrence Scientific School; he was, in other words, a member of the establishment, and he brought together some of the best minds of his time in what is one of the first and one of the best cooperative attempts to write the history of the United States.

To get at a problem in the definition of the meaning of the American tradition, let me deal with each one separately and then array them one against the other. Turner's thesis, put bluntly in his first formulation of it, was that "the existence of an area of free land, its continuous recession, and the advance of American settlement westward, explain American development." It is obvious what Turner is trying to do. He wants to turn the attention of Americans away from Europe, away from the past, and turn it toward America, toward the constant, ongoing process of the making of America. He is also arguing a kind of ecological determinism: contact with the frontier gives rise, as he put it in his essay, to "the really American part of our experience." So, he writes, "American development has been continually beginning over again on the frontier. This perennial rebirth, this fluidity of American life, this expansion westward with its new opportunities, its continuous touch with the simplicity of primitive society, furnish the forces dominating the American character. The true point of view in the history of this nation is not the Atlantic Coast, it is the Great West."

Even one not familiar with Turner's writings will recognize that he speaks out of a considerable emphasis in American thought. The notion at work in Turner's reading of American history is that the American is a man who escapes from Europe to seize the opportunity for a fresh start, the chance to begin over again. The movement out of society to a world unencumbered by form and tradition and social restraint is reenacted again and again as the characteristic American takes his way West. If one will imagine, if one will call up before one's mind's eye, a map of the Western world, one gets a sharper sense of the dramatic tableau that Turner describes. Across the Atlantic Ocean stands Europe; westward lies the New World, America. In the sequence Turner relates, Europe stands for society, tradition, restraint, the lethargy of the past, the system of classes, inequality, undemocratic and irresponsible rule by kings and aristocrats. To sum it up, Europe stands for the enervation and corruption of a decadent civilization. To the West, though, stand freedom, spontaneity, simplicity, the self-reliance of the individual, equality, innocence—no less than, to use Turner's language, a perennial rebirth. To sum it up, the beneficent power of unfallen nature.

Turner is not simply saying this is the way things went. He is saying it is good this is the way things went. He is putting forth a way of looking at the meaning of American experience and saying this is the really American part of our experience. He asks us to share in his definition of the meaning of what it is to be an American.

But if the movement out of society, away from the East when it becomes more and more like Europe, the movement toward nature and the frontier is, as Turner insists it is, the really American part of our experience, then consider what this reading of the American tradition leaves out. The world of Western frontier farmers leaves out, one hardly need be reminded, Boston and New York and Philadelphia and Charleston. It leaves out, it even gladly rejects, the contribution Europe has made to the development of our national experience. It leaves out a number of Americans: Hawthorne and Melville, Henry James, Willard Gibbs and Henry Adams. It leaves out, in other words, a range of experience and attitudes that are indispensable to the realization of our stature as fully developed human beings. It leaves out the consideration of sophisticated ideas and all art. It leaves out no less than the sense of the past itself and its embodiment in tradition. Finally, and most obviously, it leaves out the city and the technology that was implicit in the urban, industrial Chicago where Turner stood when he spoke. All these are somehow not really American.

Leaving Turner for the moment as I have described the major thrust of his thought, let me turn to my second instance,

Nathaniel Shaler's three volumes, *The United States of America*. There was another way to read the meaning of the American historical experience, one that runs counter to Turner's reading, and one that is symbolized in the physical format of Shaler's three volumes. In putting together the three volumes of which he was general editor, Shaler picked a lithograph as frontispiece for each volume. For Volume I, he chose Christopher Columbus, the discoverer of the New World; Volume II, Samuel F. B. Morse, identified as the inventor; Volume III, Henry Wadsworth Longfellow, the poet. The selection of the three figures is not accidental; the contents of the volumes are organized in the same fashion. Volume I deals with the geography of the New World and its abundant natural resources; Volume II deals with the exploitation of the land, the emergence of industry and technology, the development of America's transportation network and the maturation of its economy; Volume III deals with the political system and, finally, the achievements of Americans in literature and art.

If one considers it, one can see that Shaler, both in the illustration he chooses to put at the front of each of his three volumes and in the material he thinks appropriate to the successive volumes, has in mind a theory of history that is implicit in the format of *The United States of America*. It is, simply, a view of American history that sees it as the record of the advance of civilization through fixed stages. First, we have the discovery and the natural setting, then the economic development of the material base of society, leading to the achievement of a political order and the flowering of the arts and the imagination. The sequence is symbolized by the discoverer, the inventor and the poet. The meaning of America is the advance of civilization into higher and higher forms.

If one imagines again that map of the Western world, one will see that in Shaler's vision of American history the terms of the contrast between East and West are the reverse of Turner's. The western edge of advancing settlement no longer stands for the moment of rebirth and life-giving simplicity. Now, the western edge of advancing civilization represents the undeveloped beginnings, the rude and primitive start of a process, the culmination of which lies East, presumably all the way east in Europe where the process has achieved its full development in a rich culture of art and intelligence and sophisticated social forms.

Shaler's three volumes epitomize, in other words, a view of the meaning of America as the advance of civilization into a raw and savage continent. He is thinking within the frame of reference of a theory of progress, while Turner's interpretation of American history belongs to a species of primitivism.

Yet if, as I have said about Turner, there is in the frontier interpretation of our history a threat, even a denial, of the life of the mind, a depreciation of critical and sophisticated forms of intelligence and imagination, there is a subtler threat lurking in Shaler's reading of the meaning of America. Like many Americans, of his time and ours, he presumes that physical and economic advance will somehow inevitably result in cultural achievement. To put it vulgarly, his theory of fixed and chronological stages of advance says that you have to get the plant built first, you have to take care of the business of the world which is business, and after all that is done, then you have time for literature and thought. Then the last stage will arise inevitably. He is optimistic, of course, grandly so. But he is also a fatalist, and a theory of inevitable, fixed progress makes it possible to concentrate now on business and profit and work because sometime, sometime in the future, of course, we will have time for philosophy and art and scholarship. Fully developed intelligence comes at the end. It does not interfere in the world's work now. Despite the fact that the poet is held up to be the final goal, he is put off to the end. He is a luxury to be afforded later after men of the world finish dealing with first things first.

Turner and Shaler, therefore, present different readings of

the meaning of American history, antithetical interpretations of the meaning of what is American about America. One will quickly recognize, of course, that they are simply particular spokesmen for, representative examples of, attitudes that are much more deeply rooted in American culture than their individual instances. If this were not so, if they did not participate in a much more widely socially shared way of understanding American experience, one may presume they would not have looked at American history in the different ways they did. Because from the beginning of our history there have been two ways to read the meaning of the American experience.

As the first settlers set out from the Old World to the New, they were both leaving an old home and seeking a new one. Universally, in all human experience, the voyage or the trip has lent itself to easy translation into the metaphor of the quest, a symbolic quest for the meaning of it all. One thinks of the wandering tribes of Israel in the Old Testament, Homer's Ulysses, Bunyan's Pilgrim, Don Quixote. The metaphor is probably basic to shared human experience, but it has been especially characteristic of the American version. From Whitman tramping the open road to the adventures of Saul Bellow's Augie March, the best of our imaginative writing has been organized around metaphors of setting out and venturing forth into the new and the unknown. Until the twentieth century the metaphor seemed hardly metaphor at all. It conformed so closely to our historical experience that it seemed a fair description of American reality.

But the meaning of a journey out of the Old World into the New always had a certain doubleness to it, an inevitable ambivalence. One valuation had it, as in Turner, that the movement westward into a virgin land meant the rejection of Europe and the past. In this reading of our collective experience, the past stood for the snobbery of social classes, feudalism, rule by irresponsible aristocrats and kings, the craft of priests, institutional complexity and social decadence; the New World, the

future, stood for the equality of all men, the abolition of invidious social distinction, freedom, spontaneity, simplicity and
vigor.

Yet at the same time, as in Shaler, there was another way to
read our experience. Here, America meant the advance of the
best of civilization, choice seed sifted from the Old World for
planting in the New, as the Puritans had it, the advance of civilization into a raw and savage continent. In this reading the
American venture meant the progress of reason, order, enlightenment and cultivation, an extension of civilization into a wild,
untamed and savage continent where law was absent and barbarism posed a constant danger to the achievement of human
order.

Not only were the terms of the evaluation different; they
pointed in different directions in space and in time. For the
first the geographic locus of value was West, the frontier, and
beyond it the unfallen innocence of an Edenic world; for the
second, the point of reference was East, toward a developed
society of urbanity and sophistication. Such a stark formulation suggests an "either-or" appraisal, and one may ask impatiently, which was it? But the question is a false one historically, and it may even be a false one humanly. Americans saw
the matter of their experience both ways; they assumed the
best of both. That is, Americans have from the beginning of
their national experience affirmed their culture at one and the
same time as both a return to the harmony of a simple and
equalitarian society and an advance in the power and achievements of a complex civilization. The ambivalence runs from
the politics of Thomas Jefferson to the New Frontier of John
Fitzgerald Kennedy; it helps to account for the persistent nostalgia for a presumably better past, somehow just lost, somehow just behind us, which permeates our industrial and technological society as well as provides the theme for some of our
best imaginative literature.

All this brief excursion into the interpretation of American history has done is to suggest what starts to happen as soon as the intellectual turns to the past and begins to attempt to determine what tradition means. He discovers, as I have already said, that "tradition" is no unitary thing. He will discover and make us aware of tensions and contradictions implicit in the past of which Americans living in the past may not themselves have been fully aware. Even if he stops there, he confronts us with the need to take thought, the need to consider and to address the tension that persists into our own present and to attempt a resolution of it in some way in present action. Even as cleric of the past, even as one who holds up the past for our contemplation, the intellectual becomes troublesome.

But as I have indicated in my remarks about Turner and Shaler, the intellectual does considerably more than that. He inevitably goes on to imagine a better, a more appealing sequence of events which did not take place. He passes judgment and appeals to us to share that judgment on what at first he seems simply to describe. For example, however different the interpretations of the meaning of American experience in the frontier interpretation and in the theory of the progress of civilization, both curiously share one common attribute. They both present decerebrated views of the meaning of American history, views of history in which mind and intelligence and imagination have little or no place: Turner more markedly, of course, since intellect and feeling are not the qualities that characterize his simple society of untutored practical energy; but Shaler's view of history also implicitly relegates feeling and imagination and intelligence to some future date when we can afford the luxury of such activity. Different as they are in other ways, both participate in the constant American emphasis on practical action in the present, both are in different ways anti-intellectual, both represent a threat to the importance of intelligence in day-to-day life.

So the intellectual, and by extension the University, becomes a critic of society, not only by insisting that the study of the past raises problems for understanding in the present, but, more severely, by saying that the traditions of the past may themselves be a hindrance to the present, a source of our confusion, a block to our desire to create a humane and decent world.

The intellectual, in other words, in formulating the meaning of tradition, is led to imagine alternative lines of development that did not take place and that to him, whether aesthetically, or ethically, or politically, seem more admirable. He becomes, in other words, a critic of tradition, and, by necessity, a critic of his society. In the attempt to present, systematically and coherently, the general ground for values and beliefs, which only intermittently holds the attention and engages the passions of most men, not only in our culture but in all cultures —in this very attempt the intellectual becomes not only the conveyor of traditional values but critic of the very values he wishes to convey. So we, as intellectuals in the University, are caught finally in the unsettling posture of being inside and outside our society, passionately committed to it, yet by that very passion inevitably somewhat alienated from it. We are inside and outside our culture at one and the same time, balancing in the situation in which we find ourselves opposite and opposed demands. Little wonder that the society that supports us should be uneasy about what we are up to and little wonder we cannot easily say whether the main function of the University is the preservation of the old or the discovery of the new, whether the intellectual in the University is to be cleric or critic. What at first may seem to be opposites turn into one and the same activity. They represent not opposites, but poles which define the field of energy we name the intellectual life, the field of power we name the University.

2

THE UNIVERSITY:
THE TROUBLE WITH
HIGHER EDUCATION

BERKELEY IS NOW a symbol in the full sense of the word, that is, an image which condenses a complex range of ideas and emotions and presents it for our contemplation. Berkeley is a symbol of the necessities and the possibilities which confront higher education in the United States today. In this sense, Berkeley is now a convenient shorthand name for the internal structural strains and the external social demands which trouble every university and college in the country. If it were not, if the explosion of student unrest and the painful grinding to a halt of one of the world's great universities were purely local phenomena, Berkeley would soon have passed from the front pages of the national press and soon been forgotten. But the torrent of books and articles about the meaning of what happened at Berkeley poured forth because Berkeley dramatized a national and not a local problem. Higher education in the United States is today—always granting the fond hope that war will not obliterate all other social matters and make them inconsequential—the most important institution in American society as we enter the second half of the twentieth century. The claim is large but not extravagant. And Berkeley symbolizes the crucial fact that higher education is in trouble.

One way to measure the social importance of higher education in the United States today is simply to attend to the many voices talking about it, voices which have little in common except a subject. For examples: for the business community, Merrill Lynch, *et al.*, having learned from Fritz Machlup, the Princeton economist, that apart from defense the "knowledge industry" comprises the single largest and fastest growing sector of the Gross National Product, speak with optimism of the new and expanding "horizons" for investment opportunity in education; at the liberal center, Walter Lippmann writes in the *New Republic* that the only institution left to fill the void left by the dissolution of traditional authority in the modern world is the university; on the "new" left, the late C. Wright Mills, dismayed by the bourgeois aspirations of the laboring classes, claimed the new class of intellectuals created by advanced education as the only possible base for a new radicalism in modern politics. In short, the university is asked to bear the responsibility for economic growth, for cultural cohesion and identity, and for radical social change. The burden, however shortly named, is awesome and it is the burden which for a moment broke Berkeley, and it is the burden which weighs on the back of every institution of higher learning in the country.

At least since Quintilian took education out of the hands of the Roman *paterfamilias* and put it at the service of the Emperor Vespasian to restore the sober virtues of the early Roman Republic and to create the good citizen, education has inevitably been political. From the beginning, in our own society education has had a special task thrust upon it. Scholars like Lawrence Cremin and Bernard Bailyn have rescued the history of education in America from accounts of pedagogical and curricular changes to remind us of what we should never have forgotten: education is one of the major institutions in society to create order and to accommodate change. And change has been about the only constant throughout American history. The centrifugal force of expansion across a virgin continent, the shattering of elite leadership by an egalitarian democratic ideology, the sudden transition from an agrarian to an industrial society, the need to acculturate millions of newly arrived immigrants, all these massive forces of social history have pushed and pulled American education throughout its turbulent history, but mainly at the lower levels, in the common grade school and the public high school. Now the tides of change are washing over the colleges and the universities.

When Fitz Machlup speaks of the knowledge industry, he refers to any person employed in the production and distribution of ideas, which makes room for Madison Avenue and *Time* and *Life* and radio and television networks. In that company, most colleges and universities are small as well as uncomfortable, but however sniffish the academic intellectual may be about such enterprises, one thing is clear. However "educational" they may or may not be, they cannot survive without the pool of labor which higher education creates.

But higher education, even in its own terms, is an enormous business. In 1870, there were about 300 colleges and universities in the country with little more than 5,000 professors and 50,000 students. Less than two percent of the eighteen to twenty-one age group (conventionally used to define the potential college population) were enrolled. By World War II, the number of institutions had become 1,690, the number of students rose to one and a third million, and those in attendance to 14 percent. In 1964, there were about 2,100 degree-granting institutions of higher education, 400,000 faculty members and almost five million students, around 40 percent of their age group. Current projections for 1970 predict a student population of 7 million, almost one-half of all young men and women between eighteen and twenty-one in the United States.

Why? Partly, as President Johnson insisted recently, because one version of democracy insists that education is a right not a privilege and that all should have it. But ideals, however deeply cherished, generally produce slender results unless they are attached to significant social and economic forces, and the massive movement of young people into higher education in the United States today is no exception. Intelligence is now as important as capital in economic development and economic growth. John Kenneth Galbraith recently argued at a conference in England that the financial power of the large corporation is today less important than the quality of the organization itself and that this depends directly on the intellectual capacity, the training, and the skills of the individuals who constitute the organization. So, indirectly, let alone directly in the contract research it does for government and the consulting its faculty does for business, the university is now the chief source of innovation in the American economy. Closely related to that economic fact is the social fact that prestige in society, one's "class" in our open and "classless" society, is largely a function of one's educational level. Economic opportunity and social privilege are the engine of change, even if democratic ideology is the switchman who determines where the traffic is going.

Practical and Ideal Service

If economic and social pressures were all there were to the problem, then the problem—the sheer matter of numbers— would be enormously difficult but surely not insurmountable. Money would take care of it once society was made to see the advantage. But Lippmann's point complicates the matter. Society needs more than trained intelligence simply to serve its necessary functions. The university cannot neglect that practical need, but society finally will not allow it to neglect a still greater need. Lippmann puts it succinctly: "The dissolution of the ancestral order and the dethronement of usage and authority in modern society have left us dependent upon man's ability to understand and govern his own fate." To do so, man needs more than specialized training and marketable skill; he needs a generalized capacity to think and to judge and to see beyond the constrictions of his own moment in time. If modern man is to develop the capacity to be free in a world where customary usage and traditional ways no longer chart his course, he needs, in other words, a liberal education. Lippmann is asking the colleges and universities to do no less than to provide what Plato called the "royal science," the knowledge needed by the rulers of the state, in an age when Everyman is King. Professors may flinch from the arrogant assumption that the task is theirs, but it is hard to see who else there is to accept it. The Family? The Church? The political parties of liberal democratic politics? To ask the question is to answer it and to name the void which Lippmann thinks only an ideal liberal education can fill. Education must, if only by default, create the free intelligence which is capable of using the social and political freedom which is still our ideal if not yet our reality.

To do so, however, may serve society in the long run but challenge it in the short, and it is precisely this conflict between practical and ideal service to society which lies at the bottom of student unrest from the great urban university like Berkeley to the small private college in its pastoral setting like Amherst. "The specialization of function and knowledge," declared the Students for a Democratic Society at Port Huron, Michigan, in 1962, "admittedly necessary to our complex technological and social structure, has produced an exaggerated compartmentalization of study and understanding. This has contributed to an overly parochial view, by faculty, of the role of its research and scholarship, to a discontinuous and truncated understanding, by students, of the surrounding social order; and to a loss of personal attachment, by nearly all, to the worth of study as a humanistic enterprise." More vociferously, more directly and more indecorously, the new student left asks what Lippmann asks the university to do, but with a sharper edge because there is too much in contemporary American society these educated sons and daughters of the middle class do not like. Moving from civil-rights protests to anti-war campaigns to educational reform, they have a single goal. They are trying, in the words of one of their heroes, Robert Moses (now Parris), they are "trying very hard to be people and that is very hard." To say what follows from that estimable sentiment is also hard, but in a curious way the radicals among the students share the same view of the relation of the university to the general society as their enemy, the administrators and faculty committed to the multiversity and the purpose of serving society. SDS and the loose alliance of students around them spurn the notion of disinterested intelligence or withdrawal into the academy from the heat and dust of daily life. They want the faculty and the curriculum even more directly related to the needs of society. Only they see the real needs of society as ideal, drastically different from the practical needs they believe higher education to be serving all too well already. They want the university to accept the responsibility of being the fulcrum of change, to move contemporary America to a more just and more humane society rather than to a more powerful and more efficient version of what it now is. They want not to be prepared to play a role in society. They want to change society so they may play a role in it.

    It is such a configuration of forces—economic and social change in the structure of contemporary society, the need for direction and order in a world wracked by change, the moral demand for the achievement of a truly great society—which has imposed upon higher education today an incredible task. Whether higher education in the United States is competent to deal with the burden imposed upon it is perhaps impossible to say. At least, it is impossible to say if one stays at the level of grand historical and ideal generalization. The future may best be seen by scrutinizing the particulars of change and reform going on in higher education and guessing where they may lead. Three books provide three different angles of vision on what higher education might become. One is the report of a select committee at Berkeley, a faculty committee charged with "finding ways in which the traditions of humane learning and scientific inquiry can best be advanced under the challenging conditions of size and scale that confront" the University of California. A second, also directed primarily to faculty colleagues, in this instance at Columbia University, but not in so official a fashion as the Berkeley Report and not the product of a committee but of a single man, is Daniel Bell's *The Reforming of General Education.* The third is the publication of a series of lectures given at Princeton by James A. Perkins, the President of Cornell University, under the title, *The University in Transition.* Each complements the others in significant ways.

If Berkeley is a symbol, it is still a particular place with particular problems and the *Report of the Select Committee,* now popularly known as the Muscatine Report after its chairman, Charles Muscatine, professor of English and Chaucer scholar, is presented with an eye toward the particular. It contains forty-two specific recommendations for change at Berkeley. But it would be unfortunate, indeed, if only Berkeley were to attend to it because each recommendation is made within the context of a general discussion which argues its necessity, and the larger context applies to a larger community than Berkeley.

At one level, the Muscatine report is a capsule case study of what did happen at Berkeley. Chapter II, "The Berkeley Students," provides a sober and statistical description of the Berkeley undergraduate body and the conditions of their environment. Although it gained considerable graduate student support, the student rebellion at Berkeley began among the undergraduates and the Muscatine Report reflects the fact. There are about 17,000 undergraduates at Berkeley, roughly 10,000 upperclassmen (juniors and seniors) and 7,000 underclassmen. But students do not come to Berkeley and work four years and graduate. The pattern is remarkably different. Only about half of those who enter as freshmen graduate; the other half either drop out or transfer elsewhere. And of the graduating class of 1965, 40% were transfer students into Berkeley who had been there only during their upper-class years. There is little continuity in educational experience and, so, little chance that students will catch the sense of a shared community. The absence of community, what the Muscatine Report calls, "the missing college community," is compounded by the fact that few students live on the campus. They commute, as to any place of work, and a survey shows that two-thirds of the students at Berkeley regard the institution as "impersonal" and one-third "often feel lonely walking on campus even though there are crowds of people around."

In the place of physical community, then, Berkeley can only offer an ideal community, that is, a shared commitment to an intellectual process which defines a community of teachers and scholars and students. But, although the quality of students entering Berkeley has risen significantly, at least as measured by verbal and mathematical aptitude tests, "only four percent of [the] graduating class of 1965 had been in honors programs, and only eight percent had received any individual instruction." Further, over forty-percent of classes taken in the freshmen and sophomore years were taught by graduate teaching assistants, and throughout the entire college 65% of the classes and laboratories of 15 students or less, and 63% with 16 to 30 students, were taught by graduate students. To generalize: education at Berkeley is largely in the hands of young graduate students, themselves just out of college and just beginning their own professional preparation. The conditions under which those graduate students labor can be suggested by the fact that all seventeen graduate departments in the humanities with about 1,600 graduate students have reading rooms for them which seat 124; or, with a total graduate body of around 10,000, the Main Library at Berkeley has 415 individual study spaces assigned on a first-come, first-served basis; or, the Department of English with almost 500 graduate students has desk space for 75.

How some undergraduates reacted to what these figures barely imply can be seen in an open letter written by one during the Free Speech Movement crisis: ". . . your situation is hopeless when it comes to actually participating in serious learning. As an undergraduate you receive a four-year long series of sharp staccatos: eight semesters, forty courses, one hundred twenty or more units, fifteen hundred to two thousand impersonal lectures, and over three hundred oversized 'discussion' meetings. Approaching what is normally associated with learning; reading, writing and exams, your situation becomes absurd." Despite the split infinitive and the weakness in punctuation, the judgment is fair.

Circumventing the Departments

The Muscatine report faces the facts honestly and most of its recommendations are aimed at involving the faculty more in teaching, improving the quality and compensation of graduate assistants, and changing the curriculum and conditions as best as Berkeley can with the numbers it has. Understandably enough, the Committee would prefer to see Berkeley "change gradually and continuously rather than having to suffer the shocks of drastic adjustment." And the philosophy it offers is noble: "What will our students have in common? Our answer is that ideally they will have in common the exposure to a noble stance, both scientific and humane, that will be exemplified in the conduct of every one of us. It is not, then, what we teach that will give final validity to education at Berkeley, but what we are. We reject for Berkeley the idea of teachers who are not also scholars. . . . By the same token, we find no place on the faculty for researchers who are not teachers. . . . There is no scholarly eminence that justifies contempt of students. . . . By this central act of service—teaching—we submit our learning directly to the test of human relevance and complete ourselves as proper objects for the emulation of the young."

But the exemplary character of the faculty as noble models for the young is, to put it softly, a dubious road to reform. How to relate the advantages of a superior faculty, at the moment made economically possible by the large number of teaching graduate students, to the educational interests of the young is the crux of the matter; and the single most important reform the Muscatine committee put forward, one adopted by the Berkeley faculty, is the creation of "A Board of Educational Development." Broadly, the Board is charged with oversight of new and experimental courses and programs which do not have a place in traditional departments, perhaps even "field study" off the campus, that is, providing credit for social service and community projects which are "educational" although not in the conventional curricular sense. And the Board is given power: if departments balk, then the Board may ultimately grant a degree for a program of study which finds no departmental home. That is a radical move in higher education where, traditionally, departments have jealously guarded the degree-granting power. Naturally, the Muscatine committee trusts that the showdown will never come, but the Board it has created is probably the best measure of its intense awareness of the need to have a powerful lever to budge the vested interests of the various specialties within the particular departments of higher learning.

The Muscatine committee frankly faced the fact that Berkeley could not provide a common experience in general education for so diverse and large an undergraduate body. But neither did it dare rely simply on the goodwill of a generous faculty. As it puts it, "the needs are too great; our energies and resources too few." So the Board of Educational Development is, obviously, a middle-of-the-road solution, however radical it might first appear. What it provides, in effect, is a resource for the highly motivated and engaged student who is disenchanted with the regular course of study offered in the college. An outsider can only hazard the guess that this is, perhaps, the best that can be done. But the effect is obvious: the change will provide a safety-valve for the discontented and bright student (and it *was* the bright student who was most discontent) who can always be told to take his ambitions to the Board of Educational Development if he rebels against the quality and style of teaching in the regular pattern of instruction.

Education and the Method of Inquiry

What the reform at Berkeley may imply (and, to be honest, one at this moment has to say "may") is that the democratic ideal of mass education must find a way to provide sufficient variety within the huge student bodies it creates to allow for special education for the gifted and less than ideal education for the mass of students, those not bold enough to bitch or bright enough to care. Daniel Bell in his suggestions for the "reforming" of general education at Columbia (and the language is intentional, to suggest a never-ending, ongoing process) refuses the option, although one must remember that

Columbia college has fewer than 3,000 students to Berkeley's 17,000.

Bell's book, because it is his alone, is much more forceful, apodictic, and wide-ranging than the Muscatine report. Chapter III, "The Tableau of Social Change," is an admirable review of the outside forces playing upon the shape and structure of higher education, and the "Coda" at the end is an eloquent affirmation of the tradition of humane and liberal learning against both the technocratic specialists in our culture and the anti-intellectual assault of intellectuals themselves upon the dignity of reason. Because Bell treats Columbia College as a microcosm of the social context of education today, his book should reach a much broader audience than the in-group of academics and educators (although Bell has his own provincialism, and the non-Jewish reader may tire of the number of Talmudic anecdotes which populate the footnotes).

The heart of Bell's book is his answer to the central problem of higher education, how is it possible to be a generally educated man in a world of proliferating knowledge and necessary specialization? When, in the late 19th century, less than two percent of the potential population were going on to college, higher education was clearly for the social and economic elite who largely shared a common background and common aspirations. To provide a common body of intellectual fare was no great task. More importantly, it is now fair to say that no faculty in any college or in any university in the country can generally agree on what particular subjects would define the condition of being generally educated. At Harvard, after three years of discussion, the faculty refused to ratify a new program in general education and President Pusey had to gloss the inability of one of the best faculties in the nation to reach any general conclusion by saying that, after all, the discussion was good for everyone.

"The recalcitrance of the problem," as Bell says, "may lie directly in the structure of knowledge today." If it is no longer possible to find general agreement on what an educated man should know, should we then collapse the college at two ends, downward into accelerated secondary school education and upward into early specialization and graduate training, as the French do? Bell says no and offers, not just a necessary, but an intellectually conceived answer to the problem of general education for all students, not just for the select few.

Beneath the many particulars of his discussion, Bell's answer is that, if it is not possible any longer to say what, in terms of subject matter, an educated man should know, then education consists of an awareness of the process by which men arrive at provisional truths in the three traditional areas of inquiry, the humanities, the social sciences and the natural sciences. Not that a mode of inquiry can be taught apart from subject matter, but the emphasis is to be on the assumptions and procedures of different modes of the inquiring mind. Bell still believes in the worth of a generally shared knowledge of the history of Western civilization, but beyond that requirement the emphasis is not on content but upon the applicability of modes of knowing which relate to experience generally, both in education and in life. In essence, Bell's answer is a rejection of the widely held disjunction between specialization and general education. "One must embody and exemplify general education through disciplines; and one must extend the context of specialism so that the ground of knowledge is explicit. The common bond of the two is the emphasis on conceptual inquiry." So, the emphasis in general education, its peculiar and still vital province, "must be less on what one knows and more on the self-conscious ground of knowledge; how one knows what one knows, and the principal of the relevant selection of facts."

The Force of Inertia

At one point in his book, although there glancing at secondary school education, Bell writes that the problem of reform is not so much curricular, "it is a matter, much more difficult to achieve, of raising to consciousness the underlying values of a middle-class society in a people who do not want such a confrontation with their lives. But this is, within the compass of this book, necessarily an aside." Daniel Bell is not exactly the darling of the new student left and it is not likely that they will soon be attracted to his definition of what modern education must become. A strong threat to education's basic commitment to tradition and disciplined inquiry comes from that breed of student who demands imperiously that all education relate directly to his immediate experience. As the Muscatine report bluntly puts it, "Those who believe that there can be short cuts to social reform, mysticism, and love cannot conceive that there are no short cuts to learning." So, the impatient student will insist that Bell's stress on conceptual method is just another dodge around the dubious values of a middle-class society which he refuses to confront.

But, although he does not claim it himself and may not want to, there is a value in the proposal Bell makes, a value which is basic to the life of the mind and, perhaps more importantly, *the* value which is basic to the working of a democratic society. It is the value of the way in which agreement is reached, the institutionalization of the process by which truth is discovered, whether intellectually or politically, with the end never determined authoritatively in advance nor the search ever closed down. If one takes this view, then Bell's proposal for general education is not to train people so they may live in a democratic society, it is to create the liberal quality of mind which makes a democratic society possible, a quality of mind which insists that the ultimate value lies in how we arrive at truth and not in the particular truths we arrive at. It is a quality of mind which denies dogmatism, which is flexible and open to new experience, and has the courage to doubt that the truth is ever finally known. Such an education might result in that admirable maturity described by the late Professor Joseph Schumpeter: "To realize the relative validity of one's convictions, and yet stand for them unflinchingly, is what distinguishes a civilized man from a barbarian." But whether higher education can bring the United States to that pitch of civilization is yet to be seen.

Whether it can or not depends mainly on whether the inertia and resistance to change inevitable in any large and established institution can be overcome. To take only one example: in a discussion of the possibility of widening the definition of education to include the worth of work done beyond the confines of the regular course and classroom, the Muscatine report observes that "supervision and accreditation of field study is already open to departments by use of courses designated for special study and individual research." In other words, the legislation to achieve the reform the committee proposed was already on the books, but no one had the imagination or the impulse to use it! To overcome that failure, the Muscatine report was driven to proposing the new Board of Educational Development and the creation of a new "Council for Special Curricula," that is, two new committees, and, in order to give them access to money and power at the top, to creating a new executive officer, a Vice-Chancellor in the Administration (although the faculty exercised its political prerogative and reduced that title to Assistant-Chancellor). Whether this bureaucratic superstructure will stifle the impulse to educational reform or not, it points to the immense difficulty of moving any large institution of higher education off dead center.

Who Speaks for Society?

This brings one to President Perkins' book. His book is slender and his thesis is unadorned and direct: "the discussion of the university has now come to the point where theory and doctrine must encounter the practical problems of management and direction." The major practical problem facing the management is to see to it that the three major functions of the modern university do not get out of balance. They are the discovery of knowledge (research), the transmission of knowledge (teaching), and the application of knowledge (public service). But who is to see to it that the balance is maintained? Not the students: "The student is a student. He is at the university to learn, not to manage; to reflect, not to decide; to observe, not to coerce." Not the faculty: "Partial views which are based upon increasingly specialized interests make it difficult for the faculty to have a point of view on broad institutional matters. Consequently, the faculty's administrative stance contains elements of senatorial courtesy—maximum permissiveness with respect to individual faculty desires, combined with maximum protection if anyone would interfere with this permissiveness. Such a posture is exactly right for the protection of the classroom, but it is quite inadequate for educational or institutional management." So, since Mr. Perkins is President of Cornell, one is not exactly astonished to discover that direction must ultimately derive from the administration, the President and his staff.

Without meeting him, one catches the sense from *The University in Transition* that Mr. Perkins must be a congenial and winning man. A nice sense of humor and a wry, ironic self-depreciation run through his pages. But the manner only makes more attractive, it does not try to conceal, the essentially blunt toughness of the man. He was chosen to lead one large state university and he intends to lead it and tells other presidents they had better get busy and lead theirs. But before students and faculty decide to go about their proper business and not bother the management, they might well ask Mr. Perkins to get a bit tougher with his own criterion for making decisions.

Mr. Perkins sees, quite properly, that the single university is no longer autonomous but is part of one level in a complex structure which reaches from individual departments and the college below, to regional and federal and international organizations above. Having described this complexly interwoven structure, Mr. Perkins adds: "Now, in the long run, this structure itself matters very little to society. What society cares about is not which level of this hierarchy has the right to lead and to make decisions. What ultimately matters is that the right decisions are made at the level most competent to make them, and that these decisions are carried out successfully. The approval of society will come, in the end, not by claims of privilege but rather from results observed over time. And the desired results will be in those areas where society asks most of its educational system."

The question to ask here is obvious: who, asking most, speaks for society? Clark Kerr's now famous Godkin Lectures on the multiversity welcomed the "constructive chaos" of education and its response to the various demands society put upon it. Mr. Perkins rejects the model, but how does it differ from his own? And if the test of the success of the university is the pragmatic one of results over time in response to the desires of society, however defined, when will the time possibly come when the university through its leadership decides that American society is simply wrong? Or is that an impossible thought? What if it turns out that Lippmann is right, after all, and that the major resource for the direction of society lies within the university and not somewhere else? To whom does the management turn then?

One version of American history today has it that Americans have succeeded so well by resolutely refusing to think about what they were doing, by doing what comes naturally, by reacting practically to the exigencies of experience and adapting to the demands of the moment, unfettered by the constraints of self-consciousness and reason's imperious demand for coherence between thought and action. The version leads to different evaluations in different hands, of course. For Louis Hartz, the inability of Americans to transcend by an effort of imaginative thought the uniquely favorable circumstances of the American experience is the one great flaw in American culture. Americans have become the victims of their own good fortune. Confined within the clichés of a liberal consensus, with no significant social group to challenge its terms, Americans have been trained by their very success into a deep suspicion for systematic thought, and left, ironically at the moment of their greatest power, unable to understand themselves, let alone the rest of the changing world in which they play so powerful a part. For Daniel Boorstin, the descriptive becomes normative and pragmatic expediency is elevated into a species of philosophic naturalism, an intellectual form of anti-intellectualism, which celebrates the repudiation of systematic thought and rejects the attempt to control in advance the unforeseen consequences of social change. What has worked so well in the past will work best in the future and the genius of American culture has been its willingness to let itself be shaped by the contours of experience.

History-as-it-happens, rather than history-as-it-is-written, will have the final say about which evaluation turns out to be controlling. But as Americans move into the end of the twentieth century, there is one institution which can no longer afford the luxury of waiting to see how the story turns out, and that is the institution of education itself. Not simply because education has a stake in the notion that self-consciousness is a good thing, but because education, especially at its higher reaches, now plays a leading part in the plot, and how it plays that part will largely determine how the story turns out. If higher education decides that it will turn out "whiz kids," not just for the Pentagon but for every demanding institution in the world we live in, then we have the multiversity, straining its resources to provide the trained intelligence which society does in fact need. But, if higher education accepts the role of acting as witness against society, as well as servant to it, the burden of fostering minds which are free as well as servants, minds which may control power and not simply be victims to it, then we have the university and the ideal of a liberal education.

What troubles American higher education today is the simple fact that it has no choice between these simple alternatives. It must meet both demands. It must serve power and yet make that power humane. Whether it can or not is at the bottom of what troubles American education today.

ACKNOWLEDGMENTS

Except for the first essay, "History and the Concept of Culture," which derives from a talk given at a meeting of the American Historical Association, each of the essays in this volume has been published before. In bringing them together, I hope they may now reach the general reader, that necessary fiction for anyone who writes, and have chosen not to print again such scholarly paraphernalia as footnotes, since anyone who wishes to pursue them may find them in their original place.

I am indebted to editors and others who hold copyright on the essays for allowing me to use them again in a collection of my own. In the order of their sequence in this volume, the essays first appeared as follows:

"The Meaning of Lindbergh's Flight," *American Quarterly*, X (Spring, 1958), 3–16.

"Lindbergh, Dos Passos and History," *Carleton Miscellany*, VI (Summer, 1965), 20–46.

"Nature and Civilization: James Fenimore Cooper," as an

"Afterword" to the New American Library's Signet edition of Cooper's *The Prairie* (1964).

"The Meaning of History in *Uncle Tom's Cabin*" as an "Afterword" to the New American Library's Signet edition of *Uncle Tom's Cabin* (1966).

"Empiric of the Imagination: E. W. Howe and *The Story of a Country Town*," as an "Afterword" to the New American Library's Signet edition of *The Story of a Country Town* (1964).

"James Gould Cozzens and the Condition of Modern Man," *American Scholar*, XXVII (Winter, 1957–58), 92–99.

"Benjamin Franklin: The Making of an American Character," appeared under the title, "Who Was Benjamin Franklin?" *American Scholar*, XXXII (Autumn, 1963), 541–53.

"John F. Kennedy and the Meaning of Courage," was recorded in 1968 for broadcast by the Voice of America.

"Some Reflections on Freedom," *American Scholar*, XXVIII (Autumn, 1959), 500–14.

"Frederick Grimke: The Dynamics of Freedom," appeared as my introduction to the John Harvard Library edition of Frederick Grimke, *The Nature and Tendency of Free Institutions* (Cambridge, Mass.: The Belknap Press of Harvard University Press, 1968).

"Mill, Marx, and Modern Individualism," *Virginia Quarterly Review*, XXXV (Autumn, 1959), 527–39.

"The Ideal of Individualism and the Reality of Organization," in *The Business Establishment*, ed. Earl Cheit (New York: John Wiley and Sons, 1964).

"The Politics of Design" appeared in *The Massachusetts Review*, VI (Autumn, 1965), 661–88; and in *Who Designs America?* ed., Laurance B. Holland (New York, Anchor Books, 1966); permission by the Trustees of Princeton University for the program in American Civilization.

"Herbert Croly: The Promise of Constructive Individualism," appeared as my introduction to the Bobbs-Merrill Company's edition in "The American Heritage Series" of Herbert Croly, *The Promise of American Life* (1965).

"The Intellectual: Cleric or Critic?" *American Scholar,* XXXV (Winter, 1965–66), 101–13.

"The Trouble with Higher Education," *The Public Interest,* I (Summer, 1966), 76–88.